The Scottish Parliament under Charles II, 1660–1685

Gillian H. MacIntosh

Studies presented to the International Commission for the History of Representative and Parliamentary Institutions

LXXXIII

Études présentées à la Commission Internationale pour l'Histoire des Assemblées d'États

Edinburgh University Press

In memory of my grandparents

© Gillian H. MacIntosh, 2007

Edinburgh University Press Ltd
22 George Square, Edinburgh

Typeset in Adobe Sabon
by Servis Filmsetting Ltd, Manchester, and
printed and bound in Great Britain by
Biddles Ltd, King's Lynn, Norfolk

A CIP record for this book is available from the British Library

ISBN 978 0 7486 2457 7 (hardback)

CONTENTS

ACKNOWLEDGEMENTS

This monograph began life as a Ph.D. thesis researched in the School of History at the University of St Andrews between 1998 and 2002. Neither this book nor my postgraduate studies would have been possible without the generous financial assistance of the Scottish Parliament Project, set up in 1997 by the Scottish Office and subsequently funded by the Scottish Executive. Many thanks are due to my Ph.D. supervisor Professor Keith Brown, who has been a constant source of helpful advice, encouragement and assistance both while I was writing my doctoral thesis and subsequently under his employment as a research fellow at St Andrews. Numerous conversations with my project colleague Dr Alastair Mann on various aspects of late seventeenth-century Scottish history have proved very rewarding and I have benefited immensely from his in-depth knowledge of the parliamentary records in the period covered by this book. Dr John Young at the University of Strathclyde initially introduced me to the early modern Scottish parliament as an undergraduate and I am extremely grateful to him for his assistance in my honours year and his subsequent interest in my work. Many thought-provoking discussions with other colleagues, past and present, on the Scottish Parliament Project – Dr Alan MacDonald, Dr Alison McQueen, Dr Derek Patrick, Dr Pamela Ritchie and Dr Roland Tanner – have significantly broadened the perspectives of my initial research and this book can only have been improved as a result. Thanks are due to all my fellow editors on the project for making the lengthy task of producing a digital edition of the records of the pre-1707 Scottish parliament a largely genial and rewarding experience.

In researching this book friendly and helpful assistance has been provided by the staff of the National Archives of Scotland, the National Library of Scotland, the Scottish National Portrait Gallery, Glasgow University Library, St Andrews University Library and the Mitchell Library, Glasgow. I am especially grateful to the Earl of Dalhousie, Mr Archibald Stirling of Keir and to Mr D. Maxwell

Macdonald of Pollok and Corrour Ltd for kind permission to consult and quote from their family papers. Gracious acknowledgement is due to the Duke of Buccleuch for granting me permission to visit the Queensberry archives at Drumlanrig Castle and to his archivist Mr Andrew Fisher for his helpful assistance with the collection.

My greatest debt is to my family, especially my parents Jim and Frances MacIntosh, for their support, financial and otherwise, throughout my education. My sister Fiona and brother David have always provided a welcome diversion from academic study. Sincere thanks are also due to Alan Black, my uncle, for the many enjoyable summer jaunts around deepest darkest Sussex and the innumerable Dorset cream teas. I am fortunate enough to have inherited his instinctive curiosity and enthusiasm for archival research, albeit a few centuries separate our particular interests.

Gillian H. MacIntosh
St Andrews, May 2006

ABBREVIATIONS AND CONVENTIONS

Personal names and place-names have been modernised where identified. Personal names conform to G. F. Black, *The Surnames of Scotland* (New York, 1946) and place-names to *The Ordnance Gazetteer of Great Britain* (London, 1987). Punctuation and capitalisation have been modernised in all contemporary quotations but the original spelling remains. All monetary values are in Scots unless otherwise specified. From 1601, the rate of exchange was at a fixed rate of £12 Scots to £1 sterling; a merk was approximately two thirds of £1 Scots. Dates have been altered according to modern usage, with the new year taken to begin on 1 January.

The reference system used in the forthcoming digital edition of *The Records of the Parliaments of Scotland to 1707* [*RPS*] has been adopted in preference to the superseded *Acts of the Parliaments of Scotland* [*APS*] page numbers. Each record in the digital edition is given a reference number (for example, '*RPS*, 1669/10/6', which refers to the sixth act of the October 1669 parliament) and the *RPS* references in this book follow the same style and logic. Parliamentary minutes, committee proceedings and additional sources are reflected in reference numbers with the prefix of M, C and A respectively. To assist identification of material prior to publication of the digital edition, manuscript references have also been provided for all records that will appear in *RPS*.

With the exception of those abbreviations given below, sources are cited in full when first mentioned and then given in abbreviated form thereafter.

APS	*The Acts of the Parliaments of Scotland*, C. Innes and T. Thomson (eds), 12 vols (Edinburgh, 1814–75).
BL	British Library, London.
Burnet, *History*	G. Burnet, *A History of His Own Time*, O. Airy (ed.), 2 vols (Oxford, 1897–1900).

CSPD	*Calendar of State Papers, Domestic Series.*
HMC	Historical Manuscripts Commission.
Lauderdale Papers	*The Lauderdale Papers*, O. Airy (ed.), 3 vols (London, 1884–5).
Mackenzie, *Memoirs*	Sir George Mackenzie of Rosehaugh, *Memoirs of the Affairs of Scotland from the Restoration of Charles II*, T. Thomson (ed.), (Edinburgh, 1821).
NAS	National Archives of Scotland, Edinburgh.
NLS	National Library of Scotland, Edinburgh.
PER	*Parliaments, Estates and Representation.*
RPCS	*The Register of the Privy Council of Scotland*, third series, 10 vols (1661–85).
RPS	*The Records of the Parliaments of Scotland to 1707*, K. M. Brown et al. (eds), (St Andrews, forthcoming).
Scots Peerage	*The Scots Peerage*, Sir James Balfour-Paul (ed.), 9 vols (Edinburgh, 1904–14).
SHR	*The Scottish Historical Review.*
SHS	Scottish History Society.

FIGURES

INTRODUCTION

Until relatively recently, the Restoration era was one of the murkier corners of Scottish history. Previous studies of Scotland in the reign of Charles II (of which there have been a limited few) have tended to focus exclusively on the religious conflict between presbyterian dissenters and a government-supported episcopal church, as if this was the only subject-matter of note for historians of the Restoration period. Until the latter half of the twentieth century, it was Robert Wodrow's portrayal of an age of brutality, in which the people were involved in a godly struggle in defence of presbyterianism, that dominated the bulk of research.[1] Whereas Wodrow did much to establish the covenanting tradition of martyrdom, it was later published accounts which inexorably linked the Restoration period with religious persecution in the popular imagination. The emergence of the Free Church of Scotland in the mid-nineteenth century prompted a plethora of sympathetic and hagiographical biographies of persecuted covenanters, which for some years remained the dominant output concerning the Restoration. Whilst contemporaneous episcopalian writers challenged such an interpretation, the unerring concentration on the ecclesiastical dimension of the Restoration period only served to confirm an entrenched view of the era as one marked solely by fanatical rebellion and state oppression.[2]

The publication in the early twentieth century of a number of biographies of the chief political figures of the period – such as W. C. Mackenzie's partisan study of the historical reputation of John Maitland, second earl and first duke of Lauderdale, Andrew Lang's commentary on the career of Sir George Mackenzie of Rosehaugh, lord advocate, and John Willcock's life of Archibald Campbell, ninth earl of Argyll – were to be welcomed, even if they also showed signs of the religious bias that had marked so many previous studies of the Restoration era.[3] It was not until the 1960s, coinciding with a general renaissance in Scottish historical writing, that a number of studies reconsidered the Restoration period in much less emotive terms, although these too were similarly focused on ecclesiastical matters. Nevertheless, Ian Cowan's revisionist appraisal of the later phase of the covenanting movement did much to advance a more balanced historical understanding of government policy on religious dissent, eschewing mawkish sentimentality in favour of a more dispassionate approach.[4] The lone pioneering efforts of Julia Buckroyd in the 1970s and 1980s, specifically focusing on the remarkable fluctuations between repression and conciliation which marked government strategy in the years 1661–81, likewise provided fresh insight into the political alliances of the period, convincingly arguing that ecclesiastical policy had less to do with religious convictions than with political power struggles within the Restoration regime.[5]

Apart from a recent number of historical accounts of the Restoration which include Scotland as part of a 'three-kingdoms' approach to British history, there has been no comprehensive published attempt to study political events in Charles II's northern kingdom from a non-Anglocentric perspective.[6] In 1994, Allan Macinnes and Michael Lynch identified several conspicuous lacunae in the study of Scottish history, 'none more striking than the "black hole" in the Restoration period.'[7] In the intervening period, some valuable work has been produced that has done much to shift the focus away from traditionalist studies of religious dissent. A number of articles on particular aspects of Restoration politics, such as government policy towards the Highlands and a brief study of the origins of the opposition to Lauderdale in the parliamentary session of 1673, whilst illuminating, have tended to raise more questions than provide answers.[8] Perhaps the most useful work undertaken recently on Scotland in the reigns of Charles II and James VII has been by Clare Jackson, whose detailed and intelligent reconstruction of late-seventeenth-century intellectual culture, particularly regarding royalist ideas and theories, has injected Restoration history with a much needed dose of political thought.[9]

Nevertheless, despite the past decade witnessing a renewed interest in the study of Scottish parliamentary history in particular, the Restoration period has not been well served by current published historiography.[10] For example, John Young's exhaustive account of the political and constitutional development of the mid-seventeenth-century Scottish parliament ends at 1661, albeit with a short analysis of the first session of the newly restored parliament.[11] Although the role and significance of the Scottish parliament has been briefly discussed in the aforementioned British studies of Charles II's reign, the institution has often been unfavourably contrasted with its English equivalent and subsequently dismissed as feeble and ineffective in comparison. For example, Tim Harris, despite seeking to promote a more inclusive and integrated British approach in his recent study of Charles II's kingdoms, seems content to sum up Scotland's parliament as a 'relatively weak institution, unable to offer the same sort of counterbalance to the political authority of the crown as their English counterparts.'[12] Such a view has been endorsed by Scottish historians themselves, with the Restoration Scottish parliament being described as 'pliant' and 'emasculated' because it passed legislation to strengthen the powers of the crown.[13]

As a result of the limitations identified in currently published historiography, it is still Robert Rait's 1924 book on the Scottish parliament that remains essential reading on constitutional matters, even though this thematic study devotes only thirteen pages to the period 1660–85.[14] For the modern reader, however, Rait's generally harsh and Whiggish conclusions about the Scottish parliament's historical significance, derived once again from comparisons with its English counterpart, mars what still remains the only attempt at a general history of the institution. If Rait is to be believed, Scotland's parliament 'never established the claim upon national gratitude and reverence which, at the date of the union, Englishmen proudly acknowledged to be the inheritance of the two houses that sat at Westminster.' Nor, according to Rait, did it 'give to the world that example of, and inspiration to, representative government which is perhaps the greatest English contribution to the development of civilization'. In attempting to justify his very reasons for studying the institution at all, Rait concluded that, despite 'its defects and its impotence', the Scottish parliament had value chiefly as a historical 'curiosity', if nothing more.[15]

Rait's unflattering assessment of the historical significance of the Scottish parliament was so effective that it killed off interest in the subject for much of the last century. It was not until the late twentieth century that systematic attempts were made to question Rait's judgements and rescue the reputation of the early modern Scottish parliament. This revisionist approach, best seen in the work of David Stevenson, Julian Goodare and John Young amongst others, revealed the hitherto overlooked complexity and highly developed nature of the institutional processes at work in the late-sixteenth to mid-seventeenth-century parliament.[16] Building on these foundations, a recent reassessment of the early history of parliament undertaken by Roland Tanner and other late medievalists has prompted a radical rethinking of the respective power of the estates between the thirteenth and sixteenth centuries, comprehensively deconstructing the notion that assemblies in late medieval times were wholly passive affairs, controlled entirely by the monarch, and instead demonstrating that a robust and developed parliament played a significant role in government and often kept the crown in check.[17] As a result of this reappraisal of parliament's historical significance, the new shared consensus is that the Scottish estates were at least as powerful as many comparable European institutions, if not more so.

Despite the recent renaissance in the study of Scottish constitutional history, the role and function of parliament under Charles II has until now awaited a detailed study. This book therefore seeks not only to provide an analysis of the political and legislative role of the estates throughout the Restoration era, but an explanation of why they were called together, who attended and what they did. Individual sessions of parliaments have been placed in the context of the time in which they sat. Only then is it possible to ascertain if the predominant and traditional view of the Scottish parliament as a weak and ineffective institution is a well-deserved assessment or an unfairly harsh one.

Notes

1 R. Wodrow, *The History of the Sufferings of the Church of Scotland from the Restoration to the Revolution*, R. Burns (ed.), 4 vols (Glasgow, 1828–30).

2 Of the many such works published at this time, see, for example, P. Walker, *Biographia Presbyteriana*, 2 vols (Edinburgh, 1827), J. K. Hewison, *The Covenanters: a History of the Church of Scotland from the Reformation to the Revolution* (Glasgow, 1908) and A. Smellie, *Men of the Covenant: the Story of the Scottish Church in the Years of the Persecution* (London, 1909).

3 W. C. Mackenzie, *The Life and Times of John Maitland, Duke of Lauderdale* (London, 1923); A. Lang, *Sir George Mackenzie, His Life and Times, 1636–1691* (London, 1909); J. Willcock, *A Scots Earl in Covenanting Times: being Life and Times of Archibald, 9th Earl of Argyll (1629–1685)* (Edinburgh, 1907).

4 I. B. Cowan, 'The Covenanters: a revision article', *SHR*, 47 (1968), pp. 35–52; I. B. Cowan, *The Scottish Covenanters, 1660–1688* (London, 1976).

5 J. Buckroyd, 'The dismissal of Archbishop Alexander Burnet, 1669', *Records of the Scottish Church History Society*, 18 (1973), pp. 149–55; J. Buckroyd, *Church and State in Scotland, 1660–81* (Edinburgh, 1980);

J. Buckroyd, 'Anti-clericalism in Scotland during the Restoration', in N. Macdougall (ed.), *Church, Politics and Society: Scotland 1408–1929* (Edinburgh, 1983), pp. 167–85; J. Buckroyd, *The Life of James Sharp, Archbishop of St Andrews, 1618–1679: a Political Biography* (Edinburgh, 1987).

6 See, for example, R. Hutton, *Charles II: King of England, Scotland and Ireland* (Oxford, 1991) and T. Harris, *Restoration: Charles II and his Kingdoms, 1660–1685* (London, 2005), which both focus largely on England but give admirably inclusive attention to the fringes of the British Isles.

7 A. I. Macinnes, 'Early modern Scotland: the current state of play', *SHR*, 73 (1994), p. 43; M. Lynch, 'Response: old games and new', *SHR*, 73 (1994), p. 47.

8 A. I. Macinnes, 'Repression and conciliation: the Highland dimension, 1660–1688', *SHR*, 65 (1986), pp. 167–95, and J. Patrick, 'The origins of the opposition to Lauderdale in the Scottish parliament of 1673', *SHR*, 53 (1974), pp. 1–21.

9 C. Jackson, 'Restoration to Revolution: 1660–1690', in G. Burgess (ed.), *The New British History: Founding a Modern State, 1603–1715* (London, 1999), pp. 92–114; C. Jackson, *Restoration Scotland, 1660–1690: Royalist Politics, Religion and Ideas* (Woodbridge, 2003).

10 A number of unpublished doctoral theses have, however, provided fresh insight into various aspects of late-seventeenth-century Scottish government, such as R. W. Lennox, 'Lauderdale and Scotland: A Study in Restoration Politics and Administration, 1660–1682' (University of Columbia, Ph.D., 1977), K. M. Colquhoun, ' "Issue of the late civill wars": James, duke of York and the government of Scotland, 1679–1689' (University of Illinois at Urbana-Champaign, Ph.D., 1993) and R. A. Lee, 'Government and politics in Scotland, 1661–1681' (University of Glasgow, Ph.D., 1995).

11 J. R. Young, *The Scottish Parliament, 1639–1661: a political and constitutional analysis* (Edinburgh, 1996).

12 Harris, *Restoration*, p. 25.

13 C. Kidd, *Subverting Scotland's Past: Scottish Whig Historians and the Creation of an Anglo-British Identity, 1689–c.1830* (Cambridge, 1993), p. 131.

14 R. S. Rait, *The Parliaments of Scotland* (Glasgow, 1924).

15 Rait, *Parliaments of Scotland*, pp. 125–6. C. S. Terry's earlier study, *The Scottish Parliament: its Constitution and Procedure, 1603–1707* (Glasgow, 1905), reached the same damning verdict. According to Terry, the early modern Scottish parliament 'failed to secure for itself . . . the respect, popularity and authority of its English contemporary', p. 162.

16 For an example of this approach, see D. Stevenson, *The Scottish Revolution, 1637–44: The Triumph of the Covenanters* (London, 1973);

D. Stevenson, *The Revolution and Counter-Revolution in Scotland, 1644–1651* (London, 1977); J. Goodare, 'The estates in the Scottish parliament, 1286–1707', *Parliamentary History*, 15 (1996), pp. 11–32; J. Goodare, *The Government of Scotland, 1560–1625* (Oxford, 2004); J. R. Young, 'Seventeenth-century Scottish parliamentary rolls and political factionalism: the experience of the Covenanting movement', *Parliamentary History*, 16, 2 (1997), pp. 148–70; J. R. Young, 'The Scottish parliament in the seventeenth century: European perspectives', in A. I. Macinnes, T. Riis and F. G. Pederson (eds), *Ships, Guns and Bibles in the North Sea and the Baltic States, c.1350–c.1700* (East Linton, 2000), pp. 139–49; and Young, *Scottish Parliament*.

17 For a small example of this revisionist output, see R. J. Tanner, *The Late Medieval Scottish Parliament: Politics and the Three Estates, 1424–1488* (East Linton, 2001); K. M. Brown and R. J. Tanner (eds), *The History of the Scottish Parliament, volume I: Parliament and Politics, 1235–1560* (Edinburgh, 2004); and K. M. Brown and A. J. Mann (eds), *The History of the Scottish Parliament, volume II: Parliament and Politics, 1567–1707* (Edinburgh, 2005).

Chapter 1

TURNING BACK THE CLOCK: THE RESTORATION SETTLEMENT OF 1661

When the news of the beheading of Charles I reached Edinburgh in early February 1649, the Scottish parliament, sitting in session, immediately declared his son lawful successor as king of Great Britain, Ireland and France. The proclamation of kingship, however, was laden with a number of weighty qualifications: before Charles II would be admitted to power, he must take the covenants and agree to establish presbyterianism in all three kingdoms.[1] Despite initial refusal to acquiesce in the demands of the Scots, the failure of the royalists to capitalise on military advances made in Ireland and the routing of James Graham, first marquis of Montrose's army on its invasion of Scotland gave the exiled king little room for manoeuvre. On 23 June 1650, with the Scottish coast visible from his ship anchored in the Moray Firth, Charles could delay no longer and he grudgingly appended his signature to the covenants. In joyous celebration of their covenanted king, on 26 June, the Scottish parliament ordered the general of artillery to 'shoott the haill cannon of the castell' and the provost of Edinburgh to 'sett on bonfyres and ring all the bells presentlie'.[2] Charles's often-delayed coronation eventually took place at Scone on 1 January 1651, ceremonially confirming the return of the monarchy. When parliament met in Stirling in May 1651, Charles, present at all but one of the diets, quickly assumed the king's traditional position of authority within the chamber. He successfully argued for the repeal of the 1646 and 1649 'Act of Classes', thus enabling former Engagers and royalists to resume positions of public trust. An act outlawing the Western Remonstrance was easily approved by parliament, albeit in the face of dissent from John Campbell, first earl of Loudoun, and Archibald Campbell, first marquis of Argyll, and their faction. By the summer of 1651, Charles and his royalist supporters were in a position of ascendancy, the kirk rent by internal divisions.[3] However, just as the king seemed to be on the brink of political success, his military position was rapidly deteriorating. The defeat of the royalists at the battle of Worcester on 3 September 1651 followed on from the capture of the committee of estates at Alyth in Perthshire in August, leaving the English forces unimpeded to complete their conquest of the rest of the country. Scotland's political and military independence was virtually destroyed, ushering in almost a decade of occupation and a form of union radically different to that proposed by the covenanters in 1638.

The majority of Scottish people thus welcomed the restoration of Charles II in the spring of 1660 with considerable enthusiasm. Contemporary accounts tell of the proclamation being greeted at the Mercat Cross in Edinburgh on 14 May 'by ringing of bellis, settling out of bailfyres, sounding of trumpetis, roring of cannounes, touking of drumes, dancing about the fyres and using all uther tokins of joy for the advancement and preference of thair native king to his croun and native inheritance.' It was the occasion for much celebration, albeit largely orchestrated by the government itself. In Edinburgh 'the spoutes of the croce [were] ryning and venting out abundance of wyne, placed thair for that end; and the magistrates and counsell of the toun, being present, [were] drinking the kinges health and breaking numberis of glasses.'[4] Naturally, provision of free alcohol was an ideal way to procure enthusiastic public support. Yet away from the public celebrations, the political elite had for some months been making preparations for the return of monarchical government after nearly twenty years of internal upheaval. Eager to be rid of the large numbers of English soldiers garrisoned throughout the nation, the king was welcomed back unconditionally, with no Scottish equivalent of the declaration of Breda. However, the fundamental questions regarding the respective powers of crown and parliament remained unanswered.

The collapse of the Protectorate in April 1659 meant that the administration of Scotland was left in turmoil. The presbyterian church still remained divided down the same party political lines of the 1650s, split between sympathisers towards the commonwealth, best represented by the Protester party who were fiercely antagonistic to the Stewart monarchy, and the Resolutioners, who supported the return of the king provided the covenants were upheld. The struggle between the two opposing groups was still unresolved when events in England signified a major upheaval north of the border.[5] The reinstatement of the Rump parliament in England made void all proceedings regarding union with Scotland that had taken place since April 1653. The matter was referred with some urgency to a committee of the council of state, but its deliberations were impeded by the speed of political events, and when the army forcibly dissolved the Rump in October 1659, the issue of the union remained unresolved. In Scotland itself, the judicial system had collapsed, forcing the army to deal with issues of law and order in addition to its peacekeeping role. Fear of unrest amongst a lawless population, perhaps with a political dimension akin to Booth's rising in England, at last hastened the settlement of affairs north of the border.[6]

On 27 October 1659, the Cromwellian leader, General George Monck, sent letters to the magistrates of burghs and sheriffs of the shires asking them to assemble the leading noblemen and gentlemen of their region. Monck invited both groups to send one of their number to attend a meeting in Edinburgh on 15 November, to 'speake with them about some affaires that concerne the countries att that time.'[7] One of the first measures undertaken when the meeting duly convened was the election of two presiding representatives from both the shire and burgh membership. The burghs elected as their leader Sir James Stewart of Coltness, lord provost of Edinburgh, a known Protester who was soon to be imprisoned on a charge of countenancing the execution of the earl of Montrose and who was to be fined heavily under the forthcoming indemnity act.[8] The shires conversely elected William Cunningham, eighth earl of Glencairn, a staunch supporter of the king who had gained royal favour through his involvement in an abortive royalist rising in 1653. Following the election of the two shire and burgh representatives, Monck made a short speech declaring his intention to march into England. He entrusted those present with the maintenance of order in his absence. Each had a duty to help preserve the peace of the commonwealth and to suppress all signs of disturbances, Monck told the gathered commissioners.[9] The commissioners agreed to these initial demands, but in a letter to Monck of 16 November requested more concrete proposals on how to prevent disorders in the localities. Monck's reply was highly unsatisfactory: he had no time to consider specific measures but would welcome suggestions by their next meeting.[10]

Before the conference was adjourned, the commissioners were asked to hold new elections for representatives to meet in Berwick on 12 December. The resulting election contests provided the first indications that the initial consensus between the three estates was beginning to break down. Some shires complained about the actions of their chosen representatives, as Robert Baillie, a Resolutioner minister, noted: 'After Monck's march [into England in late 1659], some stickling there was in the west to have had meetings in shyres for new commissioners.'[11] Although the exact objections are unknown, it is possible that certain shires disliked the dominance of the nobility, who had, in effect, hijacked almost every shire seat. There had also been criticism from individuals in the localities who felt that they were given no further consultation as to matters now under discussion. Sir Andrew Bruce of Earlshall, a resident of Fife, wrote to Monck bitterly complaining that he had been summoned to Cupar by Sir Alexander Gibson of Durie to approve a series of proposals that Durie and his followers had already written, 'as if the gentlimen in this shyre had bein meer dolts'. Bruce was also indignant that Durie had been chosen as one of the commissioners: 'I wes of lait desyred by your lordship to discover the practises of malignants, and now they [seem] to be the men on whom your lordship doeth repoise and mainlie trust.'[12] It was thus evident that the coalition of widely differing viewpoints that the first meeting successfully united was but a temporary state of affairs.

Prior to the Berwick meeting, it had been decided that, owing to their poverty, each burgh was to send any comments on the particulars decided at the November conference to the provost and bailies of Edinburgh, who would be responsible for bringing all submissions to Berwick. However, before the estates met, it was resolved that the burghs of Linlithgow and Haddington were to be added to the burgh representation.[13] Thus, at the new election, the burghs returned only four representatives, with Sir James Stewart of Coltness, president of the estate in November, notably absent.

When the meeting at Berwick convened on 12 December, it was the nobility who overwhelmingly dominated proceedings. The commissioners from the shires elected five of their number to personally attend Monck. Those chosen – the earl of Glencairn, John Leslie, seventh earl of Rothes, David Wemyss, second earl of Wemyss, Alexander Montgomery, sixth earl of Eglinton and Alexander Bruce of Broomhall – had all been opponents of the Cromwellian regime and were all members of prominent noble families.[14] In response to Monck's request for suggestions on how to ensure the peace of the country, the five representatives submitted a number of proposals. Their primary request was for the shires to be permitted to regulate their own affairs and to raise a force for their defence. Monck, however, only authorised the basic arming of a few key personnel, much to the chagrin of Glencairn and others. Thus, the meeting broke up on a sour note.[15]

Both the conferences at Edinburgh and Berwick revealed that, despite such disagreements, General Monck did at least intend to involve the chief men of Scotland in his plans to march south. Furthermore, Monck was prepared to offer the nobility the opportunity to return to their traditional position of political superiority. The nobility's domination of the shire membership of both meetings is striking, and it was they, rather than the gentry or lairds, who personally met with the general to offer proposals. Yet Monck was careful to ensure that the nobility did not act too independently. His refusal to allow the Scots to take up arms either for his own assistance or in defence indicated that he was wary of allowing them too much autonomy. This unwillingness on Monck's part was a tacit acknowledgement that he feared the Scots were capable of taking an independent initiative, endangering planned action in England.[16]

The royalist nobility's increasing ascendancy was demonstrated when the shires and burghs met again in early 1660. Only about half of the shires and burghs in Scotland sent representatives to the meeting in Edinburgh on 2 February 1660, but the nobility's success in the election contests (in which the shires elected one noble or laird, while each burgh elected one burgess) indicated that within the localities the nobility were in the process of reasserting political power. From October 1659, General Monck had permitted the nobility to take part in elections and their influence is reflected in the noble domination of shire representation at the meetings.[17] To illustrate this point, the first business dealt with by the meeting was the issue of a disputed election in Edinburghshire, where James Richardson of Smeaton was in competition with George Ramsay, lord Ramsay. Richardson's commission was refused, perhaps the most significant reason for this being that 'Ramsay's commission is subscribed by the most considerable noblemen and gentlemen of the shires and Smeaton's is subscribed only by a few considerable gentlemen and no nobleman.' Noble representatives were returned for all but four shires.[18]

Correspondence from Scottish nobles in London reveals that the nobility was all too aware of the danger of alienating the gentry in the shires. It was recommended that 'some of the greatest interest' (presumably members of the nobility) 'meet . . . to keep correspondence with meetings of honest men in every shire.' This was vital, since 'the great means of preserving the liberty and restitution of Scotland' lay in achieving 'hearty concurrences in such friendly and necessary meetings.'[19] Yet relations between the nobility and shires was less of an alliance than was perhaps at first intended, certainly from the shires' point of view. Indeed, the almost total noble dominance of the shire representatives was possibly one of the reasons why there had been demands in November for new elections to be held.

The main issue under discussion at the February meeting was the English parliament and the fact that it had no Scottish representation. As it was likely that decisions made by the House of Commons would affect Scotland, the commissioners were eager to draw up a variety of demands that would be sent with a delegation to London. Various measures were agreed, such as encouraging trade, protecting shipping, releasing prisoners of war and the establishment of a stable currency. However, soon a number of serious differences emerged between the shires and the burghs. The burghs were anxious to enforce the law of debtor and creditor and, by implication, collect what was owed to them by the nobility. The shires, however, wanted to continue the system of deferment sanctioned by the Cromwellians.[20] Shire opposition was voiced at the burghs' proposal for the speedy setting up of law courts (and thus, by implication, the legal enforcement of the laws of debt). In reaction, the burghs complained of the shires' proposal for the revocation of gifts and annuities. The issue of union, although the subject of some disagreement, was not as contentious an issue as perhaps should have been expected. Squabbling over domestic issues, especially concerning financial reparations to be offered to those who had suffered in the last twenty years, turned out to be the main item on the agenda. In the end, both parties decided to send separate messengers to London with their individual requirements. Such a move only served to weaken Scotland's voice.[21]

The nobility's dominance was again apparent when the shires chose their commissioners to be sent to London to meet with the English parliament. The earl of Glencairn was again selected as part of the membership, and James Home, third earl of Home, Sir Alexander Gibson of Durie, Archibald Stirling of Garden and Mungo Murray, brother to John Murray, second earl of Atholl, completed those appointed. Their instructions outlined a number of mainly economic and political grievances: trade and fishing were to be promoted, public judicatories were to be reconvened and the assessment and excise was to be made proportional to England. The burghs sent only one representative, William Thomson, clerk of Edinburgh council.[22]

By the time the messengers reached London, the republican regime was crumbling. Monck therefore had little time to consider the particulars of a Scottish government, and so, in March 1660, five commissioners for managing the affairs of Scotland were appointed. Monck chose to completely ignore those who had been elected as commissioners to the two meetings in late 1659, preferring instead to appoint trusted military colleagues. General Thomas Morgan and Colonels Philip Twistleton, William Daniel and Molyneux Disney (replacing the initial members Colonels Nathaniel Whetham and Henry Markham) arrived in Edinburgh in May 1660, and, with the king's approval, acted as the government of Scotland until August 1660. Ten judges were also appointed in March – four Englishmen and six Scots. The appointments were not well received. Monck had promised to treat Scotland on an equal footing with England, but the appointment of this influential group looked instead like an attempt at subjection.[23] Insult was only added to injury when it became apparent that for the first time since the 1653 Barebones parliament, there would be no Scottish representation at the Convention parliament. Scotland had regained its independence, but by default rather than design.

The Scottish nobles were increasingly worried by the turn of events. Anxious to play an important part in the ongoing English negotiations, it was at first suggested that John Maitland, second earl of Lauderdale and John Lindsay, seventeenth earl of Crawford-Lindsay should act on the nobility's behalf since they were presently in London. This, however, was rejected, and on 5 or 6 April 1660 the noble members, along with some of the gentry, assembled without the permission of Monk to choose representatives to send to London.[24] Claiming the right to convene by virtue of the warrant granted to the shire commissioners in February, the meeting was attended by thirteen noblemen and ten shire representatives. Under the presidency of the earl of Rothes, the commissioners drafted correspondence to the king indicating that they were waiting for instructions on how they could best serve him. The commissioners appointed in February to travel to London were again re-appointed, this time with the addition of two burgesses, Robert Murray of Cameron and James Borthwick of Stow.[25] The commissioners left Edinburgh on 20 April with a draft letter for the king, but once again they reached London too late to influence English opinion. The elections to the Convention parliament were already under way and were producing results in favour of the restoration of the monarchy. Nevertheless, summoning their own meeting without Monck's approval indicated that the royalists in Scotland were exercising significant power even before the king returned from the continent.[26]

In England, parliament convened on 25 April 1660 to lay the groundwork for the Restoration settlement. The bitterness of civil war and regicide had left serious political divisions that hampered the attempt to come to a unanimous agreement on the role of the monarchy and its relationship to parliament. As in Scotland, south of the border there was a split between those who had remained committed royalists since Charles I's reign, those who had sided with parliament or who had collaborated with the republican regimes and neutral or new men. Charles II recognised this when he included all three groups in his reconvened privy council and ministerial and household offices. Despite the divide, the Convention parliament soon agreed that the monarchy should return unconditionally, disregarding the Nineteen Propositions, the Newcastle Propositions and the treaties of Oxford, Uxbridge and Newport. The declaration of Breda was accepted instead, a package which contained something for every political faction in England. Once the royal assent had been received to a bill declaring it to be a full and legal parliament, the Convention proceeded to arrange the terms for land and fiscal arrangements under the new regime, followed on 29 August by a generous act of indemnity. Bloodletting was kept to the minimum, with only thirty-three individuals excepted from the pardon, of whom only a third were to be executed. The main task of sorting out the fine details of the Restoration settlement was left to the Cavalier parliament, which was to sit from 8 May 1661.[27]

The restoration of the monarchy produced much the same reaction in Ireland as in Charles's other two kingdoms. The king's return was widely celebrated since it brought to an end a decade of military occupation, often characterised by the brutal suppression of both religious and political views divergent from the English republican regime. Even before the king had reached London, the Irish convention sitting at Dublin in February 1660 decided upon the restoration of episcopacy as a symbol of national order and unity. The subsequent meeting of the Irish parliament in May 1661, its membership carefully managed to exclude radical presbyterians and Catholics, issued a series of proclamations requiring obedience to the new church settlement and outlawing all forms of resistance. The most controversial aspect was the land settlement question, which was eventually resolved in the terms set out in Charles's initial proclamation of November 1660: owners of land seized from Catholic rebels in the 1640s and royalists in the 1650s should keep their acquisitions or be compensated for any land they were to restore to those unfairly implicated in rebellion. Problems were to be inevitably expected but the Irish estates continued to be constitutionally restrained by Poynings' law of 1494, which dictated that all legislation agreed upon by the Irish parliament would have to be first approved by the English privy council.[28]

Until an English settlement had been successfully thought out and implemented, Charles and his chief ministers refused to call a meeting of the Scottish parliament. Instead, the newly restored monarch asked for proposals for the administration of Scotland in the interim. Since March, the government of Scotland had lain in the hands of the four commissioners appointed to that task by the republican regime. The majority of the nobility and gentry advocated the recall of the 1651 committee of estates as the simplest solution, which would sit until a full session of parliament could meet. Such a proposal from the Scottish estates recognised that the power of summoning parliament rested solely with the king, therefore ignoring the constitutional legislation of 1639–41, despite the fact that this legislation was still legally viable.[29] The committee of estates was scheduled to meet on 23 August 1660 and act as a provisional government until the holding of parliament on 23 October 1660.

In August 1660, Charles began to appoint his chief officials in Scotland. John Middleton, first earl of Middleton, a professional soldier who had gained the king's favour in the 1650s with a futile royalist rising, had latterly been employed by the exiled king in various schemes to raise money and troops. As his reward, at the Restoration he was appointed commander-in-chief in Scotland, governor of Edinburgh Castle and, most significantly, lord high commissioner to the Scottish parliament. It is clear from contemporary evidence that Middleton was not a popular choice, especially amongst those who were hoping for a presbyterian church settlement.[30] Humiliated in 1651 by James Guthrie, minister of Stirling, by being forced to perform public penance in sackcloth for his involvement in military action against the kirk party, he is said to have harboured an intense personal hatred of presbyterians for the rest of his life.[31]

The post of secretary of state went to John Maitland, earl of Lauderdale, who, for his adherence to the royalist cause, had been imprisoned in various English fortresses for the last nine years. Understandably eager for political power and favour on his release in March 1660, Lauderdale had immediately travelled to the exiled court in Breda where he struck up an instant rapport with the king. Vilified by contemporaries such as Gilbert Burnet and Edward Hyde, earl of Clarendon, it is their portrait of an arrogant, ruthless and unprincipled politician that has shaped Lauderdale's historical reputation.[32] Whig historians such as Osmund Airy condemned Lauderdale as being 'brutalised . . . by the rank exercise of irresponsible power', a 'bad man, even for that bad time', who, under the influence of his second wife, Elizabeth Murray, countess of Dysart, abandoned himself 'to the worst vices of irresponsible despotism'.[33] Recent studies, however, have been more kind, emphasising a natural, skilful and adaptable politician forced into adopting increasingly savage measures in response to a religious problem spinning out of control.[34] Lauderdale's long imprisonment was reason enough for him to expect a compensatory position in the new government, but Charles soon recognised him as a man of great ability, by far the most intelligent of the Scottish nobles who were clamouring for office. Returning to Britain with the post of gentleman of the bedchamber, it was not long before the higher office of secretary was bestowed on him. Based in London, with direct access to the king's ear, Lauderdale had been well rewarded for his long years of incarceration.[35]

The remaining offices of the Scottish ministry were also soon filled. The earl of Glencairn was appointed chancellor, Rothes secured the post of president of the privy council and the earl of Crawford-Lindsay was retained in his post of treasurer. Completing the list was Sir John Fletcher as king's advocate, Sir Archibald Primrose of Carrington as clerk register, Sir William Bellenden as treasurer depute and William Keith, seventh earl Marischal as lord privy seal. The majority of officers of state had all demonstrated their royalist credentials at some point in the past. However, Charles tried to ensure that the administration appointed was both amenable to the royal interest whilst maintaining a balance between the various factions of the 1640s and the collaborators. Notably absent from the most influential positions were the kirk party leaders John Campbell, earl of Loudoun and William Kerr, third earl of Lothian, although they were compensated in kind with patronage for their families and pensions. Charles felt no affection for those who had tried to control him in 1650. Instead, power had been lodged firmly in the hands of moderate covenanters, those who had supported the Engagement in 1648 and who had made a favourable impression on the king himself.[36]

With the major offices now filled, the committee of estates, which was to provisionally govern the country until parliament convened, met in Edinburgh on 23 August 1660. Although technically based on the committee of estates from 1651, large numbers of the 1651 committee did not attend, either because of death, withdrawal from politics or fear amongst former radicals of political retribution from the new royalist regime. To replace those absent members, a number of individuals gained admittance to the committee despite holding no commission, with six nobles, fourteen shire and nine burgh commissioners in attendance who were not official members of the 1651 committee.[37] Sitting for forty-eight diets in total, sessions were relatively well attended over all three of the estates. Five of twenty-nine nobles attended between twenty-five and forty diets: the earl of Glencairn (who took on role of president in the first session, replacing Loudoun who had been president in 1651), the earl of Rothes, John Fleming, third earl of Wigtown, James Murray, second earl of Tullibardine and William Crichton, second earl of Dumfries. Of the remaining nobles from 1651, twenty-four did not attend at all. Some of these absences can be explained given that ten had died, seven were heavily in debt and one, the marquis of Argyll, was in prison. The earls of Crawford-Lindsay and Lothian, two notable radicals, stayed away.[38] There was a similar level of absence from the other two estates. Nineteen shire and fourteen burgh commissioners who were members of the 1651 committee of estates were absent. Again, many of these vacancies were caused by the death of the original committee member, the king ordering vacancies to be filled with 'persons . . . who have not by remonstrance or any public act' disclaimed royal authority.[39]

The political intentions of the newly reconvened committee of estates were immediately made clear to those who were in opposition to the restored monarchy. On 23 August 1660, a rival gathering of Protesters convened in Edinburgh and issued a declaration emphasising the obligation of Charles II to the covenant throughout the British Isles and detailing their hostility towards the restoration of episcopacy in England.[40] The committee of estates, in response to the Protesters' declaration, established a sub-committee for the 'dischargeing of all conventions or extra judiciall meitings in any sort within any place of this his majesties kingdome of Scotland, not being authorized by his majesties commission and warrand.' Warrants were immediately issued for the arrest of all those ministers who were found to be present at the rival assembly.[41]

The committee's reaction to the Protester meeting only heightened for some the fear of retribution from the fledgling royalist administration. For those who had aided the republican regimes in any way, the return of the king posed delicate problems. George Maule, lord

Brechin, writing to his father, Patrick Maule, first earl of Panmure, informed him that the committee had been given 'such a large power that thei mey doe what they will with any and so bring under lesh all thei please to pick at.' Even those who were 'forced to give passive obedience' to the English purely for 'selfe preservation' may 'expect little favor of them'. Brechin was undoubtedly concerned, since, despite his family's support of the royalists in the past, they had made their peace with Monck soon after the battle of Dunbar. 'If I see business like to goe wrong', wrote Brechin, 'I mind to see what I may doe.' With arrangements for Scots affairs still relatively unresolved, it seems that many who had co-operated with the English were waiting until their particular position became clear before declaring their loyalties.[42]

Throughout August to December 1660, the committee of estates established a number of sub-committees to deal with a wide scope of business. The most significant dealt with the punishment and imprisonment of Protesters, the banning of unapproved political and religious meetings and the levying of excise and cess. Appointments to these committees were mainly distributed to a number of key personnel, all of whom were amongst the top attendees at the diets. Of the nobility, Wigtown, Rothes and Tullibardine were given the highest number of appointments. Sir Archibald Stirling of Garden, James Foulis of Colinton, Robert Hepburn of Keith, Robert Innes, younger, of that ilk and Robert Nairn of Strathord dominated the shire membership. Of the burghs, Sir Robert Murray of Cameron, Sir Andrew Ramsay of Abbotshall, Archibald Sydserf of Ruchlaw and John Bell of Hamilton Ferme were given the most nominations. A relatively small clique of trusted personnel dominated the committee of estates, with non-commissioned membership (John Bell, representing Glasgow, and Sir George Mackenzie of Tarbat) also securing admittance to this group. In the sessions of parliament that were to follow, these individuals again rose to significant prominence and were to be vitally important in securing royalist dominance.[43]

The majority of the committee's time was spent in ensuring that those who opposed the restored monarchy and the likely outcome of the parliamentary settlement were unable to gain public office or to hold unauthorised meetings. On 24 August, a proclamation was issued to sheriffs of the shires and magistrates of the burghs to ensure that no 'dangerous meitings be permitted'. A further sub-committee was established on 28 August for 'making a list of persons to be cited' who were 'remonstrators or have bine complyers with the enemyes of his majestie and this his ancient kingdome' to be 'summoned to appeare at such dyets as the committie shall appoynt'. On 18 September, a proclamation was issued against Samuel Rutherford's *Lex Rex* and James Guthrie's *The Causes of God's Wrath*, popular covenanter texts, whose purpose, the committee claimed, was to 'corrupt the minds of his majesties loyall subjects, to alienate and withdraw from that duety of love and obedience that they ow unto his sacred persone and greatnesse . . . laying the fundation and seeds of rebellion for the present and future generations.' It required that the two books 'aught not to be read, perused nor keept in the houses or custode of any of his majesties leidges.' An additional proclama-tion on 20 September was made against 'seditious ralliers and slan-derers whither civill or ecclesiastick of the king's majestie and his government.' Any found guilty of such crimes, the committee warned, were to be punished according to the relevant acts of parliament or imprisoned until the authorities saw fit.[44]

As one of his first actions as chancellor, Glencairn had sent a letter to a meeting of the burghs ordaining that

in the inshewing election of magistratis, counsellours and all wther office bearers within burgh . . . no persone or persones who contryvved or sub-scryvet the remonstrance or associatiounes, or concured in the prosecu-tione of ony cours for promoving the ends therof, or protested against any publict judicatories their determinatioune, or ony wtherwayes disaffected to his majesties government, or indeavoured by factioune or seditioune to the disturbance of his majesties peace . . . be admittit to any place of mag-istracy, counsell or ony office of any deaconrie within any burgh.[45]

Another letter from the chancellor to the town councils had previ-ously ordered that magistrates who had held office in 1648 and who had since been dismissed were to be restored to their original posi-tion. The chancellor's instructions suggest that the crown was taking steps to ensure a proven royalist presence in the localities. Combined with the recent action taken by the committee to exclude opposition from offices of public trust, secure royalist personnel was being estab-lished in the localities even before parliament had first convened.

The committee of estates, acting before an indemnity had been issued, was faced with the problem that the majority of the Scottish elite (indeed many of its own present membership) had been guilty of being 'complyers with the enemies of his majesties and this ancient kingdome.' To avoid this delicate issue, the committee indicated to the king in a letter on 30 August its desire to 'abstaine from medling with the lyves, estates or fyning any persone . . . and lykwayes abstein from ceiting those persons your majesties hath bine gratiously pleased to pardon.' The estates resolved not to admit 'any of those to sit [on the committee] whom his majesties hath not pardoned, or any such as hath bine shirrefs and exercised that office under the late usurpers . . . Nor doe wee intend any shall sit who have by remonstrance or any publict act disclaimed his majesties authority.'[46] Only those individuals who had received a special dispensation from the king could take up office. The remainder would be dealt with by parliament under a forthcoming indemnity act.

Despite the committee's forceful action against the more radical supporters of the covenants, the realisation that presbyterian church government secured by the covenanters in the 1640s was under threat seems to have dawned slowly on the Resolutioners. Preoccupied with the fate of their presbyterian brethren in England and jubilant over the subjugation of their Protester rivals, it was not until the late summer of 1660 that James Sharp, trusted with presenting the case of the Resolutioner ministers in London, sent the disturbing news north that the Scots nobles jostling for position at court had veered towards a form of moderate episcopacy as the favoured form of church government. With the recall of the committee of estates, the civil administration had been quickly revived, but no corresponding steps had been taken to settle the ecclesiastical administration of the church through the summoning of a general assembly, despite constant pleas for a new meeting.[47] As a result, the ministers were placed in limbo, left to decipher every scrap of information from London for positive news. Robert Douglas, a prominent Resolutioner who had preached at the coronation of Charles II, wrote in his treatise *A Brief Narration of the Coming In of Prelacie* that Sharp had previously reassured him that 'we needed not doubt the king's favour to our established presbyterial government . . . bishops would be kept in England, but we need not fear episcopall government in Scotland for the king had given assurance to the contrare.'[48] To bear this out, in August, a letter was received from Charles addressed to the presbytery of Edinburgh that was intended to reassure the kirk of the king's commitment to preserve the government of the Church of Scotland.[49] Douglas, however, hinted at division within the ministry over the perceived meaning of the letter. Some argued that it indicated that episcopal government 'was to be the setled government by law' whilst others thought that 'it could have no other meaning yt the present presbyteriall government because it makes mention of good services done to his majestie, and makes mention of the generall assemblie at St Andrews contravened by his majesties commissioners and afterwards by himself.'[50] The letter was probably designed to allay suspicion, but the actions of the committee of estates over the previous three months had already indicated the nature of the parliamentary settlement to come.[51]

The first meeting of Scottish parliament for ten years began on 1 January 1661. Seventy-five nobles, fifty-six commissioners representing thirty-one shires, sixty-one commissioners representing sixty burghs and five officers of state were to sit in session for over six months due to the large amount of governmental and private business which the re-establishment of a monarchical constitution entailed.[52] Elections to the parliament had taken place during late November and December 1660, under close scrutiny from the crown, who were openly controlling elections in certain burghs and shires to ensure that the commissioners returned to parliament were amiable to a strengthening of royal authority. Although a numerical analysis of the membership has revealed that 45 per cent of the nobility, 25 per cent of the shire representatives and 20 per cent of the burgh commissioners had served in previous parliamentary sessions from 1639–51, the vast majority of commissions were given to 'new men', individuals who had no previous experience of serving in parliament.[53]

On 4 January, parliament considered four cases of disputed elections in the shires of Peebles, Dumfries, Elgin and Inverness, all of which were settled in favour of the crown. In the instance of Dumfries it is apparent that the crown openly intervened in the election to ensure a royalist victory. The subsequent parliamentary investigation into the election of James Crichton of St Leonards and Robert Ferguson of Craigdarroch found that Sir William Douglas of Kelhead, convener, had called another meeting to choose rival commissioners after the first had taken place. A number of 'dissatisfied barrons and some others', unhappy with the initial choice of commissioners, had 'removed themselves without voycing' at the first election, and at a second meeting fourteen freeholders subscribed a commission in favour of Alexander Jardine of Applegarth and Robert Dalzell, younger, of Glenae. Papers submitted to parliament in support of the competing commissions show that the main contest was between James Crichton and Alexander Jardine, with objections being directed against Jardine for his past involvement in military action against the king.[54] Legally Jardine's commission should have been preferred since Crichton (whose commission was signed by only seven freeholders) was elected despite being a non-resident who possessed no land in the shire, both of which made him incapable of holding office.[55] Crichton, however, had valuable connections, chiefly that he was brother to William Crichton, earl of Dumfries, himself present in parliament as a member of the nobility and a key member of Middleton's faction. Prior to the election, Crichton had secured a pardon and remission by the king for his 'complyance with the late usurpers', for which, he assured the estates, he was deeply remorseful.[56] When parliament pronounced its verdict on 4 January, Crichton's election was unsurprisingly accepted.[57] The remaining three cases of disputed elections in this crucial session were also settled in the crown's favour.

Unofficial candidates involved in disputed elections who had not been approved by the crown were an obvious risk to the royalists in parliament. According to Mackenzie of Rosehaugh, effective management of elections was secured by the use of gentry in each shire who were favourable to the royalist cause:

> Letters were directed to such a gentleman in every shire as stood best affected to his majesty's service and whom they wisht should be elected as one of the members to serve; and order was given to him for convening the shire, to the end they might choose their commissioners.[58]

Baillie likewise notes that 'the chancellor so guided it that the shyres and burroughs should chose none but those that were absolutely for the king. Divers were cited to the parliament that they might not be members.'[59] Throughout November 1660, Rothes had been courting the burghs to procure political support for Lauderdale and had secured the services of Sir Alexander Wedderburn of Blackness from Dundee, prominent in burghal circles, to promote that cause.[60] Rait argues that 'the delay in the summons of a new parliament was connected with a desire to obtain royal control over the elections.'[61] In England, the situation was broadly similar. Commissions to the 1660 Convention parliament were distributed according to candidates' previous record of allegiance. Borough patrons aggressively controlled corporate seats and the result was, as in Scotland, a relatively young and inexperienced chamber. In the 1661 Cavalier parliament, half of the commissioners who took their seat in the Commons had previously shown sympathy for the royal cause and nearly a quarter had been punished for their former loyalty to the crown.[62]

When parliament first assembled, the prominent Resolutioner Robert Douglas was given leave to preach to the gathered commissioners. In his sermon, Douglas reiterated many of those demands that had troubled the Edinburgh ministry in the previous year: 'Let

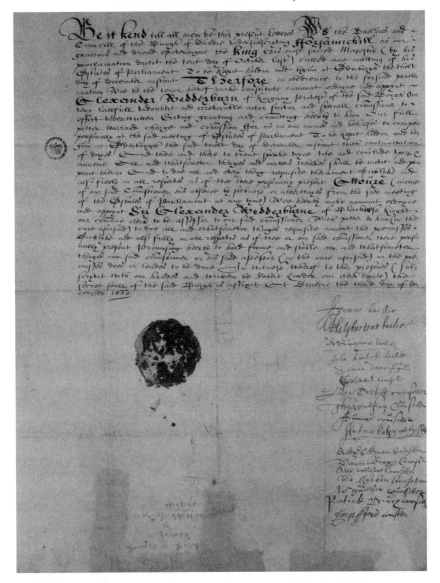

Figure 1.1 *The parliamentary commission to Alexander Wedderburn of Kingennie and Easter Powrie, elected to represent the burgh of Dundee at the first session of the newly restored Scottish parliament in 1661. In case of the original commissioner's 'absence or seekness' from parliament, an alternative representative was often chosen, in this case Sir Alexander Wedderburn of Blackness. The Wedderburn family (originally from Berwickshire) was prominent in Dundee from the fifteenth century, taking an active role in town councils and burgh affairs. (National Archives of Scotland – NAS, PA7/25/56/2.)*

the rubbish of seditions and rebellions wherewith the covenant hath been covered, if not buried, be thrown away', Douglas argued, 'but the covenant be preserved . . . take heed what ye do with the oath of God.' Recognising that many of those in parliament blamed the covenanting revolution on insurgent presbyterian ministers, Douglas appealed for parliament to 'distinguish the time of war from the time of peace, [for] in every civil war there are parties who speak and do things for mutual defence and justification, which would seem very irrational in time of peace.' In his conclusion, by calling for those present to uphold the work of the reformation and maintain a presbyterian church, Douglas presented to parliament the true demands of the Resolutioners. The result, however, was all too familiar, as parliament during the subsequent session went on to disregard Douglas's supplication.[63]

Not all submissions presented to parliament on behalf of the ministry echoed Douglas's opinions. Petitions from Aberdeen, an area that had been extremely hostile to the covenant, considered the uprising against the monarchy an unjust war. John Paterson, in a sermon which was sufficiently to the government's liking to be published, stated that the restrictions placed on the king before he was allowed to exercise his royal power had been unlawful and a 'principle and practice inconsistent with the safety of any nation'.[64] The address of the synod of Aberdeen, signed by the ministers of the region, advised that subjects should 'engage ourselves never to be accessory to any disloyal practice or principle, but declare utter abhorrence thereof . . . obliging our selves to subjection, obedience and submission to the royal authority and commands.' The government of the church, therefore, should be settled in accordance with 'the practice of the ancient primitive church in such a way as may be most consistent with royal authority.'[65] The episcopal sympathies of the north-east were to be later confirmed when two ministers, including John Paterson, were given bishoprics.

After a fulsome speech from the earl of Middleton, in which he urged parliament to condemn the invasions that had been made on the regal authority and to restore the king's prerogative powers, one of the first items of business on the opening day of parliament was the act constituting the chancellor president of parliament.[66] In the absence of the king's commissioner in the 1640s, the post had been seized by the covenanters as a means of ensuring that the estates controlled the house in debate. An elected president did not, however, survive the Restoration. As Baillie observed, 'the parliament's pulse was quickly felt, for when [John Kennedy, sixth earl of] Cassillis moved that the election of a president should be by vote of parliament, the commissioner obtained that the chancellor should preside by virtue of his office, as before it wont to be.'[67]

The chancellor was to be responsible for administering the oath of allegiance, arguably the first measure that would test the mood of parliament. On 4 January, all members were ordered to publicly declare their adherence to the oath and acknowledge 'my said soverane only supream governour of this kingdome over all persons and in all causes'.[68] Although not explicitly mentioning royal authority over ecclesiastical affairs, for some within parliament itself subscribing the oath was tantamount to signing away the independence of the kirk. On its initial reading, supported by a number of other members, the earl of Cassilis immediately asked for an official interpretation of the wording of the oath. Sir John Fletcher, lord advocate, assured the earl that the supremacy applied only to civil proceedings, but refused, as Cassilis suggested, to attach this provision to the oath. Cassilis and a small but vocal group of opponents refused to take the oath and walked out of parliament, thus sidelining themselves from future proceedings.[69] Refusal to sign the oath not only excluded the dissenters from parliament, but from all public offices.[70] Cassilis wrote to Lauderdale of his dismay at withdrawing from his official positions, but he remained steadfastly determined in his refusal to subscribe the oath, even though he would be forced to 'leave his majesties counsels and dominions'. This, he noted, was 'as ill as anie thing Oliver [Cromwell] ever threatened mee with, tho he knew I abhorid him and his way.'[71] It is likely that Cassilis was hoping the king would except him from having to subscribe the oath. Instead, by leaving the chamber voluntarily, those most likely to vote against controversial legislation aimed at reasserting royal authority had actually made life much easier for the commissioner.

The royalists were making full use of the covenanting tradition of oaths to ensure that those who refused to pledge their allegiance to the royalist administration were removed from, or were unable to take up, public office.[72] Further legislation throughout February, which incorporated the constitutional enactments of the past month, declared that all those who refused the oath 'shall not only therby render themselffs uncapable of any publict trust, but be lookt upon as persones disaffected to his majesties authority and government.' Statutes in the second session of parliament concerning a declaration to be signed by all persons in positions of public office stated that employing persons of 'sound principles and entire loyaltie' in all offices of trust and places of public administration would be conducive to the peace of the kingdom.[73] With legislation requiring all of those who had supported the Western Remonstrance to remain ten miles outside Edinburgh for the duration of parliament, along with the ruling that no subjects could convene to determine any matter of state, civil or ecclesiastic, any opposition to the royalists, both in parliament and in the localities, had been severely curtailed.[74]

On 8 January, the lords of the articles were officially revived with only the bare minimum of protest.[75] Recent research has convincingly questioned the long-held assumption that this key committee was merely an instrument of royal power, instead demonstrating that it was often a tool of the estates, reflecting the balance of political power in the nation at large.[76] The notion that there was a long tradition of crown domination of the articles has been shown to have a very short pedigree indeed, being confined almost entirely, and in varying degrees, to developments from around 1584 onwards. James VI tried repeatedly to control the membership of the articles, but it was not until 1621 that he successfully forced his own nominees on an unwilling parliament. In 1633, Charles I's control of the articles (and therefore the preparation of parliamentary business) was such that those members of the estates not on the committee were effectively excluded from any participation in the legislative process. The outrage this caused was one of the main reasons why the covenanter parliaments had dispensed with the committee altogether.[77] It was, however, the 1633 session that the Restoration settlement looked to for inspiration. Thus, on its revival, although the format of the committee differed from that which sat under Charles I, its function was the same: to ensure royal control over debate in parliament.

The membership of the articles consisted of Middleton, who, as king's commissioner, was to preside, the officers of state and twelve from each of the three estates. The method of nomination also differed from previous parliaments. Each estate separately elected its own representatives, who were then personally approved by the commissioner. This ensured that the articles were only staffed with approved royalist personnel. As had been the case in the 1660 meetings of the committee of estates, power was concentrated in the hands of a trusted few. All noble members (except the earl of Dumfries, who was later added to the council), including officers of state, were to be appointed privy councillors, as were eight of the twelve shire commissioners and one burgh commissioner.[78]

The lords of the articles reconstituted in 1661 did not adhere to the conventional tradition of presenting legislation en bloc to the parliament for enactment in one day. Instead, the new committee was to receive all papers, overtures, processes and indictments for weekly preparation prior to being presented to the full parliament and king's commissioner. If the articles did not present an overture, proposal or petition to parliament which had been requested by a member, it could then be presented for consideration to the commissioner and the estates, who met twice per week during the sitting of the articles (or oftener if the commissioner required). Nevertheless, preparation of parliamentary business firmly lay with the articles, who dictated the content of proposed legislation that came before the full parliament.[79]

On the same day the articles were revived, an additional committee was appointed to deal with the large amount of private petitions that were presented to parliament because the justice courts were in abeyance. The commission for bills and trade had a membership of twelve from each estate, thirty-six in total, and throughout the session dealt with various claims for reparations for damages incurred throughout the civil war and interregnum periods.[80] When the court of session was restored, the commission was rendered unnecessary and it was not revived in later sessions of parliament.

The restoration of the royal prerogative began with the 'Act asserting his majesties prerogative in the choise of his officers etc.', passed on 11 January. The legislation declared that before the covenanters had unlawfully taken power, it was an 'inherent priveledge of the croun' to have sole right in choosing personnel. Next, the 'Act for his majesties prerogative in making of lawis' stated that no parliament could lawfully sit without the express warrant of the king, who could summon, prorogue and dissolve a session at will. In a precursor to the rescissory act, no act, sentence or statute passed in an unlawful parliament could thus be binding on the people. The 'Act for his majesties prorogative in the milita', approved on 16 January, completed the reassertion of the prerogative. Under the pain of treason, it was forbidden for subjects to rise in arms or make any treaties amongst themselves, or with foreign powers, without the king's special authority.[81]

As a supplement to these acts, on 22 January, steps were taken to revoke all enactments from the 'pretendit' conventions and parliaments that met under the covenanters. The 'Act annulling the convention of estates [of] 1643' also rescinded any acts ratifying the same. Not explicitly named in this statute, the importance of the

Solemn League and Covenant warranted a separate enactment. Thus, on 25 January, the 'Act concerneing the League and Covenant' stated that the future renewal of the covenant required the king's approval. The legislation stipulated that there was no obligation on the kingdom to endeavour by arms, or any other means, a reformation of religion either in England or Ireland. This proved to be a controversial measure, and to 'shun voting in this, many absented themselves', with a number, including John Elphinstone, third lord Balmerino and James Elphinstone, first lord Coupar absolutely retiring from parliament rather than submitting.[82]

In February 1661, the commission of the privy council was issued. The council was to sit as two different sections, with Lauderdale joined in London by the earl of Clarendon, General Monck (now duke of Albemarle), Edward Montagu, second earl of Manchester and James Butler, first duke of Ormonde. The council sitting in London was to act as an advisory committee on the affairs of Scotland, whilst the privy councillors in Edinburgh dealt with the routine matters of administration. The commission lists thirty-seven nobles and twelve lairds, virtually all of whom were royalists and, with the exception of the earl of Cassilis (who never sat on the council because of his refusal to take the oath of allegiance), had participated in the fight against Cromwell. The majority had sided with the radical regime in the 1640s, but none of the most influential covenanters were included. In July, the privy council finally convened with a membership of thirty-six nobles, fourteen shire and one burgh commissioner. A number of influential radical nobles, including Lothian and Loudoun, were excluded.[83]

In parliament, proceedings were still taken up by the technicalities of rescinding and approving legislation passed during the 1640s. On 9 February, an act approved the Engagement of 1648 as a 'most noble and pious testimony of the loyaltie of his majesties good subjects of his antient kingdome'. An act condemning the delivery of the king to the English in 1647 was put before the chamber on 20 February. In this, parliament acknowledged that there had been a loyal opposition to the sale of the king, whilst many others were 'in the simplicity of their hearts draune along for the tyme'. A minority faction, and not the kingdom of Scotland as a whole, carried out the incident.[84] The act approving the Engagement simultaneously annulled the parliament and committees of 1649. All legislation passed by the radical regime was declared unlawful, and the measure was passed successfully because it was established that all those who had sat in the 1649 session and any of its committees were not to be proceeded against, except those who were to be specified in a future act of indemnity. As much of the legislation from 1649 had dealt with the ministry, it was ordained that no minister or parish who had benefited, for example, from the increase in stipends, or from the sale of church land, was to be punished.[85] This seems to have been a hasty addition to the act, as James Sharp told of how initially 'the augmentations granted by that parliament were the other day in the meeting of the articles voted down, but the commissioner by his negative interposed, and so far the time the ministers may scape that blow.' Noting that 'generally all joyn in bringing contempt upon the ministry', Sharp no doubt had guessed at the hostility of the administration towards his brethren, ironically noting that 'if church government did depend upon the vote of this parliament it would undoubtedly be overturned.' For the time being, however, Middleton had decided to take a more cautious approach in parliament, thus avoiding an open demonstration of his dislike of the ministry.[86]

In order to secure the prerogative powers of the crown, it was necessary to ensure adequate financial backing. This was achieved on 22 March with the 'Act and offer of 40,000 lib. sterline to be payed to the king's majestie yeerly dureing his lifetyme by this kingdome.' The committee of estates had previously agreed this sum in 1660, to be raised by a customs duty and excise on domestic and imported alcohol, and parliament was all too willing to approve this generous grant.[87] The restoration of unfettered royal power was finally completed with the passing of the 'Act rescinding and annulling the pretendit parliaments in the yeers 1640, 1641 etc.' on 28 March. Parliament was to abolish the very legislation that guaranteed not only the legal basis of the presbyterian church system in Scotland, but also that which determined its own standing in the constitution.

The momentous act rescinded as a whole the parliaments of 1640, 1641, 1644, 1645, 1646, 1647 and 1648. Passed after earlier legislation in the session had sorted out the technical points of the Engagement, the rescissory act rescinded all legislation from the 1630s and 1640s that protected the presbyterian church.[88] Another enactment of the same day, the 'Act concerning religion and church government', suspended temporarily the effect of the first act, but promised that the king would settle the government of the church so as to make it 'most agreeable to the word of God, most suteable to monarchicall government and most complying with the publict peace and quyet of the kingdome.'[89]

Middleton's instructions from the king prior to the meeting of the parliament make no mention of such an act being planned, and it seems the commissioner, encouraged by the ease in which the annulling legislation of January and February 1661 had been passed, decided to press ahead with a general repealing act without waiting for royal approval.[90] Certainly the act had caught the majority of the ministers off guard. According to James Sharp, the act had first been suggested in the articles as a joke:

> The account I had was this: that at first it moved by way of ralliery with Crafurd, but after they came to earnest, and, though they waved the determining of it for the time, yet by vote of all the committee saif four it was marked to be takin into consideration before the rysing of this parliament.[91]

Sharp's account is confirmed by Burnet, who tells of how Archibald Primrose, clerk register, suggested a general act 'half in jest', although he was perhaps under direction from Middleton. The commissioner was determined to outdo Lauderdale, who had insisted that the king should proceed with caution over religious matters. The passage of the act would ensure a considerable victory over his rival if the legislation guaranteeing presbyterianism could be repealed without protest. After some discussion, the idea was at first abandoned. 'Yet within a day or two', Burnet continues, 'when they had drunk higher, they resolved to venture on it.' Primrose's draft bill, so badly written it was originally laid aside, was later copied out and introduced to parliament without alteration.[92]

The storm of opposition that greeted the passing of the act proved that Middleton had misjudged the mood of the parliament. Forty individuals, including such prominent figures as Crawford-Lindsay and William Douglas, third duke of Hamilton, are said to have voted against the commissioner, taking particular exception at the annulling of the 1641 parliament which had been legally summoned and attended by Charles I in person. The act displeased not only the radical minority in parliament but also those who had taken part in the Engagement, since that parliament also fell under the same condemnation. When the act was initially introduced into the chamber, the duke of Hamilton immediately voiced concerns that it implicitly condemned all those who had been members of the 1648 parliament. Rather than being unlawful, this session, Hamilton argued, 'had done as much as they could to relieve his late majestie and to establish him upon his throne.' Yet Middleton insisted that the session of 1648 had acted against the king, and he was seconded by the earl of Tullibardine, who told the gathered estates that he had been present at the disputed session and had personally witnessed the passage of the Engagement declaration in support of the covenant. He saw 'nothing they went in for but to set up a covenanted religion'. This argument won the day and the act passed by a majority. Privately, however, there were concerns that those present members of parliament who had attended the Engagement parliament were assigned the blame for past actions. Hamilton, in a private conversation with Glencairn after the passage of the act, insisted that the majority of those present in 1648 had only attempted to 'relieve their king and to restor the kingdoms, and that it was so, some of them had sealed it with ther blood.'[93]

Middleton's risky gamble had richly paid off. Despite harbouring misgivings about the timing and scope of the act, and conveniently overlooking the fact his commissioner had acted independently without royal consent, Charles was delighted with what had been achieved. The earl of Clarendon was so impressed that he demanded the act be published south of the border to serve as a fitting example of how a loyal parliament should behave.[94] The act was greeted with considerably less enthusiasm within the localities. In the church, it became necessary for government interference in meetings of synods to prevent them from making their discontent public. The Resolutioner leader James Wood threatened Middleton with the mob if the act was passed and a number of petitions from various presbyteries were suppressed. Rothes, Glencairn and James Sharp were soon dispatched from Edinburgh to reassure the king in person that any dissent was minor and to persuade Charles that the time was ripe for the return of the bishops. Once again English events were crucial. The Cavalier parliament, meeting in May 1661, set out from the beginning to wreck Charles's programme of toleration of non-conformity regulated by the monarch.[95] The eventual triumph of episcopacy in England encouraged the government to take further action in Scotland.

On 18 June, a proclamation from the king concerning church affairs praised parliament for its work over the session, declaring Charles's desire to 'make good what our parliament have declared in our name as to maters of religion'. In the next session the king would 'imploy our royall authoritie for setling and secureing the government and the administration therof in such a way as may best conduce to the glorie of God', and would encourage 'the exercise of religion' and protect all ministers who refrained from meddling with the government of the church and submitted to royal authority.[96] The extensive prerogative powers that had been restored to the monarchy during the session meant that, without fear of insurrection, it could now be openly stated that episcopacy was to be reintroduced. The parliamentary legislation of the past six months had all but silenced the critics of the crown. Any remaining opposition could safely be disregarded and episcopacy imposed on an unenthusiastic nation.

The first session of the Restoration parliament adjourned on 12 July, and amongst the closing enactments was the king's proclamation concerning the indemnity, which stated that an act was to be passed at the next parliamentary session.[97] Many in parliament had already taken it upon themselves to mete out punishment to those guilty of involvement in the late regimes, undoubtedly for their own financial gains. So much so that on 22 March 1661, Charles was driven to write a letter of complaint to Middleton, protesting about the

> strange cours [which] is taken there with many of those who were appointed to be cited to the parliament. Privat barganes I heare are driven and money receaved from too many who are represented to have been abominable complyers . . . the sole power of pardoning resides in me, and that fines and forfaultures are wholly at my disposall . . . I am cleirly of opinion that pardoning and punishing is to be caryed above boord, and that no privat bargaines are to be driven to make sale of my grace and mercie.[98]

Despite the king's complaints, a delay in the drafting of an indemnity act also worked to the crown's advantage, as fear of royal reprisals for past crimes had undoubtedly made parliament more yielding than it would otherwise have been. The act of adjournment declared that there were to be no new elections in shires or burghs except in cases of death. This was to ensure that the commissioners who had proved amenable to the strengthening of the royal prerogative in the first session were present in the second.[99] Measures passed during the first session had indicated that loyal royalists were to be rewarded, in particular those whose estates had been confiscated. From February to May 1661, eleven forfeitures enacted in 1640s were rescinded, the most notable being that of James Graham, marquis of Montrose and his successors. In addition, on 5 July, an interval committee was appointed to consider the losses and debts of those who had been loyal to the royalist cause.[100]

With the indemnity delayed until the following year, there needed to be some public demonstration of the kingdom's repentance. There was no significant desire for blood within Scotland, but scapegoats were needed and a number of prominent covenanters were singled out for punishment. The marquis of Argyll, who had placed the crown upon the head of Charles II at his coronation in 1651, had been unceremoniously seized in July 1660 while awaiting an audience with the king and shipped to Leith for confinement in Edinburgh Castle. Treason proceedings began against him and Archibald Johnston of Wariston, John Swinton of that ilk and James Guthrie when parliament met in early 1661. The lengthy trials of all four, conducted before parliament, were a farce, the outcome of which was never in doubt. The most able advocates could not be induced to represent Argyll and there was no significant support in the chamber for a stay in his execution.[101] Argyll was beheaded on 27 May 1661; Guthrie met the same fate by hanging on 1 June. Thus the blame for the covenanting revolution was directed at a relatively small number of individuals, with most elites relieved that the bloodletting was to be kept to a minimum.[102]

From the time of King Charles II's restoration to the Scottish throne in May 1660, the Scottish political nation had undergone massive and drastic upheaval. The nobility gradually resumed their traditional role at the head of society, unequivocally welcoming the king back since securing royal favour represented the best means of financially repairing their enervated personal estates. Since General Monck's departure, marking the end of the Interregnum, the nobility, in co-operation with sympathisers from the shires, had sought to control affairs, first by ensuring that the king knew of their demands by sending commissioners to London. They were granted, as they had wished, the recall of the committee of estates from 1651, and this meeting was used as a launch pad for an offensive against their main opponents, the Protesters. By ensuring that the Protesters were given no forum to express their opposition to the crown, when parliament met in January 1661, any opposition had already been silenced. A cooperative chamber was guaranteed through careful control of elections and through the imposition of oaths that removed those who would not pledge allegiance to the monarchy. Apart from a small rump of mainly old covenanters who opposed crown control over parliament, Middleton was faced with very few obstacles to block his radical legislative programme. All innovations introduced in the 1640s were swept away within a matter of days and the stage set for the reintroduction of episcopacy in the ensuing parliamentary sessions, something that looked impossible at the beginning of the Restoration. It seems fair to say that parliament, staffed mainly with 'new men' who had little previous experience of serving in office, overwhelmingly rejected the radical innovations of the civil war period in favour of stability and order under a strong monarchy.

Notes

1 NAS, PA2/24, ff. 97r–v; *RPS*, 1649/1/71.
2 Hutton, *Charles II*, pp. 43–8; Harris, *Restoration*, pp. 104–5; J. R. Jones, *Charles II: Royal Politician* (London, 1987), pp. 19–20; NAS, PA3/2, ff. 21v–22r; *RPS*, M1650/5/38.
3 NAS, PA3/2, f. 203r; *RPS*, M1651/5/11; NAS, PA3/2/12, ff. 213r–215v, 220r–220v, 222r; *RPS*, A1651/5/4–5, A1651/5/7, A1651/5/10; Buckroyd, *Church and State*, pp. 8–9; F. D. Dow, *Cromwellian Scotland* (Edinburgh, 1979), pp. 10–11.
4 John Nicoll, *Diary of public transactions and other occurrences, chiefly in Scotland, from January 1650 to June 1667*, D. Laing (ed.), (Edinburgh, 1836), p. 283.
5 J. Buckroyd, 'The Resolutioners and the Scottish nobility in the early months of 1660', *Studies in Church History*, 12 (1975), pp. 245–6.
6 Dow, *Cromwellian Scotland*, pp. 241–2, 245–8; Hutton, *Charles II*, p. 116; Jones, *Charles II: Royal Politician*, pp. 35–7.
7 C. H. Firth (ed.), *The Clarke Papers*, 4 vols (London, 1901), iv, pp. 78–9; J. Buckroyd, 'Bridging the gap: Scotland 1659–1660', *SHR*, 66 (1987), p. 8.
8 M. D. Young (ed.), *The Parliaments of Scotland: Burgh and Shire Commissioners*, 2 vols (Edinburgh, 1992–3), ii, pp. 664–5.
9 Firth, *The Clarke Papers*, iv, pp. 113–16, 120–1; C. S. Terry (ed.), *The Cromwellian Union: Papers relating to the negotiations for an incorporating union between England and Scotland 1651–1652, with an appendix of papers relating to the negotiations in 1670* (Edinburgh, 1902), pp. xciii–xciv; Dow, *Cromwellian Scotland*, pp. 255–6. Dow's study is the most comprehensive account of events in Scotland from Monck's exit from Scotland in January 1660 to the sitting of parliament in January 1661. For a similarly extensive account of the situation in Ireland, see A. Clarke, *Prelude to Restoration in Ireland: the End of the Commonwealth, 1659–1660* (Cambridge, 1999).
10 Firth, *The Clarke Papers*, iv, p. 115; Thomas McCrie (ed.), *The Life of Mr Robert Blair, minister of St Andrews, containing his autobiography, from 1593 to 1636; with supplement to his life, and continuation of the history of the times to 1680, by his son in law, Mr William Row* (Edinburgh, 1848), p. 340. For an example of the response to Monck's

request, see Glasgow City Archives, Stirling-Maxwell of Pollok Collection, T-PM108/40, 'Reply by the nobility and gentry of Lanarkshire to General Monck's letter to the shires and burghs, November 1659'.

11 R. Baillie, *The letters and journals of Robert Baillie, principal of the University of Glasgow, 1637–1662, edited from the author's manuscripts*, D. Laing (ed.), 3 vols (Edinburgh, 1841–2), iii, p. 446.

12 Firth, *The Clarke Papers*, iv, p. 223.

13 Forty-four replies were eventually received from the burghs around the country. Dow, *Cromwellian Scotland*, p. 255.

14 Dow, *Cromwellian Scotland*, pp. 255–6. Bruce was kinsman to Alexander Bruce, second earl of Kincardine.

15 Firth, *The Clarke Papers*, iv, pp. 190–1.

16 Dow, *Cromwellian Scotland*, pp. 256–7; Buckroyd, 'Bridging the gap: Scotland 1659–1660', pp. 11–12.

17 Nicoll, *Diary*, p. 299; NAS, Papers of the Edmonstone family of Duntreath, GD97/3/150 (RH4/124/1). The address to the localities giving permission to elect shire commissioners was addressed to the 'noblemen, gentillmen and burgesses', despite the nobility being excluded from elections by a number of previous acts of parliament, most significantly 'The kingis majesties declaratioun concerning the voittis of small baronis in parliament' of 29 July 1587. NAS, PA2/13, ff. 145r–v; *RPS*, 1587/7/143.

18 NLS, Dalrymple Mss 3423, 'Sederunt, with an abstract of the proceedings of the noblemen and gentlemen, 2 February 1660', f. 25.

19 NLS, Dalrymple Mss 3423, 'Lords Crawford, Lauderdale and Sinclair to their friends in Scotland', April 1660, ff. 33–4.

20 Buckroyd, 'Bridging the gap: Scotland 1659–1660', p. 13. The shire of Renfrew was in fact supportive of the burgh's stance, and in their instructions to their representative, the earl of Glencairn, ordered him to ensure that Renfrew's economic grievances received a speedy redress. Glencairn, however, gave notice that he would refuse to carry out the instructions. In a letter to Sir George Maxwell of Nether Pollok, he informed him that 'though I needed the act of debitor and creditor als much as other, yet I thought it mor suitable . . . [to act] in the guid of the publick.' Such blatant disregard of shire demands by the nobles that represented them gives further credence to the notion that the nobility had, in effect, hijacked the shire membership. Glasgow City Archives, Stirling-Maxwell of Pollok collection, T-PM108/41, 'Instructions from the noblemen and gentlemen of the shire of Renfrew to William, earl of Glencairn'; T-PM113/872, Glencairn to Sir George Maxwell of Nether Pollok, 28 January 1660.

21 NLS, Dalrymple Mss 3423, ff. 25–6; *Records of the Convention of the Royal Burghs of Scotland, with extracts from other records relating to the*

affairs of the burghs of Scotland, J. D. Marwick (ed.), 4 vols (Edinburgh, 1866–80), iii (1615–76), p. 492; Dow, *Cromwellian Scotland*, p. 259.

22 Dow, *Cromwellian Scotland*, p. 259; NLS, Watson Mss 597, f. 21, 'Instructions to the commissioners of the shires in London'; NLS, Watson Mss 597, f. 50, 'Instructions for the commissioners in London'.

23 Dow, *Cromwellian Scotland*, p. 261; Buckroyd, *Life of James Sharp*, p. 50. On 22 March 1660, two of the commissioners sent to London, the earl of Glencairn and Archibald Stirling of Garden, drafted a letter to Monck asking him to summon a new series of meetings in which the shires and burghs could address the 'manie and daylie growing troubles this nation has long and still does lye under.' The request was ignored. NLS, Watson Mss 597, f. 22.

24 Buckroyd, 'The Resolutioners and the Scottish nobility in the early months of 1660', pp. 247–50; Dow, *Cromwellian Scotland*, p. 262. For the minutes of this meeting, see NLS, Dalrymple Mss 3423, f. 28.

25 NLS, Dalrymple Mss 3423, f. 28. The noble members of the meeting had probably vetted both men. Robert Murray was to become a key figure in the recalled committee of estates, a privy councillor and a prominent member of the ensuing session of parliament. Young (ed.), *Parliaments of Scotland*, ii, p. 524.

26 NLS, Customs Accounts Mss 2263, 'A History of Events, 1635–1661', f. 239; Buckroyd, 'Bridging the gap: Scotland 1659–1660', pp. 20–1; Dow, *Cromwellian Scotland*, pp. 262–3.

27 Harris, *Restoration*, pp. 47–8; Hutton, *Charles II*, pp. 130–1, 134–5, 140; Paul Seaward, *The Restoration* (Basingstoke, 1991), pp. 46, 47–8.

28 Clarke, *Prelude to Restoration in Ireland*, Chs 7–8; Hutton, *Charles II*, pp. 146–9, 173–5; Harris, *Restoration*, pp. 88–95.

29 Young, *Scottish Parliament*, p. 305; NLS, Customs Accounts Mss 2263, 'A History of Events, 1635–1661', f. 240; NLS, Dalrymple Mss 3423, 'Petition of the nobility and gentry of Scotland then at London, July 1660', f. 52; *Lauderdale Papers*, i, pp. 32–3; M. Wood (ed.) *Extracts from the records of the burgh of Edinburgh, 1655–1665* (Edinburgh, 1940), pp. 208–9. At a meeting of the nobility held at the earl of Crawford-Lindsay's house to discuss the proposal of reconvening the 1651 committee, Sir George Mackenzie of Tarbat was the only dissenting voice. Mackenzie, *Memoirs*, pp. 11–12.

30 The Resolutioner minister Robert Baillie of Kilwinning notes in his journal of the period: 'For a commissioner, by our nobles' consent, least strife should be for it, the Lord Middleton, earl of Fettercairn was nominat; who was not very acceptable to many', Baillie, *Letters and Journals*, iii, p. 443.

31 Buckroyd, *Church and State*, p. 20.

32 See, for example, Burnet, *History*; Edward Hyde, earl of Clarendon, *The Life of Edward, Earl of Clarendon . . . written by himself*, 3 vols (1759).

33 O. Airy, 'Lauderdale, 1670–82,' *English Historical Review*, 1, 3 (1886), pp. 445, 469; O. Airy, 'The Lauderdale Mss in the British Museum, 26 vols', *The Quarterly Review*, 57 (1884), p. 439. For a similar disapproving view, see also T. B. Macaulay, *The History of England from the Accession of James II*, 6 vols (London, 1913–5), *passim*.

34 See Mackenzie, *Life and Times of John Maitland, Duke of Lauderdale* for the first attempt at a more balanced view, with limited success. For a much more effective reappraisal of Lauderdale's place in British history, see R. C. Paterson, 'King of Scotland: Lauderdale and the Restoration north of the border', *History Today*, 53, 1 (January 2003), pp. 21–7 and R. C. Paterson, *King Lauderdale: The Corruption of Power* (Edinburgh, 2003). Ronald Hutton's article 'John Maitland, duke of Lauderdale (1616–1682)', in *Oxford Dictionary of National Biography*, 60 vols (Oxford, 2004), vol. 36, pp. 218–25 gives a brief but complete overview of Lauderdale's career and later reputation.

35 Hutton, *Charles II*, pp. 136–7.

36 Burnet, *History*, i, pp. 184–91; Hutton, *Charles II*, p. 137.

37 Young, *Scottish Parliament*, p. 307; NAS, PA11/12, 'Register of the committee of estates, 23 August–13 October 1660', ff. 1r–67r; NAS, PA3/2, ff. 206v–208r; *RPS*, M1651/5/18–19.

38 NAS, PA11/12, ff. 1r–67r; NAS, PA11/13, 'Minutes of the committee of estates, 9 October–8 December 1660', ff. 1r–18v. Of the radical nobility who had been named on the 1651 commission, some did attend (for example, John Kennedy, sixth earl of Cassilis) but Robert Balfour, second lord Balfour of Burleigh was the only radical in frequent attendance at the committee. Amongst the shires, David Beaton of Creich, who had advanced £500 sterling to the government in 1645 to help with the war effort, and Sir James MacDowall of Garthland, active in both the covenanting and Cromwellian regimes, were the most conspicuous absentees. Young (ed.), *Parliaments of Scotland*, i, p. 52 and ii, pp. 450–51.

39 NLS, Dalrymple Mss 3423, 'The king's answer', f. 53.

40 For the text of the declaration, see Wodrow, *Sufferings of the Church of Scotland*, i, pp. 68–71.

41 NAS, PA11/12, ff. 4r–v.

42 NAS, GD45/14/110 (2) Dalhousie Muniments, 'Letter from Lord Brechin to his father concerning news of arrangements for Scotland after the Restoration', 6 July 1660; *Scots Peerage*, vii, p. 21.

43 NAS, PA11/12, ff. 4r, 6r–8r, 19v–20r, 51r; NAS, PA11/13, ff. 2r–v, 6r–v, 9r–10r; Young, *Scottish Parliament*, p. 309.

44 NAS, PA11/12, ff. 5v, 8r, 28v–29r, 32v–34r.

45 *Extracts from the records of the Burgh of Glasgow*, J. D. Marwick and R. Renwick (eds), 6 vols (Edinburgh, 1876–1911), ii, pp. 449–50.

46 NAS, PA11/12, ff. 11v–12v.

47 Cowan, *Scottish Covenanters*, pp. 36–49. For more on Sharp's visit to London to press for the complete restoration of the presbyterian church, see Buckroyd, *Life of James Sharp*, pp. 45–8.

48 Robert Douglas, *A Brief Narration of the Coming In of Prelacie* in NLS, Wodrow Quarto LXIII, f. 110. See also Glasgow University Library, Mss Gen 210, Robert Wodrow's transcription of correspondence principally between James Sharp and Robert Douglas, 1659–61. For an in-depth account of the re-establishment of episcopacy in Scotland, see G. Davies and P. Hardacre, 'The restoration of the Scottish episcopacy, 1660–1661', *The Journal of British Studies*, 1 (1962), pp. 32–51; Buckroyd, 'Bridging the gap: Scotland 1659–1660', pp. 24–5; Buckroyd, *Church and State*, pp. 22–40; and Buckroyd, 'Anti-clericalism in Scotland during the Restoration', pp. 168–71.

49 Jackson, *Restoration Scotland*, pp. 105–6. For a copy of the letter, see Nicoll, *Diary*, p. 299.

50 NLS, Wodrow Quarto LXIII, *A Brief Narration of the Coming In of Prelacie*, f. 111.

51 See Wodrow, *Sufferings of the Church of Scotland*, i, p. 81, who tells of how the letter was designed to 'lull all asleep till matters were ripe for a thorough change'.

52 NAS, PA2/26, ff. 1–3; *RPS*, 1661/1/2.

53 Young, *Scottish Parliament*, pp. 309–10; J. R. Young, 'Seventeenth-century Scottish parliamentary rolls and political factionalism: the experience of the Covenanting movement', *Parliamentary History*, 16, 2 (1997), pp. 162–5.

54 NAS, PA7/25/11/5/2, 'Commissione to the lairds of Apillgirth and Glennae'; NAS, PA7/25/11/5/4, 'Protestation of the freeholders of Nithsdale and Annandale, 20 November 1660'; NAS, PA7/25/11/5/8, 'Reasons humblie offered . . . against a pretendit commission alleged granted in favours of Robert Dalzell, younger, of Glenae and Alexander Jardein of Aplegirth'; NAS, PA7/25/11/5/10, 'Enscriptions against James Crichton why he aught not to be commissionar to the parliament for the shire of Dumfreis'.

55 NAS, PA7/25/11/5/1, parliamentary commission to Crichton and Craigdarroch.

56 NAS, PA7/25/11/5/9, 'Articles to render James Crichtoun incapable of being a member of parliament'; NAS, PA7/9/1/2, 'Ansuers for the commissioners elected for the sheriffdom of Drumfreis to some pretendit reasons given in to the honorable and high court of parliament why the saids commissioners there election is alleged voyd'.

57 NAS, PA3/3, ff. 2r–2v; *RPS*, M1661/1/4. Crichton was later to be chosen as one of five trusted royalist agents employed by Middleton to browbeat other parliamentary commissioners into voting against Lauderdale in the billeting affair. *Lauderdale Papers*, i, p. 111.

58 Mackenzie, *Memoirs*, p. 12.

59 Baillie, *Letters and Journals*, iii, p. 463.

60 *Lauderdale Papers*, i, pp. 37–8; Young, *Scottish Parliament*, p. 310.
    See NAS, GD 90/2/260, 'Scroll Warrant Book of the earl of Rothes,
    1660–70', f. 4r for a list of the persons 'intrusted' by the king for con-
    vening the shires to make election of their commissioners to parliament,
    all prominent royalists.

61 Rait, *Parliaments of Scotland*, p. 76.

62 Paul Seaward, *The Cavalier Parliament and the Reconstruction of the
    Old Regime, 1661–1667* (Cambridge, 1989), pp. 36–8.

63 Robert Douglas, *A sermon preached at the down-sitting of the
    Parliament of Scotland, January 1 1660/1* (Edinburgh?, 1661),
    pp. 20–4; *Lauderdale Papers*, i, p. 61.

64 John Paterson, *Tandem Bona Causa Triumphat, or Scotland's Late
    Misery bewailed, and the Honour and Loyalty of this Ancient Kingdom
    asserted in a Sermon preached before His Majesties High Commissioner,
    and the Honourable Parliament of the Kingdom of Scotland. At
    Edinburgh the 17 day of February 1661* (Edinburgh, 1661), p. 19. For
    more on the contents of Paterson's sermon, see Jackson, *Restoration
    Scotland*, pp. 108–9.

65 Anon., *To His Grace His Majesties High Commissioner and the High
    Court of Parliament, the humble address of the synod of Aberdeen*
    (Aberdeen?, 1661), pp. 2–3.

66 Burnet, *History*, i, p. 207; NAS, PA2/26, f. 6; *RPS*, 1661/1/7.

67 Baillie, *Letters and Journals*, iii, p. 463; O. Airy (ed.), 'Letters
    addressed to the earl of Lauderdale', in *The Camden Miscellany vol.
    VIII* (London, 1883), pp. 2, 4–5.

68 NAS, PA2/26, f. 6; *RPS*, 1661/1/7.

69 The earls of Crawford-Lindsay and Alexander Leslie, third earl of
    Leven, James Elphinstone, first lord Coupar and John Elphinstone,
    third lord Balmerino, son of the prominent covenanter, joined Cassilis
    in his protest. The exact number who dissented is unknown, but of the
    group named, all were former radicals. Balmerino and Coupar left par-
    liament later on in the month. *Lauderdale Papers*, i, pp. 62–3;
    Mackenzie, *Memoirs*, p. 23; Airy (ed), 'Letters addressed to the earl of
    Lauderdale', pp. 6–7; Buckroyd, *Church and State*, p. 29.

70 Cassilis was removed from his positions of justice-general, lord of
    council, session and exchequer. Baillie, *Letters and Journals*, iii,
    pp. 463–4; *Lauderdale Papers*, i, p. 63.

71 NLS, Dalrymple Mss 3423, f. 112. There was more opposition to the
    oath in the localities when it came to be subscribed by the local coun-
    cils. In Dumfries, the majority first refused to sign the oath, although
    some eventually relented. New elections had to be held because two
    bailies and many councillors resigned rather than submit. *Records of*

the Convention of the Royal Burghs of Scotland, iii, (1615–76), p. 545.

72 For more on the use of oaths in Scotland in the Restoration era, see Jackson, *Restoration Scotland*, pp. 67–8, 147–52.

73 NAS, PA2/26, ff. 61–3; *RPS*, 1661/1/88; NAS, PA2/28, ff. 36v–37r; *RPS*, 1662/5/70.

74 NAS, PA2/26, ff. 12–14; *RPS*, 1661/1/22–3; NAS, PA3/3, ff. 4r–v; M1661/1/9–10. As part of this clampdown on independent views, the fledgling broadsheet *Mercurius Caledonius* was effectively suppressed in March 1661 after twelve issues. J. Buckroyd, '*Mercurius Caledonius* and its immediate successors, 1661', *SHR*, 54 (1975), pp. 11–21.

75 Only John Hay, second earl of Tweeddale, seconded by another unnamed person, opposed the revival of the lords of the articles. Burnet, *History*, i, p. 209.

76 R. J. Tanner, 'The lords of the articles before 1540: a reassessment', *SHR*, 79 (2000), pp. 189–212; A. R. MacDonald, 'Deliberative processes in parliament, c.1567–1639: Multicameralism and the lords of the articles', *SHR*, 81 (2002), pp. 23–51; A. J. Mann, 'Inglorious revolution: administrative muddle and constitutional change in the Scottish Parliament of William and Mary', *Parliamentary History*, 22 (2003), pp. 124–30; J. Goodare, 'The Scottish Parliament in its British context, 1603–1707', in H. T. Dickinson and M. Lynch (eds), *The Challenge to Westminster: Sovereignty, Devolution and Independence* (East Linton, 2000), pp. 23–4.

77 MacDonald, 'Deliberative processes in parliament', pp. 41–4, 47–9.

78 NAS, PA2/26, ff. 8–10; *RPS*, 1661/1/13; Rait, *Parliaments of Scotland*, pp. 380–1; *RPCS*, third series, i, pp. 1–4.

79 NAS, PA2/26, ff. 8–10; *RPS*, 1661/1/13.

80 Rait, *Parliaments of Scotland*, pp. 384–5; Mackenzie, *Memoirs*, p. 21; NAS, PA2/26, ff. 8–10; *RPS*, 1661/1/13. For the surviving reports of the commission, see NAS, PA6/16, collated in date order, or *RPS*, A1661/1/7, 9–14, 17–19, 23, 25–6, 28–9, 34–5, 37–40, 43–5, 52–3, 55–7, 87, 94–5.

81 NAS, PA2/26, ff. 10–11, 14; *RPS*, 1661/1/16–17, 1661/1/24.

82 NAS, PA2/26, ff. 18, 21; *RPS*, 1661/1/32, 1661/1/36; Mackenzie, *Memoirs*, p. 23.

83 *RPCS*, third series, i, pp. i–xx, 1–4; Young, *Scottish Parliament*, p. 313.

84 NAS, PA2/26, ff. 38–42, 46–7; *RPS*, 1661/1/67, 1661/1/74.

85 NAS, PA2/26, ff. 38–42; *RPS*, 1661/1/67.

86 *Lauderdale Papers*, i, p. 72; Buckroyd, *Church and State*, pp. 30–55.

87 NAS, PA2/26, f. 112; *RPS*, 1661/1/144; Young, *Scottish Parliament*, p. 316. Shortly after the Restoration, William Cochrane, lord Cochrane (later first earl of Dundonald) obtained an audience with the king, and suggested that the government was in a position to acquire an annuity

of £40,000 sterling. The committee of estates was given permission to commence collection until parliament met. Mackenzie, *Memoirs*, p. 18.

88 NAS, PA2/26, ff. 124–6; *RPS*, 1661/1/158.

89 NAS, PA2/26, ff. 126–7; *RPS*, 1661/1/159. In a letter to Primrose, Middleton admitted that the crown needed the legislation to be pushed through without debate: 'The act that is now before you is of the greatest consequence imaginable and is like to meet with many difficulties if not speedily gone about. Petitions are preparing and if the thing were done, it would dash all these bustling oppositions.' NLS, Wodrow Octavo XI, f. 42.

90 *Lauderdale Papers*, i, pp. 39–40; Hutton, *Charles II*, pp. 161–2; Jackson, *Restoration Scotland*, p. 107.

91 *Lauderdale Papers*, i, pp. 76–7. Sir John Gilmour of Craigmillar, Sir Peter Wedderburn of Gosford and another unknown (possibly Sir James Lockhart of Lee) were the other members within the articles who sided with Crawford-Lindsay against the act. McCrie (ed.), *Life of Mr Robert Blair*, p. 378.

92 Burnet, *History*, i, pp. 213–15; Buckroyd, *Church and State*, p. 34.

93 NAS, Hamilton Papers, GD406/2/M9/148, 'Memorandum concerning the parliament 1661'; Burnet, *History*, i, pp. 215–16; Mackenzie, *Memoirs*, pp. 28–9.

94 Lee, 'Government and politics in Scotland, 1661–1681', pp. 20–3; Hutton, *Charles II*, pp. 161–2, 178.

95 Buckroyd, *Church and State*, pp. 34–7; Davies and Hardacre, 'The restoration of the Scottish episcopacy', p. 45; Burnet, *History*, i, p. 217; Hutton, *Charles II*, pp. 178–80.

96 NAS, PA2/27, ff. 37v–38r; *RPS*, 1661/1/362.

97 NAS, PA2/27, ff. 99v–100r; *RPS*, 1661/1/471.

98 *Lauderdale Papers*, i, pp. 92–3.

99 NAS, GA12/05, printed acts of parliament (1661), p.118; *RPS*, 1661/1/497; Young, *Scottish Parliament*, p. 318.

100 NAS, PA2/26, ff. 37–8; *RPS*, 1661/1/66; NAS, PA2/27, ff. 57r–v; *RPS*, 1661/1/405; Buckroyd, *Church and State*, p. 40; Young, *Scottish Parliament*, p. 316.

101 NAS, PA2/26, f. 35; *RPS*, 1661/1/64; NAS, PA3/3, f. 24v; *RPS*, M1661/1/73; NAS, PA6/16, collated in date order; *RPS*, A1661/1/15, A1661/1/67–9, A1661/1/71–2, A1661/1/81–2, A1661/1/86, A1661/1/90, A1661/1/98; *Lauderdale Papers*, i, p. 72; Hutton, *Charles II*, p. 171.

102 Baillie, *Letters and Journals*, iii, p. 467; Lee, 'Government and politics in Scotland, 1661–1681', pp. 17, 23–4.

Chapter 2

OSTRACISM BY BALLOT: PARLIAMENTARY INTRIGUE AND FACTION, 1662–3

Soon after the first session of parliament had risen, on 14 August 1661, Charles wrote to the privy council in Edinburgh declaring that the form of church government practised in Scotland during the past twenty-three years was unsuited to monarchical authority and in violation of the royal prerogative. For better stability, unity and order within the kirk, and to bring Scotland into harmony with the churches of England and Ireland, bishops were to be immediately restored. The privy council made proclamation of the fact on 6 September, assuring the king in an accompanying letter that they would keep 'a watchfull eye' for any public displays of dissent.[1] The wary councillors need not have worried. The confirmation of the return of episcopacy surprised no one given the proceedings of the first session of parliament and the initial announcement seems to have been greeted with little more than sullen resignation. Charles now sought to recruit the leading presbyterian clergy as bishops, since their acceptance of episcopacy would prove an ideal symbol of reunification in the troubled kirk. In this task the king and his ministers were much less successful. The mere existence of bishops proved to be unacceptable to a significant number of presbyterians who chose rather to remain outside the re-established episcopal church. Whether the crown would long tolerate such dissent remained to be seen.

Notably unenthusiastic in the discussions regarding the revival of episcopacy in the summer of 1661, Lauderdale had also expressed doubts that many of the Resolutioner ministers could be persuaded to accept bishoprics.[2] Indeed, by October 1661, James Sharp had only succeeded in recruiting Andrew Fairfoul and James Hamilton as the bishops of Glasgow and Galloway respectively, both minor figures in the Resolutioner ranks who appear to have secured position because of their connections to prominent nobles or favour with the king rather than through merit. But despite opposition from hard-liners like Robert Douglas, who dismissed the offer of a bishopric from Sharp with 'the curse of God [on him] . . . for his treacherous dealings', in December 1661 the first four bishops were consecrated: Sharp, Fairfoul, Hamilton and Robert Leighton, principal of Edinburgh University, again another candidate with little influence in the Resolutioner ranks to commend him.[3]

The new bishops at their ordination declared their intentions to be agents of reconciliation in the church in Scotland. The next appointments, however, did nothing but antagonise the supporters of a presbyterian church. Thomas Sydserf, the only surviving bishop from the pre-covenant church, was rewarded for his long devotion with the bishopric of Orkney. David Mitchell, now named bishop of Aberdeen, and George Wishart, chosen as bishop of Edinburgh, had both been condemned as heretics for their refusal to sign the covenant. A further seven appointments completed the episcopate: John Paterson, bishop of Ross, Patrick Forbes, bishop of Caithness (both from anti-covenant Aberdeen), George Haliburton, bishop of Dunkeld, Robert Wallace, bishop of the Isles, Murdo Mackenzie, bishop of Moray, David Strachan, bishop of Brechin and David Fletcher, bishop of Argyll. With the sole exception of Sharp, not one of the nominees had played any distinguished part in the history of the kirk since 1638.[4] Thus it is difficult to see these appointments as anything but an attempt by the royalists to increase their grasp of power. Church rule by bishops was favoured because it would act as a controlling influence in the localities and the bishops' influence as first estate in parliament would also be vital to the crown for controlling the chamber. However, the reconciliation of disparate elements within the kirk, much talked of by the king and supported by Lauderdale and others in the summer of 1661, had failed miserably. Without the moderating influence of the Resolutioners as part of the episcopate, Middleton was free to press ahead with a ferocious campaign aimed at rooting out dissent and non-conformity both within the localities and inside the parliamentary chamber itself.

The Scottish parliament reconvened for its second session on 8 May 1662. Attendance levels for both the nobility and the shire commissioners remained relatively static when compared to the first session, with seventy-four nobles and forty-seven commissioners representing thirty shires recorded in the rolls. Burgh attendance, however, dropped dramatically, from sixty-one commissioners present in 1661 to thirty-nine in 1662, prompting an act on the second day of the session fining members for their absence.[5] The majority of burghs who sent no representative were situated in the north, indicating that the geographical distance to Edinburgh may provide an explanation for the non-attendance of commissioners from these areas. Certainly the burghs, more so than the wealthier shires, struggled in financial terms to fund the expenses of their commissioners. In 1661, Mr George Dunbar of Castlefield, representing Cullen, was granted 30 shillings Scots a day for his parliamentary expenses, a sum that may have become too uneconomical to maintain in the long term, especially as the first session sat for a full six months.[6]

Widespread hostility to the legislative programme of the second session of parliament can almost certainly be ruled out as a cause of low attendance. Most absent members were still active in their localities, indicating that they had taken all the necessary oaths to occupy offices of public trust. Only two absentees came under censure from the crown and were excepted from the indemnity act passed later in the session. John Ewart of Mulloch, present for Kirkcudbright in 1661 and fined £360 under the act, was a somewhat prolific offender in the eyes of the government, being refused office as provost in 1662, blamed for riots in Kirkcudbright in 1663, imprisoned for a time in the tolbooth of Edinburgh, before being finally condemned to banishment in 1663 (this sentence was later mitigated). Also fined the sum of £3,600 was Sir Archibald Douglas of Cavers, elected for Roxburghshire in the first session, who had been active under both the covenanting and Cromwellian regimes. One other absent burgh commissioner, Alan Dunlop of Craig, returned for Irvine in 1661, was on trial for his involvement in a raid on James Douglas, second earl of Queensberry's lands in 1650.[7]

Crown support in parliament was boosted when the fourteen bishops were invited to resume their ancient place as first estate in parliament by an act passed on the opening day of the session, and nine bishops were immediately added to the membership of the lords of the articles without election. Episcopacy was formally restored on 27 May with the 'Act for the restitution and re-establishment of the antient government of the church by archbishops and bishops', which returned to the bishops the rights they had enjoyed in 1637 in relation to their position within the church, their jurisdictions and properties. The act explicitly declared that the 'ordering and disposall of the externall government and policie of the church doth propperlie belong unto his majestie as ane inherent right of the croun', and soon Middleton was making full use of these powers by bringing before parliament a number of other controversial measures concerning the church.[8] On 11 June, an enactment (possibly brought in at the behest of Middleton himself, not being mentioned in his instructions from the king) required ministers admitted since 1649 to obtain not only a presentation from their patron but also confirmation of this presentation from their respective bishop in order to collect their stipends.[9] On the same day, a similarly contentious act declared that all ministers who refused to obey an order of the 1661 session for services of thanksgiving and commemoration of Charles II's birthday and return from exile (both on 29 May) would lose their benefices unless they sought repentance before the archbishop or bishop of the diocese in which they lived.[10]

The effects of these acts, although not immediate, were far-reaching. By 1663, around 270 ministers had been deprived of their livings as a direct result of the legislation, representing some 25 to 30 per cent of the total. Disproportionately, most were concentrated in the covenanting heartland of the south-west. Galloway was particularly badly affected, with thirty-four of its thirty-seven ministers resigning or being ejected rather than accept rule by bishops. In the largest synod of Glasgow and Ayr, only thirty-five ministers remained from a total of 130.[11] Overwhelmed by the unexpected desertion of so many parishes, a search for suitable replacements was undertaken in earnest by Sharp but, predictably, met with no great success. Ministers from the conservative north who had failed to obtain position within their own localities ('the dreg and refuse of the northern parts', as Burnet put it) were induced to take up many of the vacant charges.[12] In response, their new parishioners simply stayed away from church services altogether, leading to the rapid growth of illegal house assemblies and field conventicles, occasionally approaching attendances numbering in the thousands.[13] The increase in such unauthorised large-scale gatherings, and their resulting threat to public order, were to prove altogether more troublesome a prospect for the royalist administration than any number of non-conforming ministers.

Additional legislation for removing from public office any remaining opponents to the crown was next to come before parliament. On 24 June, the 'Act for preservation of his majesties person, authoritie and government' condemned the National Covenant, the Solemn League and Covenant and the general activities of the covenanters during the 1640s as rebellious and treasonable. Subjects had no obligation to keep to these oaths or to uphold the actions of the general assembly held in Glasgow in 1638. Any opposition to 'his majesties royall prerogative and supremacie in causes ecclesiastick or of the government of the church by archbishops and bishops as it is now setled by law' was expressly forbidden.[14] As presbyterian ideologues had provided justification for the constitutional limitations imposed on the crown in the 1640s, it was now episcopal government that was to serve as a bastion for the defence of monarchical authority.[15]

To further strengthen royal authority, yet another oath to be signed by those in positions of public trust was put before parliament on 5 September. Based on the text of the act of 24 June condemning the covenants, the declaration was to be imposed on all office-holders, including those who already held position.[16] The Corporation Act, passed by the English parliament in December 1661, clearly provided inspiration for the Scottish act, also excluding from local government those who refused to subscribe a declaration against the Solemn League and Covenant, with a second oath against the principal of resistance to the king. These same measures were enacted against the clergy in the Uniformity Act of the following year.[17]

As in Scotland, the measures passed by the Commons were intended to eliminate grassroots dissent and ensure local allegiance to the crown. However, the English legislation was much less draconian than the Scottish equivalent. Forced to water down the initial draft in the face of widespread opposition, the Corporation Act was significantly more limited in scope than that originally intended by the king. Crown appointed commissioners were granted wide powers to purge corporations of known or potential dissenters, but they had to act within a limited time. In addition, each group of commissioners operated autonomously, following their own judgement of the local situation, with wide variations in practice resulting. A lack of suitable replacements and the tendency of the displaced to find their way back into power ultimately reduced the act's effectiveness.[18] North of the border, there was little opportunity for such compromise. Subscription of the various oaths was mandatory for all kinds of public office, however minor. Effectively the entire political nation was to be bound to the person of the king. In the 1640s, the subscription of the National Covenant had been a prerequisite for the exercise of civil power; in 1662, this situation had been reversed, with the imposition of oaths instead demonstrating adherence to royal authority.

By September 1662, having successfully overseen the passage of a whole series of legislation aimed at rooting out dissent within the church and local government, Middleton now turned his attention to the tricky problem of how to exclude his remaining rivals from office, thus removing the last barrier to his total domination of Scottish government. Since late 1660, the earls of Middleton and Lauderdale had been battling to secure the position of the king's favourite. Charles had certainly been impressed with the legislative programme enacted in the first session of parliament, delighted to find his royal prerogative extended far beyond what even the most fervent royalist could have wished for at the outset of the Restoration. Yet Middleton, the architect of this transformation in kingly power, increasingly found himself isolated in Edinburgh. The commissioner had already once been forced to send Glencairn and Rothes to court to reassure the king that he had been acting in the royal interest by proceeding with the rescissory act against instructions: Lauderdale had been implying otherwise.[19] Residing at Whitehall, the secretary had, in Middleton's eyes, a dangerous advantage. A fairly consistent opponent of the commissioner's policy in the section of the Scottish privy council which met in London, Lauderdale had opposed both the manner in which episcopacy had been revived and had spoken out at the proposed use of indemnity fines to bolster the crown's income.[20] It had so far proved fortunate that both these schemes had met with the king's approval, but, nevertheless, continued criticism of Middleton's ministry in Charles's presence could no longer be tolerated.

Like so many of his contemporaries, the earl of Lauderdale had played a significant role in the government of Scotland under the covenanters, although he had languished in prison throughout the 1650s for his loyalty to the exiled king. Since an indemnity act had not yet been passed by parliament, no one had yet been formally punished for involvement in the previous regimes. Thus, amongst many prominent individuals there remained a degree of nervousness over the exceptions from the act, although few expected the king's appointed ministers to be directly implicated in the covenanting rebellion. Middleton, however, viewed the indemnity act as a useful tool not only to purge public offices of former radicals, but also the perfect opportunity to remove his political rivals from their positions.

The declaration to be imposed on those holding positions of public trust, condemning the covenanters and their actions, was the first step in a campaign engineered by Middleton and his supporters to dislodge Lauderdale and his allies from office. The influence of the secretary and others such as the earl of Crawford-Lindsay, treasurer, and Sir Robert Moray, justice clerk, on the king made the group an obvious target if Middleton wished to strengthen his position at court. There had already been some prominent casualties amongst the secretary's allies: Cassilis, forced into early retirement in 1661; Archibald Campbell, lord Lorne, charged before parliament with the

Figure 2.1 *John Middleton, first earl of Middleton (c.1608–74) by David Scougal (active 1654–77). A distinguished soldier in the civil war period, Middleton gained royal favour by an abortive rising in support of the monarchy in the 1650s. On Charles II's restoration in 1660, he was rewarded with the position of king's commissioner to the first meeting of the Scottish parliament in over ten years. He was eventually dismissed in 1663 after an attempt to exclude his political rivals from office spectacularly backfired.*
(In the collection of Glamis Castle.)

crime of lease-making, at the express opposition of the secretary; and the earl of Tweeddale, later linked to the Maitland family through the marriage of his son to Lauderdale's daughter, imprisoned on a spurious charge of objecting to the execution of James Guthrie. One by one

Lauderdale's old friends were being ostracised.[21] Middleton believed that Lauderdale, long suspected by his enemies of harbouring private presbyterian sympathies, would consider the text of the oath too extreme in its condemnation of the covenants, but it soon became apparent that the secretary would, if necessary, take the declaration to keep his place. Yet, in spite of this setback, Middleton's scheme met with some early success. Crawford-Lindsay, one of the original covenanters who had formed a close bond with Lauderdale during their imprisonment at the time of the Cromwellian occupation and the only close ally of the secretary with political office in Scotland, declined to take the oath. His refusal made him relatively easy to remove, the king obeying the new law and dismissing his treasurer from office.[22] Although frustrated that Lauderdale had thwarted his initial attempt to secure his resignation, Middleton remained determined to oust his great rival from office. A more devious means of attack was clearly necessary. The secretary's closeness to the king meant that Middleton had to find a means of making Lauderdale's position untenable; his former involvement in the covenanting rebellion would be the perfect weapon.

When it became evident that Lauderdale had no qualms about subscribing the declaration, Middleton devised what he regarded as a masterpiece of policy. Making full use of his control over the drafting of legislation, to the indemnity act would be added a clause for incapacitating from public trust twelve individuals, to be chosen in parliament by a secret ballot. The draft would be sent to the king with the assurance that this was the wish of the estates of parliament; conversely, parliament would be told that this innovation was at the desire of the king. Charles had demanded to see the draft version of the act of indemnity before it was put before parliament to give it his final approval.[23] Knowing that this would give Lauderdale forewarning of the controversial clause on incapacitating those who were to be fined, Middleton, in an inspired piece of political scheming, sent Sir George Mackenzie of Tarbat in the summer of 1662 to London with two copies of the draft act. Lauderdale's copy conveniently failed to include the clause on exclusion, mentioning only that those who were named were to be fined. Despite Middleton's best efforts, Lauderdale soon discovered that the king had been supplied with a different copy of the act, his including the controversial exemption clause. Despite reassurances from Tarbat that 'parliament intended only to incapacitate a small number of the most guilty', Lauderdale immediately protested how 'heinous a punishment incapacitating was, a punishment worse than death'. Lauderdale had probably learnt by now from his correspondents in Scotland the likelihood of him being named by parliament, thus he attempted to persuade the king of the immorality of billeting as a method of punishment, given that the historical precedent of ostracism was the 'oystershell billeting' practised by the Athenians, 'who were governed by that cursed sovereign lord the people'. 'Any man's honour, his life, his posterity may be destroyed without the trouble of calling him, hearing his answer, nay without the trouble of accusing him . . . this is a stranger engine than white gunpowder, which some fancy, for sure this shoots without any noise at all,' remonstrated the secretary.[24] Along with Crawford-Lindsay, Lauderdale sent an appeal to the king desiring that those named should at least be punished legally, as those named by ballot were condemned in an entirely arbitrary manner. But Charles supported the measure, signed the draft act and agreed to grant warrant to except those whom parliament named, unaware that office bearers might be included.[25]

Middleton's instructions for the second session of parliament concerned only the act of indemnity and those who were to be excepted from it. The king had agreed in January 1662 that former kirk party leaders, Protesters and collaborators with Cromwell could be fined a maximum of one year's rent and the proceeds used to compensate loyal royalists for their wartime losses. Middleton and his supporters were, of course, prominent beneficiaries of the scheme. Yet this did not go far enough to satisfy a pervasive thirst for revenge amongst certain impoverished nobles, thus necessitating the need for the additional clause for punishing the most pernicious offenders and those who had been most active in the late rebellion.[26]

The idea of incapacitating certain individuals by a secret ballot seems to have been first formally proposed by Sir George Mackenzie of Tarbat in the commission of fines, a committee set up prior to the meeting of parliament in order to deal with the vast amount of preparation necessary before a final indemnity act could be presented to the estates for their approval.[27] Joining Tarbat on the committee were the earl of Rothes, James Graham, second marquis of Montrose, John Hamilton, fourth earl of Haddington, James Livingstone, first earl of Callander, Sir Alexander Falconer, first lord Falconer of Halkerton, Sir John Gilmour of Craigmillar, president of the court of session, Archibald Stirling of Garden, Sir John Scougall of Whitekirk, both senators of the college of justice, and John Bell of Hamilton Ferme, provost of Glasgow. Its remit was to collate the names of those to be excepted from the indemnity and calculate the proportions of their fines.[28] It is interesting to note that this committee was not exclusively staffed with Middleton's supporters; indeed, only Tarbat and John Bell can be identified as being part of Middleton's faction.

The motion for holding a secret ballot was at first rejected, but 'when it was better prepared' it appeared before the articles. Although again meeting with opposition when Middleton spoke for the idea, 'it was believed that he had good warrant for it' and so the proposal was passed onto the full parliament.[29] The anonymous vote in parliament to compile a list of those to be excepted from a future indemnity took place on 9 September. Each member was given a slip of paper, or billet, on which they were to write the names of up to twelve people. Prior to the voting, in order to assist the estates with their difficult task, Middleton distributed his own voting slip, making no secret that if others went with his suggestions they would be performing the king's service. Contemporary reports also allude to a pre-prepared list of names read out in parliament by James Livingstone, first earl of Newburgh containing the individuals he had voted against.[30] Meetings were 'kept at Masterton's tavern and elsewhere for carrying that which was called the right list.'[31] In parliament, 'agents' of Middleton were set to work, publicising the names to be billeted, engaging 'all friends, relations, interests and dependents . . . to follow their good example . . . not sparing to tell some that this wes the commessioner's list and would now be a test of their honestie to doe in this what wes so comanded.'[32] John Bell, provost of Glasgow, attended a meeting of the burghs and offered pre-prepared billets to several members. Mungo Murray, brother to the earl of Atholl, performed a similar duty at a meeting of shire commissioners.[33] As a direct result of such intrigue, Lauderdale and Sir Robert Moray were included on the final list of twelve selected by the estates, although 'some were ashamed to mention' them, 'bot many did it in heat and too many through fear'. Others, such as Archbishop James Sharp, gave in blank billets rather than risk the wrath of either faction.[34] The suggestion circulated by Middleton that the king had grown weary of Lauderdale had an obvious effect on the voting, as did the bribing and cajoling of members. Eager to please, parliament accepted the suggestion that Charles was dissatisfied with his Scottish secretary.[35]

When the votes of the estates had been cast and counted, Lauderdale found himself overwhelmingly excepted by eighty-two votes. Sir Robert Moray was also chosen by a large majority, although the exact voting figures in his case are unknown. Different sources give a contradictory account of the fate of the secretary's other allies. According to Burnet and Rosehaugh, Crawford-Lindsay was also named, although letters directed to Lauderdale state that he, along with Tweeddale, narrowly avoided being included as one of the final twelve.[36] The result of the vote was to be kept secret from parliament until Charles Stewart, sixth duke of Lennox, the earl of Dumfries and Tarbat, sent immediately to London with the draft act, had secured the king's signature of approval. However, barely hours after the vote had been held, a letter was on its way south to Lauderdale from William Sharp, his agent in Edinburgh, containing the startling news. Sharp seems to have been fed information from his brother James, archbishop of St Andrews, one of the nine scrutinisers who were entrusted with counting the votes.[37] Some three days before Middleton's cronies reached court, Lauderdale, supplied with a running commentary of events in Edinburgh by Sharp, relayed to the king the result of the ballot.[38]

Lauderdale knew exactly how to appeal to the king, letting Charles imagine that it was he who took the initiative in Scottish affairs. Lauderdale delighted in pointing out that 'the commissioner had not so much as ask'd his majesty's advice in pulling his servants from him.' Was this not an encroachment on the king's prerogative powers, he argued? Was it not also a blatant and deliberate deceit of both the king and parliament? Charles wholeheartedly agreed, and, 'highly offended' at the outcome of the vote, he immediately renounced the decision. Imagining the ballot would be used to punish unruly presbyterians, an attack on trusted, appointed servants was unwarrantable.[39] When Middleton's messengers arrived with the draft containing the result of the ballot, Charles threw the act, unopened, into his cabinet. Telling them that they were either drunk or insane to attempt such a scheme, Dumfries and Tarbat were 'severely check'd . . . for their rashness in billeting . . . his majesty's present servants' and told to depart immediately for Scotland. Middleton was to remain there for the meantime, the king instead summoning to court the earl of Rothes to give him an account of events in parliament, who had been careful to remain aloof from the whole affair. The influence and support of Clarendon temporarily ensured that Middleton kept his place as king's commissioner, though this was not expected to last indefinitely.[40]

Middleton was eventually summoned to London in February 1663 to defend his actions before the king. At a packed meeting of the Scots council at Worcester House, Lauderdale drew out with great skill each step of the fraud committed upon the king and parliament. Middleton's response was both evasive and unconvincing. In answer to the charge that he had passed legislation without the king's knowledge, Middleton maintained that it was impossible to send draft acts to the king before they were presented to the estates and had received parliamentary assent. Arguing that his commission was 'full and unlimited' and allowed him to exercise 'sovereign power', Middleton stressed that he had only consented to billeting and was not the contriver of it. At all times he believed he was acting in the royal interest. The king appeared reluctant to make any formal decision regarding his commissioner's fate and the meeting adjourned without any action being taken. Barely a few weeks later, however, Middleton hastened his own political demise by yet another disastrous miscalculation that gave new substance to Lauderdale's litany of charges.[41]

In spite of the furore surrounding the billeting affair and exclusion clause, parliament had approved the indemnity act on 9 September 1662 without much fuss. A total of 896 people were named in the accompanying 'Act containing some exceptions from the act of indemnitie', only a handful of which were actually sitting in parliament, and fines varied greatly, to a maximum of one year's rent.[42] Because of a delay in calculating the proportions of the fines, Charles only received the final list of those to be excepted in January 1663. Whilst he took time to consider the complete act, he ordered the privy council to suspend the first term's payment of the fines. Yet, a few weeks later, in a further act of folly, Middleton instructed the council to begin collection, assuring them he had discussed this issue in person with the king, who had now decided to reverse his earlier decision. The council sent a dispatch to London seeking clarification, only to find that the king knew nothing of the second order. Operating behind the king's back was intolerable and Middleton's refusal to implement the royal proclamation provided a legitimate excuse for his dismissal. In May 1663, he was forced to resign his commissionership, and, effectively banished, he retired to England to resume a minor military career.[43]

There were to be relatively few other casualties amongst Middleton's allies in the aftermath of his resignation. Tarbat was dismissed as a lord of session and exchequer, and Sir John Fletcher, lord advocate, was likewise removed from office, as much in reaction to allegations of corruption as for his links to Middleton's faction. Glencairn, perhaps the fallen earl's greatest supporter, was retained as chancellor, with most of the other co-conspirators escaping public censure.[44] Indeed, apart from forcing Middleton into political obscurity, the billeting affair had little real long-term impact on either personnel or policy within Scotland. Those who had opposed Middleton in the first two sessions of parliament – Cassilis, Crawford-Lindsay and Balmerino – were not to be reinstated, nor was there to be any radical change in government policy.[45] If anything, when Lauderdale and Rothes arrived in Edinburgh in the summer of 1663 for a third session of parliament, Middleton's work in strengthening the powers of the crown and episcopal kirk was continued and augmented, not reversed.

Parliament met for a third session on 18 June 1663, with a respectable turnout of ten bishops, seventy nobles and forty-eight commissioners representing twenty-eight shires. Although attendance of the other three estates was down slightly on the sessions of 1661 and 1662, burgh attendance rose to forty-two commissioners representing forty-one burghs, perhaps in reaction to the 1662 act fining absent members.[46] The earl of Rothes took on Middleton's role as commissioner, but it was Lauderdale who was the architect of much of the legislation, using his trusted friend Sir Robert Moray at court to liaise directly with the king.[47]

After a sermon from Alexander Burnet, bishop of Aberdeen, the first legislative measure of the session was the 'Act concerning the constitution and election of the lords of the articles'. The committee was now modified to include the bishops, and a reformed method of election made the articles as stringent as it had been under Charles I. Reverting to the 'ancient' method of election (in fact this dated only from 1633), the clergy first chose eight noblemen, the nobility then chose eight bishops, and these sixteen selected eight shire commissioners and eight burgesses. The list was then shown to the king's commissioner for approval, who, if satisfied with the choices made, then added the officers of state. The chancellor was ordered to preside in all meetings.[48] Since the bishops chose first, and they themselves held position purely at the king's pleasure, theoretically the entire membership could reflect the monarch's wishes. This was rarely the case, but the revived method of election ensured that the majority of the committee would consist of those who were well disposed to royal policy.

The change of personnel in parliament from Middleton as king's commissioner to Rothes was reflected in the membership of the articles. The former commissioner's ally the earl of Dumfries was absent from the new committee, as were Tarbat, Sir John Urquhart of Cromarty and John Bell for the burgh of Glasgow. However, the eight

clergy provided enough leverage on the other estates to resist inter-
fering further in the membership of the committee. Lauderdale could
confidently boast to the king that 'nothing can come to the parliament
but through the articles, and nothing can pass in articles but what is
warranted by his majestie, so that the king is absolute master in parliament both of the negative and affirmative.'[49]

The king had ordered a formal parliamentary inquiry into the billeting affair, and on 26 June, ignoring any pretence of impartiality,
parliament appointed an investigative committee staffed solely by
crown supporters and allies of Lauderdale.[50] The earl of Haddington,
Sir John Gilmour of Craigmillar, Sir James Lockhart of Lee, Sir Robert
Murray of Cameron for Edinburgh, Alexander Wedderburn of
Kingennie for Dundee (all lords of the articles) and Lauderdale himself
undertook investigations. After a month of sifting through a number
of depositions taken from various members of parliament, the commission's findings were summarised in a letter sent to Charles on
28 July. From examining the evidence, it was clear that an additional
clause excepting twelve individuals from public trust had not been at
the request of parliament, that Middleton had deceived Charles by
sending a contrary instruction to court and had misled both king and
parliament into accepting billeting as the most expedient way of
voting. The letter was approved unanimously, only the earls of
Dumfries, Aboyne and William Douglas, eighth earl of Morton, the
rump of Middleton's faction, abstaining from voting.[51] The 'examining of divers noblemen' in a more widespread investigation was
rejected, with the commission content to recommend only that the earl
of Middleton be removed from his position as general of the armed
forces and Tarbat as a lord of session and exchequer. Excluding
Middleton in particular from any further office, Lauderdale informed
the king, would 'unite the nobilitie and gentrie of the kingdome as one
family'.[52] On 9 September, exactly one year since the passing of the
indemnity act, the 'Act concerning persons to be excepted from publict
trust' and the 'Act appoynting the maner of voteing by billets' were
rescinded and ordered to be permanently erased from the parliamentary register. Lauderdale reported to the king, with satisfaction, that
'billeting is dead, buried and descended'.[53]

On 10 July, parliament passed an 'Act against separation and
disobedience to ecclesiasticall authority', endorsing the episcopal
settlement that had been overseen by the now disgraced Middleton
and approving a number of controversial measures against non-
conformity that were included at the behest of the bishops.[54] Since

early 1663, the privy council had received a number of worrying reports of unauthorised conventicles being held by ministers who had not obtained collation, mainly in the covenanting heartland of the south-west.[55] The earls of Glencairn and Dumfries, pushed increasingly to the sidelines as Middleton's fortunes waned, drafted a paper to the king suggesting that the declaration against the covenant should be forcefully imposed on all heritors and ministers. Whether hoping to benefit financially from the use of troops, from fining of dissenters or possibly seeking to incite overt opposition against the government, thus making Lauderdale's and Rothes's position more difficult, their approach was rejected as being too provocative. Yet some sort of clampdown against dissenters was clearly necessary, with the majority of the bishops demanding action against recusant ministers.[56] Lauderdale's response was the legislation put before parliament in July 1663. For Lauderdale, forthright action against non-conformity would have additional benefits, putting to an end rumours that he held a lingering sympathy for the presbyterian kirk, disarming Glencairn and the remainder of Middleton's party and demonstrating to the king that he too could be as useful as his predecessor had been.

Under the act passed on 10 July, persistent offenders who conducted or attended religious services outwith the established church were to be subject to fines amounting to a fourth part of a year's rent or the seizure of a proportion of moveable goods.[57] The act passed unanimously, with Lauderdale receiving plaudits from the bishops and the king for his accompanying speech in favour of the episcopal settlement.[58] On 7 August, an additional act ordering all office-holders to subscribe the declaration against the covenants before 11 November 1663 decreed that those within burghs who refused were not only to be barred from holding positions of public trust but would also forfeit all trading privileges.[59] The public execution of Sir Archibald Johnston of Wariston, who had finally been captured in France after fleeing in July 1661, concluded parliament's assault against the remaining supporters of the covenant. Brought before the chamber on his knees to seek repentance, he struck a pathetic figure, 'so disorded both in body and mind' that it was, in Lauderdale's words, 'a miserable . . . spectacle.'[60] Nevertheless, despite murmurings of disquiet within parliament that such an obviously ill man be put to death, the secretary spoke against any delay in his execution. On 22 July, after a long speech defending the covenant but repenting of his association with the Cromwellians, Johnston was hanged at the Mercat Cross in Edinburgh. His head was affixed to the Netherbow alongside James Guthrie's.[61]

Although it seemed from the action already taken against dissenters that few additional measures were necessary, on 23 September, to further ensure the security of the country, an act was passed to raise a militia of 20,000 foot and 2,000 horse. The appointment of commanding officers was to be remitted to the king himself, with the privy council taking responsibility for organisation of the levies. Uniquely, the act ordained that the king could call upon his new militia to serve him in 'any parte of his dominions of Scotland, England or Ireland for suppressing of any forraigne invasion, intestine trouble or insurrection, or for any other service whairin his majesties honour, authority or greatness may be concerned.'[62] This met with the full approval of the king, who saw it as a possible means of putting pressure upon his southern kingdom in particular. Unsurprisingly, the measure caused great offence in England, where the act was greeted with vocal hostility. In Scotland, parliament approved the act without any such controversy, few imagining that these powers would ever be tested or even whether such a force would exist apart from on paper. The inclusion of the controversial clause was merely another gesture to Charles that Scotland, under Lauderdale, would be a staunch defender of the royal interest, thus reassuring the king that the policies pursued to such success by Middleton would be continued under the new leadership.[63]

To reward parliament for its loyalty to the crown, before the third session was dissolved, Lauderdale was mindful to introduce legislation to address some long-standing concerns. Early in the session the articles had received complaints from several shires and burghs that their proportions of excise were excessive. In response, an act of 2 September sought to regulate the division of the burden.[64] To counter English protectionism, which had been increased further with the Commons' approval of the Staple Act in July 1663 requiring all goods imported into England or its colonies to be either in English ships or ships of the country of origin, parliament approved an act setting a tax of 80 per cent on English cloth and other commodities. These measures were intended to bring England by treaty to some equality in trade and, in a following act, parliament agreed that the king was free to order this as he saw fit in the interval between sessions.[65] However, on 9 October, the last day of the session, an act was brought in empowering the king to impose upon or restrain all trade with foreigners as he pleased. Under these proposals, the full control of Anglo-Scottish trade was brought under the royal prerogative.[66] This extraordinary innovation allowed the king to make as many gifts and monopolies and to exact whatever impositions he liked upon foreign commodities. As this was now a prerogative power, parliament had given itself a minor role in future trade decisions.[67] It seems the investigation into billeting had shamed many members; if parliament could stay in the royal favour, it was now content to grant the king whatever he wished.

After the close of the final session of the first Restoration parliament on 9 October 1663, Rothes instructed Sir Robert Moray to inform the king that 'the nixt parliament wold be as intirely at his maties devotion as he can desire.' Reflecting on the inclusion of the bishops in parliament in 1662, he highlighted the importance of 'the lords spirituall and temporall . . . sitting in the same hous, [for] the king knows what influence they have.' The other estates would be equally compliant with the crown since

> the power which the officers of state and noblemen have in elections of commissioners for shires and burroughs may secure his matie of the new elections, especially seeing the declaration concerning the covenant keeps out those who are avers to the church government establisht.[68]

This was the key to the success of the first Restoration parliament. Opportunities for tension did not arise, as the king did not make any additional financial demands after the 1661 session, membership had been comprehensively purged to ensure a compliant chamber and thus controversial legislation on episcopacy and trade passed without objection. Increasingly, political favour relied on the ability to serve the interests of the king and the rivalry between the two main figures of the period, Middleton and Lauderdale, throughout the parliamentary sessions, escalated into a contest to see which of them could best serve their monarch. The billeting affair proved for Lauderdale a convenient method of gaining further control of parliament, for the estates were eager to condemn their former actions in order to re-establish themselves in the royal favour. Based on past events, the earl of Rothes was right to be confident of future royalist dominance in parliament. However, the first signs of non-conformity in 1663 regarding the church suggested that, for some, allegiance to the king had its limits.

Parliament was not to meet again until 1669, but the three sessions of the Restoration parliament had achieved more than would have been thought possible in 1660. The return of Charles II was welcomed because monarchy provided stability to a country that had suffered massive upheaval over the past twenty years. Episcopacy was restored as the preferred church government because church rule by bishops made it easier to exercise control within the localities and was therefore most compatible with monarchical authority. By sweeping aside the constitutional revolution of 1640–1, parliament had demonstrated its essential loyalty to the crown.

Notes

1 *RPCS*, third series, i, pp. 28–32.
2 NLS, Almack Collection, Mss 3922, f. 17; Buckroyd, *Church and State*, p. 41; Jackson, *Restoration Scotland*, pp. 106–7.
3 Buckroyd, *Church and State*, pp. 42–3; Cowan, *Scottish Covenanters*, pp. 47–8; NLS, Wodrow Quarto LXIII, *A Brief Narration of the Coming-In of Prelacie*, f. 113.
4 Buckroyd, *Church and State*, pp. 43–5.
5 NAS, PA2/28, ff. 1r–2r, 4r; *RPS*, 1662/5/2, 1662/5/7.
6 Young (ed.), *Parliaments of Scotland*, i, p. 210.
7 *RPCS*, third series, i, pp. 373, 402, 529–30; Young (ed.), *Parliaments of Scotland*, i, pp. 189–90, 232–3; NAS, PA2/28, ff. 51r–58r, 6v–7r; *RPS*, 1662/5/96, 1662/5/11.
8 NAS, PA2/28, ff. 3r, 4v–6r; *RPS*, 1662/5/4–5, 1662/5/9.
9 NAS, PA2/28, ff. 8r–v; *RPS*, 1662/5/15; Buckroyd, *Church and State*, p. 46.
10 NAS, PA2/26, ff. 297–8; *RPS*, 1661/1/255; NAS, PA2/28, ff. 8v–9r; *RPS*, 1662/5/16.
11 I. B. Cowan, 'The Covenanters: a revision article', *SHR*, 47 (1968), pp. 45–6; Paterson, *King Lauderdale*, pp. 148–9; R. Lawson, *The Covenanters of Ayrshire: Historical and Biographical* (Paisley, 1887), pp. 19–23; Wodrow, *Sufferings of the Church of Scotland*, i, pp. 324–30.
12 Burnet, *History*, i, pp. 267–75.
13 In some parishes there were active attempts by parishioners to stop the new ministers taking up their charges, ranging from the stealing of the tongue from the church bell to stop it being pealed for summoning worshippers to church to barricading the kirk doors to deny the new incumbent entry. *Lauderdale Papers*, i, p. 200; Wodrow, *Sufferings of the Church of Scotland*, i, pp. 330–3.
14 NAS, PA2/28, ff. 10r–11r; *RPS*, 1661/5/20.
15 Lee, 'Government and politics in Scotland, 1661–1681', p. 32.
16 NAS, PA2/28, ff. 36v–37r; *RPS*, 1661/5/70.
17 Hutton, *Charles II*, pp. 168–70, 182.
18 Jones, *Charles II: Royal Politician*, pp. 57–8; Seaward, *Restoration*, pp. 35–6.
19 Hutton, *Charles II*, p. 178.
20 Burnet, *History*, i, pp. 235–6, 258.

21 NAS, PA2/28, ff. 12v–13r; *RPS*, 1662/5/24; *RPCS*, third series, i, pp. 36–7, 41–3, 45, 57–8; NAS, GD90/2/260, f. 18r.

22 Mackenzie, *Memoirs*, pp. 64–5; Hutton, *Charles II*, p. 190.

23 NAS, GD90/2/260, f. 11r.

24 Mackenzie, *Memoirs*, pp. 86–7; NLS, Dalrymple Mss 3424, ff. 331–2; Airy, 'The Lauderdale Mss in the British Museum', p. 417.

25 Lee, 'Government and politics in Scotland, 1661–1681', pp. 33–6; Buckroyd, *Church and State*, p. 50.

26 *Lauderdale Papers*, i, pp. 103–4; J. Patrick, 'A union broken? Restoration politics in Scotland', in J. Wormald (ed.), *Scotland Revisited* (London, 1991), p. 124.

27 The parliamentary investigation into the billeting affair heard evidence that the initial idea of a secret ballot came from Charles Stewart, sixth duke of Lennox, the king's distant cousin, at a meeting held in his lodgings in Holyrood Abbey. It was then tabled in the committee. NLS, Dalrymple Mss 3424, f. 425.

28 *Lauderdale Papers*, i, pp. 104–5.

29 NLS, Dalrymple Mss 3424, f. 333; *Lauderdale Papers*, i, pp. 107–8.

30 Airy, 'The Lauderdale Mss in the British Museum', p. 417; NLS, Dalrymple Mss 3424, ff. 334, 426.

31 Sir John Urquhart of Cromarty testified to the 1663 commission investigating the billeting affair that he was present at such a meeting, as was the duke of Lennox, Charles Gordon, earl of Aboyne, the earl of Newburgh and John Bell. NLS, Dalrymple Mss 3424, f. 431.

32 *Lauderdale Papers*, i, pp. 110–13. The agents included James Crichton of St Leonards and Urquhart of Cromarty (cousin of Sir George Mackenzie of Tarbat), both victors in disputed elections in 1661.

33 NLS, Dalrymple Mss 3424, ff. 426, 428–9.

34 *Lauderdale Papers*, i, pp. 111, 109. According to Mackenzie, the earl of Haddington was the only member who refused to participate at all in the voting. *Memoirs*, p. 75.

35 There is no complete list of the twelve individuals named by the ballot. The report into the billeting affair, presented to parliament on 26 June 1663, declared that the act was sent to the king sealed and that he has 'so ordered that it shall never more come to light'. NAS, PA2/28, ff. 80r–81v; *RPS*, 1663/6/8.

36 Burnet, *History*, i, p. 264; Mackenzie, *Memoirs*, p. 76; *Lauderdale Papers*, i, pp. 109, 112.

37 *Lauderdale Papers*, i, pp. 111–12, 115; Airy, 'The Lauderdale Mss in the British Museum', p. 418.

38 Burnet, *History*, i, p. 264.

39 Mackenzie, *Memoirs*, p. 76.

40 Airy, 'The Lauderdale Mss in the British Museum', p. 418; Mackenzie, *Memoirs*, p. 76; Burnet, *History*, i, p. 265; *Lauderdale Papers*, i, p. 116;

NAS, GD90/2/260, f. 26v. The failure of the billeting scheme did not put an immediate end to Middleton's efforts to remove Lauderdale from power. In January 1663, Lauderdale was given notice that Middleton had acquired the papers of the transactions between the Scottish commissioners and the English parliament, implicating the secretary in the surrender of Charles I to the English. These proved to be crude forgeries, but Lauderdale was to be plagued by such accusations throughout his career, later forced to write a detailed account of his whereabouts at the time of the execution of Charles I to put the whole matter to rest. *Lauderdale Papers*, i, pp. 125–6; NLS, Watson Mss 597, f. 263.

41 NLS, Dalrymple Mss 3424, ff. 332–5, 342; Airy, 'The Lauderdale Mss in the British Museum', pp. 419–20; Paterson, *King Lauderdale*, pp. 157–8.

42 NAS, PA2/28, ff. 51r–58r; *RPS*, 1662/5/96.

43 *RPCS*, third series, i, pp. 329–31; NAS, GD90/2/260, f. 28r; *Lauderdale Papers*, i, pp. 132–3; Burnet, *History*, i, pp. 361–4.

44 Mackenzie, *Memoirs*, p. 115; 'Letters from John, earl of Lauderdale, and others, to Sir John Gilmour, president of session', Scottish History Society, H. M. Paton (ed.), *Miscellany of the Scottish History Society* (Edinburgh, 1933), v, pp. 147–8.

45 Lee, 'Government and politics in Scotland, 1661–1681', p. 36; Buckroyd, *Church and State*, p. 53

46 NAS, PA2/28, ff. 77r–78r; *RPS*, 1663/6/2. Nicoll notes that by the time of the riding on 9 October, the last day of the session, numbers in attendance were 'very thin' and had dwindled considerably from those seen on the opening day. Nicoll, *Diary*, p. 402.

47 See, for example, the extant letters between Lauderdale and Moray in *Lauderdale Papers*, i, pp. 135–90.

48 *Lauderdale Papers*, i, p. 134; NAS, PA2/28, f. 79v; *RPS*, 1663/6/5; Hutton, *Charles II*, p. 205.

49 *Lauderdale Papers*, i, pp. 173–4.

50 NAS, PA2/28, ff. 80r–81v; *RPS*, 1663/6/8. Despite some 'fidling opposition' from some within the chamber at the naming of the commission, their report was merely a formality. Middleton's expulsion was already decided and Lauderdale was now the butt of jokes regarding the matter, with Moray relating the king's comment on opening one of the secretary's letters: 'If you write not upon better paper and with better pens, wee will have yow billeted again.' Lauderdale joined in with relish, addressing a letter to the king with the heading '10th September 1663, being the day after Saint Billetings day'. *Lauderdale Papers*, i, pp. 136, 143, 184.

51 NAS, PA2/28, ff. 90v–91r; *RPS*, 1663/6/30; Nicoll, *Diary*, p. 395; *Lauderdale Papers*, i, p. 165.

52 NAS, PA2/28, ff. 88v–91v; *RPS*, 1663/6/27–31; *Lauderdale Papers*, i, pp. 167–8, 172. The documents gathered by the commissioners in their

investigations survive as NLS, Dalrymple Mss 3424, 'Report and depositions given in to the commission on the billeting act', ff. 425–38.

53 NAS, PA2/28, ff. 101v–102v; *RPS*, 1663/6/49; *Lauderdale Papers*, i, p. 184.

54 NAS, PA2/28, ff. 85r–86r; *RPS*, 1663/6/19.

55 *RPCS*, third series, i, pp. 312–15, 338–9, 349–50, 354–5, 357–9.

56 *Lauderdale Papers*, i, pp. 175, 181; Buckroyd, *Church and State*, pp. 52–3.

57 NAS, PA2/28, ff. 85r–86r; *RPS*, 1663/6/19.

58 *Lauderdale Papers*, i, pp. 157–8, 162.

59 NAS, PA2/28, ff. 92v–93r; *RPS*, 1663/6/33.

60 Burnet, *History*, i, p. 364; *Lauderdale Papers*, i, p. 145.

61 *Lauderdale Papers*, i, pp. 151–2, 155, 163; Nicoll, *Diary*, pp. 394–5.

62 NAS, PA2/28, ff. 110v–111r; *RPS*, 1663/6/64.

63 Hutton, *Charles II*, p. 206; Mackenzie, *Memoirs*, pp. 132–3; Burnet, *History*, i, p. 368; Paterson, *King Lauderdale*, pp. 160–1.

64 *Lauderdale Papers*, i, pp. 159–60; NAS, PA2/28, ff. 99r–100r; *RPS*, 1663/6/46.

65 NAS, PA2/28, ff. 95v–96v; *RPS*, 1663/6/40–1. A duty was also imposed on imports of Irish corn, see NAS, PA2/28, ff. 93r–v; *RPS*, 1663/6/34. For more on trade between England and Scotland in the early years of the Restoration, see D. Woodward, 'Anglo-Scottish trade and English commercial policy during the 1660s', *SHR*, 56 (1977), pp. 154–74.

66 NAS, PA2/28, ff. 132v–133r; *RPS*, 1663/6/110.

67 Mackenzie, *Memoirs*, p. 133.

68 NLS, Dalrymple Mss 3424, f. 454.

Chapter 3

THE COST OF WAR, 1664–7

౭

On its adjournment in October 1663, Charles II's first parliament had been in session for seventeen months, spanning a period of three years, so it is not surprising that the close of the last session was greeted with some relief. The earl of Rothes, for one, was glad to see the 'return to the good old form of government by his majesties privy councill', claiming that lengthy meetings of the estates were 'an unsupportable charge to the nobility in obliging them to live at a high rate and to the gentry and burroughs in maintaining their commissioners.' Rothes was no doubt thinking of the billeting affair, which had cast an ugly shadow over the proceedings of the last two sessions of parliament, when he complained to Sir Robert Moray that 'long parliaments are more unfitt for Scotland than for any other place, for, public business being done, they can only serve here for creating divisions by carry[ing] on private interests.'[1] Indeed, it had been factional divisions amongst the nobility that had disrupted parliament, the membership of the elected estates having been comprehensively purged by a succession of oaths and other restrictive measures. Yet, by the time the estates met again in August 1665, the domestic situation in Scotland had drastically changed. The demands of providing money and forces for a foreign war and the increasing hostility and violence that the religious settlement provoked were to provide the first serious test to the royalist grasp of power.

The second Anglo-Dutch war, which effectively began in the summer of 1664, was not officially declared until 4 March 1665. For decades the English and Dutch had squabbled over trade routes and importation rights, and many long-standing commercial disputes, centred largely on the East Indies, had not been resolved by the first Dutch war of 1652–4. Yet it was the setting up of the Royal African, a new chartered company to trade in The Gambia and Guinea, with the king himself as one of the major shareholders, which represented a direct threat to Dutch trading interests. The Royal African's first venture to West Africa met with strong resistance from the colonial masters already in situ. In response, the company armed its own warship, which, from the autumn of 1663, carried out a series of attacks on Dutch forts, loading up with booty at every opportunity. Growing bolder, in early 1664, the company set up another corporation in the north sea fisheries, which again struck directly at Dutch interests. Simultaneously, the government sent a force to seize New Amsterdam, a smugglers' haven in the midst of England's North American possessions, to be rechristened New York in honour of the king's brother after its successful capture. Yet none of these actions, however brazen, were intended to produce war. The English government expected the Dutch, when confronted with such open aggression, simply to concede to their demands for a greater share of colonial trade. They were thus dumbfounded when, in August 1664, against all expectations, the Mediterranean fleet of the United Netherlands set sail for African waters to reassert their supremacy.[2]

Charles I's foreign wars had failed primarily because of lack of money, his parliaments preferring as a means of supply the ineffective method of subsidy. For the meeting of parliament assembled at London in November 1664, his son proceeded with care, anxious not to make the same mistakes as his father. In an opening speech, Charles was keen to portray the Dutch as aggressors and appealed for £800,000 sterling to equip a suitable English fleet. Reflecting public opinion that was already feverishly pro-war, parliament fell into line enthusiastically, voting an unprecedented £2,500,000 sterling over three years to be raised by the more efficient means of assessment.[3] The king was delighted with such a lavish grant. It remained now the turn of his northern kingdom to prove it was equally as generous as its southern counterpart.

Unlike its neighbour, Scotland had little to gain from war with the Dutch, their biggest trading partner. With a stagnant economy already suffering from English protectionist legislation, the outbreak of hostilities merely caused a further depression in trade, with no benefits to be expected from a successful outcome. Nevertheless, the country was expected to provide her share of men and money to ensure victory. Funds were immediately needed to meet the cost of raising around 500 seamen and the hire of their ships. Significant sums were also required to upgrade and rebuild civil war garrisons to defend the coastline from Dutch attack. Thus, in September 1664, the king finally authorised the privy council to begin collection of the fines due under indemnity, the proceeds likely to be put towards the nation's defence rather than their original purpose of lining royalist pockets. In March 1665, in a vain attempt to boost the public magazines, the king ordered that all private persons in the Lowlands hand in their arms. Even Rothes, left in command when Lauderdale retreated south, recognised that relying on such a meagre supply likely to amount to 'a pistull or tuo at most' from each heritor was barely worth the logistical effort of organising such a massive search.[4]

The outbreak of full-scale hostilities with the Dutch in June 1665 could hardly have happened at a worse time for the Scottish economy. Parliament's attempts in 1663 to counter protectionism by imposing tit-for-tat impositions on English commodities had had little beneficial effect on the economy, with the flow of trade simply drying up rather than revenue from imports rising. From 1662 to 1665, income from customs and excise steadily declined, with Leith, the busiest port, seeing a marked dwindling in receipts of over 50 per cent. The dire situation was compounded by widespread corruption, with a later investigation finding that Sir Walter Seaton of Abercorn, tacksman of both customs and excise, had awarded himself massive abatements at the same time as the treasury received less than half the expected tack duty for the years 1664–5. The money collected from customs and rents was less than the total needed to settle arrears for fees and pensions, which the king kept bountifully granting to favoured individuals, despite pleas from Rothes for the need to tighten the country's purse strings.[5] While the English protectionist acts were rigorously enforced, to the detriment of Scottish exports, the retaliatory measures passed by the estates in 1663 were implemented with considerable laxity. The black market flourished, with the convention of burghs complaining to the privy council that the acts were being openly flouted. In November 1664, merchants were discovered by customs officers attempting to avoid payment of the inflated rates by bringing a quantity of English broadcloth 'over the toun wall of Edinburgh privilie in the nycht'.[6]

By the summer of 1665, it was clear that the effect of the Dutch conflict on the public revenue had been catastrophic. Contemporary accounts tell of how 'trade and traffick ceased universallie by sea' and that ships carrying goods from abroad could only sail towards Scotland accompanied by a heavy English guard, such was the risk of attack from the Dutch.[7] Rothes, as treasurer, found that he could not raise funds to pay a garrison stationed on the Shetland Isles, forcing the government to borrow money and buy arms and materials on credit.[8] The continuance of English impositions on Scottish trade prompted yet another plea from the privy council in May 1665 begging Charles to personally intervene and remove the crippling restrictions placed on his northern kingdom.[9] In light of such pressing demands for money, a meeting of the estates to grant a supply of taxation could no longer be avoided.

Rothes, Archbishop Sharp and others in Scotland greeted the prospect of summoning a meeting of the Scottish parliament with considerable dismay. To his annoyance, Lauderdale had been on the receiving end of constant reports from his deputies north of the border of religious non-conformity flourishing unabated within areas such as the south-west, this despite the measures taken by parliament in 1663 to curb the spread of conventicles. Reluctant to provide a platform for dissent, it was agreed that a proposed meeting of a national synod, scheduled for May 1665, be at first delayed to August 1665 and then postponed indefinitely.[10] A deepening economic recession made discontent more widespread and asking for additional money was dangerous. As Rothes noted, with the generous grant to the crown of £40,000 sterling yearly from customs and excise agreed in 1661, the country was contributing more to the king than ever before. The continued exaction of impositions from the civil war period and the collection of fines, both for the indemnity and for church non-conformity, would make any additional demand deeply unpopular.[11] Moreover, a moratorium on pensions (finally agreed in May 1665)[12] and the diverting of the indemnity fines to boost public revenue could possibly alienate many of the fickle nobility, whose loyalty was often secured by such material rewards. It all combined to make the king's demand in March 1665 for a meeting of the estates generally unwelcome.

Soon after the formal declaration of war between the English and Dutch in the spring of 1665, discussions began as to the method of raising funds in Scotland. The king ordered Lauderdale to arrange a meeting of six or seven of the privy council to 'advise seriously whither it be not necessarie to call a parliament, or rather a convention . . . to grant such a moderat tax as the country may bear.' In fact, despite giving the appearance of involving the council, a decision had already been made. After listening to his secretary's advice, Charles had agreed with Lauderdale that holding a full session of parliament, with the scope to discuss a wide variety of grievances, would be unnecessary, even dangerous considering the prevalence of religious dissent in the localities. Instead, the king accepted Lauderdale's advice that 'a convention which hath legally power enough for a small tax' be summoned.[13] Crucially, the convention, to meet in Edinburgh on 2 August 1665, was to be summoned solely for the purpose of granting supplies for the Dutch war, with the royal letter forbidding the discussion of any other business. Despite this constraint, Rothes continued to lament the 'dangarus nesesitie' of calling a convention, warning the secretary to expect the gathered estates to be significantly more recalcitrant than had been the case at the previous parliament.[14] Yet, whatever problems the forthcoming meeting of the estates was likely to bring, the recourse to direct taxation only a few years after parliament had agreed a generous and long-term provision to the crown represented a failure of the financial aspect of the Restoration settlement. The fact that the sums raised were to be applied towards funding what many viewed as an English war, fought solely for English interests, only served to compound the misery.

After the Restoration, conventions of estates began to be regarded as a meeting assembled solely for the purposes of taxation, this partly a reaction against the precedent set by the 1643 convention that led Scotland into the English civil war. In 1665, 1667 and again in 1678, taxation was the only topic on the agenda. In the seventeenth century in general, numbers attending conventions of estates began to increase. By 1630, conventions were beginning to approach the numbers of a parliament, with nineteen shires and thirty-one burghs sending representatives (as compared with an attendance of twenty-seven shires and fifty burghs in the parliament of 1633).[15] It was in 1643, however, that the convention began to assume the role (at least in membership) of a parliament, with the numbers attending topping 154. 'The convention was a most frequent meeting, never a parliament so great', reported Robert Baillie, and only one session of parliament in 1639–41 managed to command a higher membership.[16]

A total of 142 commissioners are recorded in the rolls of 2 August 1665, the first day of the convention, a significant number considering the brief length of time for which they sat.[17] The burgh turnout of forty-five commissioners actually exceeded the attendance for the estate in the last session of parliament in 1663, no doubt reflecting their concern at the economic situation. As merchants, the estate would have had a keen interest in any discussions on trade and on their proportion of tax. Such an increase, however, was not consistent throughout the estates. The attendance of the nobility dropped from seventy that were present in 1663 to only forty-two for the convention. It was the only time during Charles II's reign that both the burgh and shire membership (of forty-four commissioners) outnumbered that of the nobility.[18]

Although there is no explicit evidence indicating widespread governmental management of elections, given the concerns already
expressed about the convention providing a platform for dissent, it
seems likely that shire and burgh candidates would be subject to the
same close scrutiny as had been the case prior to the 1661 session of
parliament. As early as March 1665, when given first notice of the
king's demand for a meeting of the estates, Rothes had warned (in his
usual atrocious spelling) that 'taym most be alouied and cear teakin
that honiest and intrestied persons be chosien' to represent the elected
estates. Otherwise, there was a danger that 'discontentied persons in
the kingdum, tho upon severall grounds and intrests, may joayn to
obstruckt reasing of munie eather in the convension by refyousing
ther assent tu it, or by uithdrauing and so randir the miting of les
istim.'[19] By July 1665, Rothes felt confident enough to reassure
Lauderdale that if 'the borrows be for the proposals, they will go near
to have as many voices in the convention as will be against them.'[20]

When the convention assembled on 2 August, fears of an open
display of dissent proved to be groundless. Sitting for only three days,
the gathered estates were instead remarkably loyal and co-operative
with the crown's demands for finance. A committee nominated by the
earl of Rothes in his role as king's commissioner to 'consider of the
quota and the way of inbringing of the same', reported in favour of
reverting to the old, pre-covenanter method of taxation. Thus, a tax
of forty shillings Scots upon every poundland of old extent was
granted, to be raised in five yearly instalments from Whitsunday 1666
to Whitsunday 1670. The archbishops and bishops agreed to a corresponding tax on church land and benefices and the burghs paid in
proportion.[21]

Events in the convention proceeded smoothly for the crown, but this
concealed the complex and often inharmonious bargaining that had
gone on during the preparations for the meeting. In privy council, there
had been 'great debates' as to whether taxation should be raised by
cess, as had been favoured during the covenanting years, but which the
king had promised in 1661 not to use. Archbishop Sharp, along with
the earl of Dumfries, 'joyned with the west countrie lords and others
ther' to urge that cess be adopted as the means for raising the supply.
William Bellenden, lord Bellenden of Broughton warned if Sharp and
Dumfries were successful, it would 'cause much division and heate at
the convention, which lyke eneugh may be a desygne of some, rather
then to carye on the busienes with quyet and satisfaction to the countrie.'[22] The inequity of the system of old extent was likely to cause

Figure 3.1   *John Leslie, seventh earl and first duke of Rothes (c.1640–81) by*
L. Schuneman, c.1667. Imprisoned for much of the interregnum for his royalist
leanings, Rothes was well rewarded on Charles II's restoration with a number
of offices, the most significant being president of the privy council. He gained
further promotion on the fall of the earl of Middleton, being appointed royal
commissioner to the Scottish parliament in 1663 and convention of estates in 1665
and 1667. Made a scapegoat for the outbreak of rebellion in 1666, Rothes was
stripped of most of his offices, although he remained a prominent public figure,
frequently in attendance at sessions of parliament until his death.
(Scottish National Portrait Gallery.)

opposition, amongst the landed estates in particular, but cess, based largely on valuations made in the 1640s by the covenanters, placed the greatest burden on those who had remained loyal to the crown.

The debate surrounding the preferred method of raising taxation became caught up with personal and factional loyalties. Sharp, by uniting with Dumfries, further damaged his standing with Lauderdale, already at a low ebb after his complaints about the prevalence of religious dissent had reached the king, endangering the illusion much propagated by the secretary that the domestic situation in Scotland was under control. The duke of Hamilton, sensing the mounting tensions, enhanced his status as the main opponent to Lauderdale by joining with Sharp, despite a history of animosity between the two. Rothes expressed dissatisfaction with both methods of raising tax, warning that if the king expected a sum in excess of forty shillings on the poundland, 'I shall never be eabell to carie it.'[23]

Despite the lengthy discussions prior to the convention for agreeing the best method of raising funds, a tax based on old extent was unsuited to meet the pressing demands for money. The first sum was not due to be paid until Whitsunday (3 June) 1666, with the rest trickling in over the next four years. The valuations on which the taxation was based were also grossly unfair and obscure. James Douglas, earl of Queensberry would have to pay a sum ten times that of his rent, almost equal to the total for the shires of either Edinburgh or Haddington.[24] A clause in the act passed by the convention went some way to addressing the inequity, ruling that the amounts due in Lanark, Ayr, Renfrew, Dunbarton, Bute, Argyll, Wigtown, Dumfries and Peebles were to be calculated on merkland rather than poundland, saving approximately 33 per cent.[25]

If paid in full, the value of the taxation voted by the convention (£144,088 10s 10d annually for five years) was not sufficient to meet the government's financial demands. The fact that so much of the taxation was either diverted to cover incidentals or went uncollected made the eventual sum available for the government even paltrier. Some 22.7 per cent of the total raised by February 1669 went towards settling fees of collection or for exceptions. Arrears accounted for another 23.6 per cent. An audit in March 1672 of the final amount collected revealed that, after subtracting these ancillary expenses, only 44 per cent of the total voted by the convention was able to be used towards meeting the cost of the Dutch war.[26]

The disastrous performance of the supply voted by the convention in 1665 was made worse by the need for additional funds to meet the cost of raising more troops in the summer of 1666. Despite continued unease at the spread of conventicling, action against non-conformity was only finally taken when Holland formed an alliance with France in January 1666 and the English naval campaign against the Dutch began to stutter.[27] It was widely suspected that Scottish non-conformists were in correspondence with their Dutch presbyterian brethren, leading to fears of an internal rebellion organised by a foreign foe.[28] Open dissent against the crown could therefore no longer be tolerated, and, in March 1666, Rothes dispatched a troop to Galloway to seize upon the conventicle ringleaders. Archbishop Sharp was simultaneously sent to London to persuade Charles that more soldiers were needed to defend the country in the event of a Dutch attack. He returned with the king's instruction that the now-collected indemnity fines were to be used to fund troop expansion.[29]

The decision to divert the indemnity fines from the pockets of the expectant nobility to public use was greeted with dismay not only amongst those who had hoped to benefit financially, but also from the king's ministers in Scotland. Although admitting he could think of no other way to raise the necessary funds, Rothes warned Lauderdale that they must expect some of the disappointed nobles to withdraw their immediate support for their administration. Rothes was concerned that he be apportioned blame for the king's unwelcome decision, but this instead fell on Sharp, who was suspected by many to be instrumental in persuading the king to make use of the fines in this manner.[30]

The loss of revenue from the fines was yet another disappointment to those members of the nobility who had yet to be compensated for civil war losses by office or compensation in kind. The situation was not helped by the recent unpopular squeeze on pensions to boost treasury funds for the Dutch war. Yet the fact that Sharp was so readily accepted as the scapegoat for the diversion of the indemnity fines was representative of a wider distrust of the bishops in general, particularly amongst the nobility.[31] The commission for church affairs, set up in the winter of 1663–4 as a means of controlling the administration of ecclesiastical laws outwith the larger privy council, was seriously hampered by the refusal of many of the nobility to enact the commission's policies on their tenants. At meetings of the commission itself (which had a quorum of five members, only one a bishop), there were disputes centred on the legal scope and powers of a court set up by royal proclamation, 'some great men contending for nice formalities of law', complained Archbishop Alexander Burnet, who 'thought to have rendered . . . proceedings ineffectuall and wselesse'.[32]

With the enforcement of the ecclesiastical settlement in moderate terms becoming impossible due to the passive resistance of the nobility to the commission's orders, the Scottish administration had no choice but to seek other means to repress the religious dissenters. The new troops paid for from the indemnity fines were raised in August and September 1666 (doubling the size of the army) and duly dispatched in October to the west to crush, by force, the non-conformists once and for all. Simultaneously, to head off any resistance from any obstructive nobles, the privy council issued a decreet making landlords, heads of families and magistrates responsible for their dependants' attendance at church.[33] Yet it was this heavy-handed approach, in addition to the simmering resentment towards the government's disarming of the west and its use of quartered troops to raise fines and taxation, which finally led to the outbreak of armed rebellion only a matter of weeks after the additional troops arrived.

The Pentland rising of November 1666 seemed to confirm the bishops' fears of an organised rebellion against episcopacy, although contemporary accounts generally exaggerate the magnitude of the uprising. The unrest originated in Dalry in Kirkcudbrightshire, where, on 12 November, a number of soldiers stationed to exact fines for non-conformity were held captive. On 13 November, in nearby Balmaclellan, an estimated sixteen soldiers were taken prisoner after a short scuffle with locals. Two days later, a crowd of around 200 rebels marched to Dumfries and took hostage the local garrison commander, Sir James Turner. Gathering reinforcements on the way, the rebels (estimated at numbers ranging from 1,100 to 2,000 men) marched at first in the direction of Glasgow, but, on hearing that government forces were in the city, the rebels turned towards Edinburgh. Reaching the outskirts of the capital on 28 November, depleted considerably in number from the journey, the rebels faced Lieutenant General Thomas Dalzell of Binns at Rullion Green in the Pentland hills. The rising was crushed with ruthless ease. Of the 900 men assembled on the battlefield, fifty were killed and around eighty taken prisoner. In the following month, another thirty-six were tried by the privy council and executed for their part in the uprising.[34]

The suddenness of the uprising, the obvious lack of planning and the poor provision of basic supplies for the rebels' forces all indicate that the rebellion was largely a spontaneous reaction set off by the abrupt influx of yet more troops to be quartered on an already resentful population. The government itself strongly suspected a number of rebels were involved in a conspiracy with foreign enemies.

Scots presbyterian exiles in Holland were certainly in correspondence with a number of conventicle ministers in the south-west and perhaps some sort of rising was tentatively planned which would be backed by Dutch military support.[35] Yet whatever the background to the rebellion, it provided justification for the further escalation of military repression, necessitating another meeting of the estates to supply a second grant of taxation in as many years.

On 8 November 1666, prior to the uprising in Kirkcudbrightshire, the privy council received a letter from the king summoning a convention of estates to meet on 9 January 1667. Ostensibly, the reason given for calling another convention was to provide supplies for the continuing Dutch war, but, after the outbreak of rebellion, it seemed more likely that any funds raised would be siphoned off to provide for yet more troops to be quartered in troublesome areas.[36] In December 1666, prior to his attendance as king's commissioner at the upcoming convention, the earl of Rothes, accompanied with a regiment of foot, marched to Glasgow, then Ayr to undertake a thorough search for any remaining rebels. He was dismayed to find that the spread of 'phanoticks' was endemic throughout the western shires, warning Lauderdale in a letter full of dire predictions that there was scarcely 'on[e] jentillman in this uholl cuntrie to be trusted'. The only cure for this disease, he argued, was forcible persecution.[37]

The opening day of the convention on 9 January 1667 was attended by 150 commissioners in total. The turnout of forty-nine for the nobility was a marked increase on the estate's attendance at the convention of 1665 and shire and burgh representation (of forty-seven and forty-eight commissioners respectively) was also slightly improved.[38] It is likely that concern over the deteriorating domestic situation helped boost attendance, with all estates taking an increased interest in the amount of taxation that they were expected to grant.

As one of the first acts of the convention, the duke of Hamilton was appointed president, replacing Sharp who had held the same position in 1665.[39] Already under censure for his involvement in the diversion of the indemnity fines, Sharp now found the blame for the Pentland rising placed squarely at his feet. Unfairly so, perhaps, but the archbishop's continued criticism of church policy and his clear ambitions for higher office were a real threat to Lauderdale's supremacy if left unchecked.[40] The elevation of Hamilton to the post of president made public Sharp's rapid fall from grace and he was to spend much of 1667 attending to diocesan duties, absent from the privy council and ostracised by his political colleagues.

The king's letter read out to the gathered commissioners again forbade discussion of any topic except that for which they had been summoned. Alleging that the Dutch 'will this summer, in all probability, endeavour to invade our dominions', another year's supply was proposed and a committee named by Rothes to decide on the proportions.[41] On 10 January, at a meeting which barely lasted quarter of an hour, the committee voted in favour of a monthly proportion of £72,000 for one year, the sum being initially suggested by the earl of Argyll and enthusiastically seconded by the rest of the committee.[42] Despite the encouraging beginnings, at this point discussions stalled. For the next two weeks, the committee became embroiled in heated debates about the method of raising the taxation. As a result, the eventual act agreed upon later in the month was perhaps more of a compromise from the government's point of view than would have been at first desired.

Although the committee nominated by Rothes to decide on the particulars of the taxation act was staffed almost entirely with proven crown supporters, when it came to deciding on the means of raising the agreed sum of taxation, there were a number of divergent voices raised against the crown. Opposition from figures such as the earl of Dumfries, the sole relic of Middleton's party, was to be expected and his objections about agreeing a sum prior to deciding on the method by which it was to be raised were easily waved aside. Only four on the committee voted in principal against the use of a cess, joined by a further six when the act was brought before the whole estates on 15 January. It was, however, when it came to the fine details of the act that there were furious disagreements in both the committee and convention, particularly over issues such as exemptions and debt relief. Despite the fact the use of a poll-tax had been rejected in the committee, it was again raised in the convention and made its way, albeit in a watered-down form, into the final act passed on 23 January. Thus those who were principally liable for the taxation were to receive relief, proportional to status, from the other inhabitants of their shire or burgh. An additional clause dealt specifically with quartered soldiers, a long-standing grievance and, arguably, one of the major causes of the recent unrest in the western shires. Under the provisions of the act, while quartering upon deficients was authorised, there were specific instructions given for the proper payment of soldiers and their supplies.[43]

For the government, the convention had been another successful meeting of the estates, despite the fact that some significant concessions had to be made to procure the passage of the final taxation act. In light of the disastrous performance of the 1665 tax, securing the use of cess as the method of raising the new supply was the main priority. Yet, even with using this improved method of collection, the generous assessment voted by the convention did little to solve the treasury's immediate shortfall. The first instalment of cess was not due until 1 May 1667 and the current means of providing for the troops, the money raised from the indemnity fines (estimated at around £360,000 to £420,000 in mid-1666), was rapidly running dry.[44] In April 1667, Rothes, General Dalzell and the duke of Hamilton were forced to advance money on their own credit for maintaining the troops in the west. Moreover, even though the convention had sought to regulate the dispersal of soldiers on impoverished areas, free quartering became endemic in the western shires, further antagonising the local population. Five additional troops were mustered in April, despite the fact the treasury was struggling to pay the existing forces.[45] Forced to provide for the army in any way possible, troops were sent to collect taxation simply to meet their own pay demands. It was a vicious circle that plagued the royal administration throughout the mid-1660s: more soldiers were needed to collect taxation, whilst, at the same time, taxation needed to be increased to fund this expansion in manpower.

This constant drain on government finances was one of the main reasons behind the subsequent failure of the 1667 tax to provide the necessary finance. An account of February 1668 by Sir William Bruce of Balcaskie, collector-general of the tax, estimated that the army swallowed up 68 per cent of the total of £1,326,335 19s raised from the cess, indemnity fines and money that had been borrowed from the duke of Hamilton out of the 1665 taxation. Arrears accounted for a further 26 per cent of the total. In the same year, the earl of Tweeddale calculated that the crown's annual Scottish income should reach £756,000. Total crown expenditure – money spent on troops, pensions and fees – was calculated at approximately £600,000.[46] On paper, the finances looked relatively healthy, but the shortfall in the treasury told an entirely different story.

As long as a large standing army was needed to protect the country from an external invader and to quell discontent in the localities, there was little possibility of an improvement in government finances. Thus, the hastily concluded peace treaty with the Dutch in August 1667 after their surprise attack on the Medway was widely welcomed north of the border, even though it represented a humiliating defeat for the king.[47]

By the time the war had limped to its inglorious end, it had inflicted its fair share of Scottish casualties, politically the most significant being the earl of Rothes. Already the object of some suspicion by dabbling in the possibility of an alliance with the disgraced Archbishop Sharp and earl of Middleton, his downfall was eventually sealed in May 1667 when a number of Dutch ships sailed unimpeded into the Firth of Forth. After a short and ineffective bombardment of Burntisland, the squadron retreated to join the rest of the fleet on their attack on the Thames, but it emerged that, despite the large amounts spent on the military, Leith was defenceless and Rothes himself was absent.[48]

Prior to the Dutch attack, plans were already afoot to remove Rothes from power. In April 1667, Charles had been persuaded to appoint Rothes to the honorary post of chancellor, which had been lying vacant since the death of Glencairn in 1664. Rothes's vehement protests that he could neither read Latin or possessed any under-standing of law were simply disregarded. His role as lord treasurer was also diluted when the treasury was placed into commission ahead of extensive reform of the king's finances. Although Rothes retained position as one of the commissioners, effective leadership passed to Lauderdale's new favourites Sir Robert Moray and the earl of Tweeddale, who took immediate charge of the country's purse strings and began zealous investigations into the state of the treasury accounts.[49] With the disbanding of the army, Rothes was also deprived of his role of general. His disgrace was complete when Charles revoked his commissionership in September 1667, with the fallen earl meekly conceding to the king's instruction without further protest.[50]

As Archbishop Sharp before him, Rothes had been cast aside because the policies he pursued had brought unwelcome attention from south of the border. Lauderdale's position at court was precari-ous, based on the condition that the political situation in Scotland was trouble-free. The embarrassing demonstrations of military unpreparedness, first with the Pentland rising and then with the sur-prise Dutch attack in the Forth, had provided the secretary's critics in London with ample ammunition and blame needed to be appor-tioned. It was clear that the use of force against religious dissenters had been a disaster, with the country almost brought to its knees by the demands of providing for a standing army in a time of great eco-nomic depression. Thus, the repudiation of former allies was accom-panied by an about-turn in policy and recognition of the unwelcome fact that religious non-conformity was here to stay.

Central to this latest political direction were Lauderdale's new deputies, sent north in the summer of 1667 to take the reigns from the departing Rothes. Sir Robert Moray, a former soldier who had taken part in royalist risings throughout the Cromwellian era, had been denied significant office earlier because he was on poor terms with both Glencairn and Middleton. Resident in London from 1661 onwards, where he served the king as a courtier and adviser, he had formed a close friendship with Lauderdale and had become a key ally. Such was his bond to the secretary, he had been seen as a potent threat by Middleton and subsequently billeted in 1662. Moray was already establishing a reputation as a scientist (he was a founder member of the Royal Society) and his status at court was the ideal position from which to observe English opinion, this so crucial to Lauderdale's success as secretary and, later, commissioner to parliament.[51] Moray was to be joined by John Hay, second earl of Tweeddale, who had been on the ascendancy since 1663 when he was made president of the privy council. In 1666, he became closely linked with the secretary when his son John Hay, first lord Yester married Lauderdale's only daughter Mary. Tweeddale was well known for his moderation in church affairs, having objected to the harsh treatment of dissenters in the past, and this made him ideal for a prime place in Lauderdale's new administration.[52]

From mid-1667 onwards, Moray and Tweeddale were the architects behind a transformation in ecclesiastical policy. Recognising that non-conformity in religion did not necessarily mean that dissenters were a direct threat to royalist control in Scotland, a scheme by which the most moderate presbyterian ministers were appointed to vacant livings was introduced and passive and peaceful dissent indulged, albeit in the face of hostility from the bishops. To circumvent such opposition, a new session of parliament that met in 1669 sought to reaffirm royal control over church matters. Toleration for non-conformity was to replace Rothes's policy of provocation. It remained to be seen whether this new direction would meet with any success.

Notes

1 NLS, Dalrymple Mss 3424, f. 454.
2 Hutton, *Charles II*, pp. 217–19; J. D. Davies, 'International relations, war and the armed forces', in L. K. J. Glassey (ed.), *The Reigns of Charles II and James VII & II* (Basingstoke, 1997), pp. 222–3; Jones, *Charles II: Royal Politician*, pp. 69–70; Seaward, *Restoration*, pp. 79–81.

3 Seaward, *The Cavalier Parliament*, pp. 120–4.

4 Nicoll, *Diary*, p. 420; *RPCS*, third series, i, pp. 600–1, 606–7, 613–15; *RPCS*, third series, ii, p. 42; *Lauderdale Papers*, i, pp. 214, 217, 222.

5 NLS, Dalrymple Mss 3424, f. 569; Lee, 'Government and politics in Scotland, 1661–1681', pp. 112–14; *Lauderdale Papers*, i, p. 220 and ii, pp. 77–8; T. Keith, *Commercial Relations of England and Scotland, 1603–1707* (Cambridge, 1910), pp. 75–6.

6 E. Hughes, 'The negotiations for a commercial union between England and Scotland in 1668', *SHR*, 24 (1926–7), pp. 30–1; *Records of the Convention of the Royal Burghs of Scotland*, iii, (1615–76), p. 575; *RPCS*, third series, i, p. 563; Nicoll, *Diary*, p. 424. For a useful, if dated, summary of the state of Scottish trade in the Restoration era, see T. Keith, 'The economic causes for the Scottish Union', *The English Historical Review*, 24, 93 (1909), pp. 45–52. A more up-to-date account is provided by T. C. Smout, 'The Anglo-Scottish Union of 1707: The economic background', *The Economic History Review*, new series, 16 (1964), pp. 457–9.

7 Nicoll, *Diary*, p. 429.

8 *Lauderdale Papers*, i, p. 220; Hutton, *Charles II*, p. 225.

9 *RPCS*, third series, ii, p. 42.

10 Buckroyd, *Church and State*, pp. 59–60, 62–4; *Lauderdale Papers*, i, pp. 200–1, 204–9.

11 *Lauderdale Papers*, i, p. 211. Two months' maintenance, originally to be raised in 1651, was finally ordered to be collected in 1661. NAS, PA2/27, ff. 82v–83r; *RPS*, 1661/1/443.

12 Lee, 'Government and politics in Scotland, 1661–1681', p. 114.

13 NLS, Yester Mss 7023, f. 18.

14 NAS, PA8/1, ff. 152v–153r; *RPS*, 1665/8/4; *Lauderdale Papers*, i, pp. 216–17.

15 NAS, PC1/31, ff. 1r–v and PA2/21, ff. 4v–5r; *RPS*, A1630/7/1 and 1633/6/8; Rait, *Parliaments of Scotland*, p. 155.

16 NAS, PA8/1, ff. 39r–40v; *RPS*, 1643/6/1; Baillie, *Letters and Journals*, ii, p. 75; Rait, *Parliaments of Scotland*, pp. 155–8. It was the session of parliament held on 17 August 1641 that had a marginally greater total membership of 163. NAS, PA2/22, ff. 91v–92v; *RPS*, 1641/8/2.

17 Rothes reported to Lauderdale that 'scarce any [were] absent, but from two or three of [the] remotest shires and some of the meanest burghs'. NLS, Dalrymple Mss 3424, f. 671.

18 NAS, PA8/1, ff. 150r–151v; *RPS*, 1665/8/2.

19 *Lauderdale Papers*, i, p. 211.

20 NLS, Dalrymple Mss 3424, f. 660.

21 NAS, PA8/1, ff. 153v–161r; *RPS*, 1665/8/7 and 1665/8/10.

22 *Lauderdale Papers*, i, p. 225.

23 *Lauderdale Papers*, i, pp. 225–6.

24 Lennox, 'Lauderdale and Scotland: A study in Restoration politics and administration, 1660–1682', p. 56. First used as a means of assessment in 1326, old extent was based largely on land values from the remote past. There was no means of revising the assessment as values changed over the centuries, resulting in gross disparity of valuations. J. Goodare, 'Parliamentary taxation in Scotland, 1560–1603', *SHR*, 68 (1989), pp. 24–6.

25 NAS, PA8/1, ff. 154v–161r; *RPS*, 1665/8/10.

26 Lee, 'Government and politics in Scotland, 1661–1681', pp. 115–16.

27 Hutton, *Charles II*, pp. 230–3; Seaward, *Restoration*, pp. 81–3; Davies, 'International relations, war and the armed forces', pp. 223–4.

28 *Lauderdale Papers*, ii, appendix A, p. xxxi; Burnet, *History*, i, p. 382.

29 *Lauderdale Papers*, i, pp. 235–8.

30 *Lauderdale Papers*, i, pp. 237–8; Burnet, *History*, i, pp. 383–4.

31 See Jackson, *Restoration Scotland*, pp. 114–16 for a discussion of secular anti-clericalism in the period, which convincingly argues that many Restoration politicians were in favour of episcopal church government more for the benefits it brought for enforcing order in the localities than for theological reasons.

32 NLS, Papers of Charles Kirkpatrick Sharpe, Mss 2512, ff. 29, 40, 46; *Lauderdale Papers*, ii, appendix A, pp. iii–iv; Buckroyd, *Church and State*, pp. 55, 59–61.

33 Lee, 'Government and politics in Scotland, 1661–1681', p. 163; *RPCS*, third series, ii, pp. 202–4.

34 Nicoll, *Diary*, pp. 451–2; Burnet, *History*, i, pp. 417–22; *Lauderdale Papers*, i, pp. 248–52; *RPCS*, third series, ii, pp. 232–4; Buckroyd, *Church and State*, pp. 65–6; Cowan, *Scottish Covenanters*, pp. 65–9; C. S. Terry, *The Pentland Rising and Rullion Green* (Glasgow, 1905), pp. 4–8, 10–14, 24–5, 37–8, 78–82; Sir James Turner, *Memoirs of His Own Life and Times*, T. Thomson (ed.), (Edinburgh, 1829), pp. 145–88.

35 Buckroyd, *Church and State*, p. 67.

36 *RPCS*, third series, ii, pp. 206–7.

37 *Lauderdale Papers*, i, pp. 256–7, 260–2, 263–5; Burnet, *History*, i, pp. 425–6.

38 NAS, PA8/1, ff. 163r–164r; *RPS*, 1667/1/2. Two members of the clergy and four officers of state were also in attendance.

39 NAS, PA8/1, f. 165r; *RPS*, 1667/1/4.

40 Buckroyd, *Church and State*, pp. 63, 68. Sharp had made an unsuccessful bid for the post of chancellor after the earl of Glencairn's death in 1664. See *Lauderdale Papers*, ii, appendix A, pp. v–ix.

41 NAS, PA8/1, ff. 165r–v; *RPS*, 1667/1/5–6.

42 HMC, *Report on the Laing Manuscripts preserved in the University of Edinburgh* (London, 1914), i, p. 355; *Lauderdale Papers*, i, p. 270.

43 HMC, *Report on the Laing Manuscripts*, i, p. 355; *Lauderdale Papers*, i, pp. 272–3; NAS, PA8/1, ff. 167v–173r; *RPS*, 1667/1/9; C. K. Sharpe and Sir G. Sinclair (eds) *Letters from Archibald, earl of Argyll to John, duke of Lauderdale* (Edinburgh, 1829), p. 52.

44 NAS, PA8/1, ff. 167v–173r; *RPS*, 1667/1/9; Lee, 'Government and politics in Scotland, 1661–1681', p. 116.

45 *Lauderdale Papers*, i, pp. 279–80.

46 Lee, 'Government and politics in Scotland, 1661–1681', pp. 118, 122–3.

47 Hutton, *Charles II*, pp. 248–9; Davies, 'International relations, war and the armed forces', pp. 224–5.

48 *Lauderdale Papers*, i, p. 240; Burnet, *History*, i, pp. 381, 432.

49 NLS, Yester Mss 7023, f. 49; HMC, *Report on the Laing Manuscripts*, i, pp. 358, 360; *Lauderdale Papers*, ii, pp. 3–6, 16–17; *RPCS*, third series, ii, p. 294; Hutton, *Charles II*, p. 246.

50 *Lauderdale Papers*, ii, pp. 45–9, 66–8, 71.

51 Buckroyd, *Church and State*, pp. 69–70; Hutton, *Charles II*, p. 245. For a comprehensive, although dated, account of Moray's career, see A. Robertson, *The Life of Sir Robert Moray* (London, 1922).

52 Burnet, *History*, i, p. 439; *Scots Peerage*, viii, pp. 452–3, 458.

Chapter 4

ARISE KING JOHN: LAUDERDALE AND THE 1669 SESSION OF PARLIAMENT

ᖇᗢ

In the nine years since the restoration of Charles II, John Maitland, earl of Lauderdale had come to dominate Scottish politics. Although based at court, through his deputies on the ground in Scotland, Lauderdale oversaw all aspects of policy and had come to exert almost complete control over the Scottish administration. Any vestiges of opposition or independence to his supremacy were swiftly quashed, as both the earls of Middleton and Rothes had found to their cost. When appointed commissioner of parliament in 1669, he journeyed to Scotland confident that opposition to measures such as the proposed union with England and the intended redefinition of the royal supremacy in ecclesiastical matters would be easily dealt with. The oath of allegiance and declaration of public trust still regulated the membership of parliament, ensuring that no one opposed to crown policy gained election. The articles remained the principal method of crown control over parliamentary business. Thus, Lauderdale had no reason to expect that the 1669 session would be any less compliant than the previous parliament or conventions of estates. Yet it was this belief that parliament was a submissive body, easily persuaded into granting the requests of the crown, that ignited protest. The resulting opposition would prove to be the source of the most serious challenge to crown control over parliament since the Restoration.

With the full backing of Lauderdale, assuming command of the Scottish administration in mid-1667, Moray and Tweeddale's impact on policy was immediate. In August 1667, the troops raised in the aftermath of the Pentland rising, the focus for much of the discontent in the localities and a potential power-base for Rothes, were ordered to be immediately disbanded as a gesture of moderation. There was also an attempt to regulate the behaviour of the remaining forces, with the privy council setting out detailed instructions for the exigencies under which quartering was to be used.[1] Concurrent with planned reform of the treasury, there were also determined efforts to pay the troops on time, thus negating their need to live off the population. It was all aimed at increasing political control over the army to prevent a recurrence of past abuses, but, in the council especially, there was considerable resistance to the new policies from those who had benefited from military commissions. Headed by the duke of Hamilton, a faction in the council sought to obstruct the raising of funds to meet the costs of disbanding. With the exception of Archbishop Burnet, all those involved had considerable self-interest in the continuance of their troops, but the order for disbanding came directly from Charles and could not be meaningfully questioned.[2] There were similar complaints in September 1667 when a list of proposals to be sent to the king (drawn up by Moray) recommended that a general pardon be issued to those involved in the Pentland rising not under process of forfeiture. By remitting the issue to a committee staffed mainly with sympathetic crown supporters, the objections were easily laid aside and a wide-ranging indemnity for the rebels was announced in late October.[3] It was a delicate balancing act: the new administration was keen to propagate a less repressive image, without incurring the wrath of previously loyal nobles. In early 1668, the establishment of a militia was therefore proposed, which, it was hoped, would satisfy the nobility's desire for military command without the excessive costs of maintaining a standing army.[4]

The reduction in forces and offer of indemnity to the rebels also met with familiar opposition from the episcopal clergy, led by the hard-line archbishop of Glasgow, Alexander Burnet. His correspondence with Gilbert Sheldon, archbishop of Canterbury, ranting against the leniency shown towards the dissenters, and his colluding with the earl of Clarendon against Lauderdale highlighted the administration's lack of a trusted figure within the bishops who could impose order. In July 1667, Sharp had tentatively made an approach to Lauderdale seeking reconciliation, which had been cautiously welcomed by the earl.[5] Yet it was Burnet's intractability and refusal to fall into line which made Sharp's return necessary. At a meeting of the bishops to discuss 'the common interest of the church' in September 1667, Burnet attacked the moderate policies now pursued and sought to persuade his fellow clergymen to address the king directly with their concerns. Instead, Sharp manoeuvred the bishops into subscribing an innocuous letter of concern for the general welfare of the church under Lauderdale's ministry.[6] Burnet found himself at once isolated. Sharp, in a startling reversal of fortune, was welcomed back into the fold.

With reforming zeal, Moray and Tweeddale continued apace, turning their attention to the widespread corruption that had flourished under Rothes's command of the treasury. Collectors of crown revenue were ordered to bring in their accounts for audit and there was to be a series of investigations into the performance of the recent grants of taxation and cess. As part of a determined effort to reduce crown expenditure, pensions and fees were again cut, this time by another 20 per cent.[7] The treasury itself was to be reformed, with William Sharp, Lauderdale's trusted agent in Edinburgh, appointed cashkeeper. There was also a renewed sense of optimism regarding Scottish trade with the end of the Dutch war, but even Moray was surprised when, in October 1667, the customs and excise on imports was farmed (to Sir Walter Seaton of Abercorn) for the hugely increased sum of £375,600.[8] An immediate shortfall of money in the treasury and the large amounts of debts the crown had accrued during the war still made the financial situation difficult but, with the recent reforms, there was at least the prospect of improvement on the near horizon.

Moray did not wait around long to enjoy his accomplishments of the past year, permanently leaving Scotland for London in the summer of 1668 to return to his preferred calling in his scientific laboratory.[9] Soon, Tweeddale became overwhelmed by the amount of work that fell on his shoulders, and Lauderdale, at first sympathetic, rapidly grew tired of his deputy's complaints.[10] In response to Tweeddale's concerns, Alexander Bruce, second earl of Kincardine, was primed as Moray's replacement. A member of Charles II's court in exile and, like Moray, a keen amateur scientist, Kincardine had previously been deprived of significant office due to a falling-out with Archbishop Sharp over the earl's alleged support for irregular practices in the kirk.[11] However, with Sharp now bullied into subservience, such past concerns were brushed aside. Joining Kincardine was John Murray, second earl of Atholl, who had earlier been commissioned to raise an independent company for securing the peace of the Highlands, a task which he had carried out with commendable success.[12] Lauderdale's brother, Charles Maitland of Hatton, was also advancing through the ranks, having already been appointed master of the mint and a lord of session, despite his lack of legal education. Plans were already afoot to have Hatton promoted to the post of treasurer depute as soon as the office (currently held by the aged Lord Bellenden of Broughton) became vacant.[13]

Ignored for office, yet again, was the duke of Hamilton. He had been badly affected by the dissolution of the army, having invested

£3,000 of his own money on his troops just a matter of months before the decision was made to disband them, but the duke had won the support of Archbishop Burnet for his uncompromising stance against rebels in the localities. '[He] hath obliged me more then all the nobility in this countrey', Burnet wrote to the archbishop of Canterbury.[14] Hamilton's friendship with Burnet may have irritated Lauderdale, but the duke had expected to be compensated for his losses with some kind of office, perhaps the post of chancellor that Rothes had instead so begrudgingly taken, or at least as one of the commissioners of the treasury. Disappointed at being overlooked yet again, Hamilton, accompanied by Rothes, travelled to London for a personal audience with the king in October 1667, both men longing for a turn around in their fortunes.

The primary reason for Hamilton's journey south was to seek the repayment of the large debt owed by the crown to the Hamilton family since the reign of Charles I. The duke had made many appeals for reimbursement since the Restoration, with little success, and more empty promises were made at his crucial audience with the king. Charles explained that, given the shortfall in the treasury, there was no means of settling the debt until the financial outlook improved. Hamilton's subsequent offer to farm the king's entire Scottish revenue 'at much advantage and to finde most excellent security for it' was tactfully declined and the duke returned home disappointed and empty-handed.[15] Devoid of further options, the only means of securing political position lay in rapprochement with Lauderdale, and, reluctantly, he approached the secretary, asserting that 'he wold doe what earl of Tweeddale and Moray should advise; in a word he promised to be very good.'[16] It was a massive personal climb-down for Hamilton, one that Lauderdale relished. Nevertheless, by the summer of 1668, Hamilton was working with Tweeddale on the settling of a militia in the south-west shires and initial steps had been taken towards the payment of the crown's debt to his family, albeit in stages. It remained a fragile relationship, however, and perhaps Tweeddale was right when he warned Lauderdale that 'Duke Hamiltonne is lost to yow for not making him a commiss[ioner] of the treasurie.'[17] If he felt undervalued, Hamilton obviously had the potential to cause trouble.

Throughout 1668, the privy council's policy of indulging peaceful dissent whilst taking forceful action against those who continued to defy the law had met with mixed results. The administration's greatest concern was the increase of conventicles, which had spread to previously unaffected areas such as Fife. Clearly, preaching within private houses, outwith the control of the crown, could not be allowed to flourish unabated. The alternative was to allow some moderate presbyterians to preach publicly in selected parishes, without conforming to episcopacy.[18] An assassination attempt on Archbishop Sharp on 11 July 1668 nearly wrecked negotiations for such a scheme, but the proposal gathered pace, in the absence of any meaningful alternatives, until a formal indulgence was issued in August 1669.[19] All this was done against a background of staunch opposition from the clergy. The admittance of non-conforming ministers to the established church was a step too far for even the most subservient of the bishops, Sharp included. His unwelcome views that such a policy may even be illegal, passed as it was against the will of the clergy, were too significant to be ignored.[20] Therefore, to deal with any lingering questions over the legality of the new initiative, plans were made to strengthen the royal prerogative in ecclesiastical matters by a supremacy act to be brought before the forthcoming session of parliament in October 1669.

The principal reason for summoning a meeting of the estates, however, was to consider a proposed union between the English and Scottish parliaments. The idea was first rooted in the trade disputes that had characterised Anglo-Scottish relations since the early 1660s and had found increasing support in light of the downturn in Scottish trade caused by the Dutch war. In November 1667, after hostilities had ended, the English parliament agreed the king could nominate commissioners to meet with the Scots and consider their demands. It was done with reluctance, however. Even in these early debates in the Commons, it was all too apparent that there remained considerable resistance to allowing the Scots any inroads to English trading interests, in the plantations and colonies in particular.[21]

The trade commission first met on 13 January 1668, with the Scots hoping that the talks would ultimately lead to removal of the restrictions placed on their trade by the Navigation acts. The discussions, however, were plagued with disagreements. The English commissioners flatly refused to negotiate on any issue until the full scope of the Scottish propositions were known. Yet, when these demands (which included an end to the import duties on cattle, linen cloth, salt and beer and to the duties on exported horses and grain) were clarified on 3 February, they met with a distinctly unfavourable reception. In what the Scots regarded merely as a delaying tactic, the English requested a list of all Scottish ships, ostensibly to assess the level of competition that would exist if the Navigation acts were repealed. This took a number of weeks to compile and, in the meantime, arguments broke out over what was thought to be exorbitant duties on coal and salt. This seemed only to sour relations further and, before the shipping list could be brought in, the English commissioners declared that they were unwilling to allow Scottish access to colonial trade. Instead, they were prepared to open up the Baltic timber trade and the markets in the Levant, along with access to the trade in foreign salt. Rather than accept this and use it as a basis for future negotiations, the Scottish representatives immediately rejected the proposals outright. Discussions continued until September 1668, but the commissioners became side-tracked into arbitrating disputes amongst English salt merchants. Thus, when the commission was eventually wound-up in the autumn of 1668, the Scots had nothing to show for the months of debate.[22]

It has been argued that the Scottish commissioners set out determined to see that the trade negotiations would fail, thus explaining why they pitched their demands so high. In this, it was Lauderdale's true design to demonstrate that mere commercial union was unobtainable, thereby illustrating the need for full parliamentary union.[23] This seems unlikely for a number of reasons. Firstly, the failure to ensure the repeal of the Navigation acts would be viewed in Scotland as a failure of the negotiations as a whole, so the uncompromising stance of the Scots was vital if further concessions on customs duty on salt and taxes on coal were to be realised. Moreover, the breakdown of negotiations was hardly due just to the demands made by the Scottish commissioners. The English themselves were guilty of delaying tactics, querying every small detail of the Scottish proposals and demanding access to the original parliamentary records held north in Edinburgh.[24] From the Commons' initial lukewarm reception and throughout the negotiations themselves, the English had clearly demonstrated no enthusiasm for making significant concessions on trade. The Scots themselves were badly hampered by a lack of bargaining power. It remained a painful truth that there were few concessions the Scots could offer to the English that would advance negotiations to an outcome that would be acceptable to both countries.

If Lauderdale had designs for fuller union at the trade negotiations, he would have been delighted when throughout late 1668 and early 1669 the proposal gained momentum. This was due partly to the support it had from the king himself. To unite the two kingdoms and their respective parliaments, to succeed where James VI had failed, would be a great coup for Charles. More important than this, however, was the prospect of using union to wean Scotland away from commercial and political associations with the Dutch, still regarded as an enemy despite the end of hostilities. Political union would also finally solve the seemingly intractable trade problems between the two kingdoms without the need for another round of wearisome negotiations. For the king, there was a less well-publicised advantage: involving both parliaments in what was likely to be contentious discussion also diverted attention away from Charles's secret negotiations for an alliance with Louis XIV, eventually culminating in the treaty of Dover.[25]

The initial reaction to the union proposal in both countries would prove crucial to the success or failure of the whole project. Bearing in mind the recent disagreement between the trade negotiators, Lauderdale was at first cautious when informing his deputies north of the border of the scheme. In December 1668, to sound out opinion in Scotland, he authorised only a few trusted nobles to discuss the plans in secret amongst themselves. Talks continued informally at court between Lauderdale and a number of English ministers and were generally encouraging.[26] Yet, it soon became apparent that if negotiations were to progress further, it was necessary that parliament be convened to approve the proposals.

A date for the new session was to be subject to the ongoing discussions for union. Tweeddale was in favour of the English parliament meeting before the Scots, since if the idea of union 'took happily it will be best ue tak measures from proceedings ther; if otherways that the unione be not lik to succeed, it wer good peopels minds wer settlid heir as soon as possible . . . what ever fall out.'[27] Tweeddale's fear of the possible failure of the union project when it came before parliament was not unfounded. Although opposition in England was expected, when the union proposal was made public in the summer of 1669, the Scots proved to be considerably unenthusiastic about the whole idea. In July, Tweeddale reported to Moray that the 'union is mightly spoken against' in the privy council. A 'cabal' was forming against the union, with Hamilton suspected to be at the head of it.[28] This sudden rash of hostility had come about as a result of a leaked paper circulating between the peers that suggested only twenty nobles would receive a seat in a combined parliament.[29] Discord amongst the nobility had been anticipated, thus there had been blatant attempts by the crown to simply buy support. In June, the king had authorised the treasury to make payments to a number of key individuals, mainly to those who had been allies of Middleton or Rothes or were otherwise not yet reconciled to Lauderdale's ministry. Amongst the beneficiaries were the earl of Dumfries, General Dalzell and Sir William Drummond of Cromlix.[30] The gradual repayment of the duke of Hamilton's long-standing debt was thought to be enough to secure his reluctant support.

The details of the union proposal had been the subject of much behind-the-scenes discussions. Finally, though, its contents became public on 10 June when the full particulars were presented to the foreign committee of the English privy council. An inseparable union under the king and his heirs was proposed, with equal privileges for the subjects of each kingdom. The church and legal system of each country would remain separate, but a bicameral parliament of both nations would sit in London, with the Scots allocated thirty seats in the Commons. The controversial issue of the status of the Scottish peers was, for the moment, postponed with the agreement that the king could summon what Scottish peers (and bishops) he wished and determine their precedence. On the crucial economic aspect, custom rates, excise and poll tax were to be equal; other taxes were to be considered on a proportional basis, with England paying 70 per cent, Ireland 18 per cent and Scotland 12 per cent.[31]

To enact the above proposals, both the English and Scottish parliaments were summoned to convene in October 1669. In Scotland, the length of the first session would be determined purely by the ongoing union discussions. 'If the union proceed, the first session wilbe very short', wrote Lauderdale to Tweeddale, envisaging a swift quickening of pace in the negotiations after both parliaments had given their approval.[32] To ensure things went according to plan, it was proposed that the nomination of union commissioners would be left to the king; parliament would approve the commission in principle.[33] Anticipating discord at this decision, it was decided that Lauderdale should oversee events in Edinburgh himself. Rather reluctantly, the secretary left London for his homeland and for his new post as commissioner to parliament.

Lauderdale arrived in Edinburgh on 11 October, a little over a week before parliament was due to formally convene. He had come north armed with a comprehensive set of instructions already agreed with the king, for it had been decided that the first session was to be a short one so negotiations with the English could proceed. However, the king's instructions also contained proposals for a supremacy act to

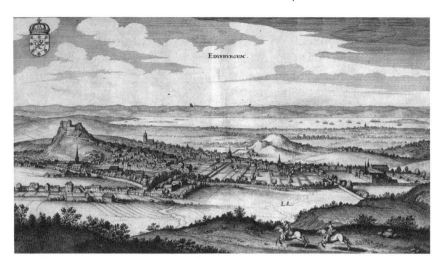

Figure 4.1   *A town plan of Edinburgh, c.1649. The Palace of Holyroodhouse is pictured at far right. This was the residence of the king or his commissioner to the Scottish parliament when in session. Holyroodhouse was also the departure point for the ceremonial procession known as the 'riding of parliament', which took place on the opening day of each session. Members of parliament on horseback accompanied the king or his commissioner up the Royal Mile to Parliament House, situated adjacent to St Giles' Cathedral, pictured to the right of Edinburgh Castle in the above engraving.*
(Reproduced by permission of the Trustees of the National Library of Scotland.)

regulate the royal prerogative in church matters, for the establishment of a national militia and for the regulating of excise.[34] These were all weighty issues that could be expected to test crown support in parliament. Nevertheless, the timetable for the session remained unchanged, the commissioner expecting little opposition and therefore little delay from parliament, believing that his position in the chamber as the king's closest advisor would overawe any possible opponents. Lauderdale was soon to discover that it was dangerous to take the subordination of parliament entirely for granted.

The second parliament of Charles II formally opened on 19 October with the traditional prayers led by Robert Leighton, bishop of Dunblane. Lauderdale's commission was then read, the rolls called and the parliament fenced. This was a slight change in procedure from the previous session, since Middleton, as commissioner, had first fenced the parliament and then read his commission; in other words, approved the parliament before the king's authorisation for its meeting was presented.[35] A total of 192 members attended on the opening day: eleven bishops, sixty-four nobles, three officers of state, fifty-six commissioners representing thirty-one shires and fifty-eight burgh commissioners representing fifty-seven burghs. This was a significant increase in attendance from the two previous conventions of estates and only slightly less than the first session of the last parliament in 1661. Yet the continuity of the membership had changed significantly since last meeting of the estates. Inevitably, increasing numbers of past attendees succumbed to old age and illness and a host of new men replaced many of those who had been present at the first Restoration parliament. Twenty-seven of the peers present in 1661 died prior to October 1669 and a further seventeen died by the last session held in 1674. Lack of information regarding dates of death for the other two estates hampers similar investigation, but the same trend of sending new commissioners exists. Of the thirty-one shires present in 1669, twenty-two had at least one commissioner who had not attended any previous sessions. Likewise, commissioners with no previous parliamentary experience represented thirty of the fifty-eight burghs.[36]

Despite the changes, the government seemingly had no difficulties in recruiting loyal subjects to take the place of those now absent. 'The commissioners for the parliament are, I heare, well-chosen', wrote Lauderdale to the king on arriving in Edinburgh.[37] There is little evidence of widespread manipulation of local elections, as had been the case at the previous meeting of parliament. It seems that the oath of allegiance and the declaration of public trust had largely succeeded in preventing any known opponents from obtaining election. Certainly there does not seem to have been the same trouble taken over managing elections, although on the opening day parliament nominated a committee to undertake investigations into instances of double commissions in the shires of Berwick, Stirling, Kincardine and the burgh of Cromarty.[38] Only the account of the election in Stirling survives, but this suggests that the dispute was not a result of a contest between a chosen crown candidate and a local opponent, but rather a dispute between two local factions over voter eligibility.[39] Thus, to further clarify the guidelines for shire elections, an act was passed on 26 October decreeing that non-residence was not a bar to voting or being elected.[40]

After all members had undertaken the oath of allegiance and the declaration, the king's letter was read in which it was declared that the purpose of summoning parliament was to bring the 'two kingdomes of Scotland and England to as close and strict an union as is possible.'[41] The estates were then dismissed to allow for the election of the lords of the articles and it was here that the pattern was set for the rest of the session. Rather than break-up peacefully, there were endeavours on the part of some unidentified members to delay the selection of the articles until the four controverted elections were determined. When Lauderdale 'cut that debate short, for it wold have made three dayes' delaye', questions were then raised as to the method of election of the articles. The king's instructions to his commissioner had stated that the bishops were to receive a list of those the king 'wold have them nam to be of the articles' so that 'they be not left to make such a choys as they mead in 1617'.[42] Partly to circumvent this rather blatant attempt at increasing crown control over the election of the articles, when the bishops had chosen the nobility and the nobility the bishops, it was questioned by some members whether only those elected should choose the shire and burgh members, or whether the whole body of the bishops and nobles present in parliament should have a vote. Although Lauderdale was convinced that only those already elected should be allowed to participate, Rothes, as chancellor, could not remember what had been done in previous sessions and Sir Archibald Primrose of Carrington, clerk register, could not find the act from 1663 that laid out the correct procedure. The duke of Hamilton 'cryed out' against any restrictions to be placed on the election and others soon joined in. No doubt angry at the unexpected uproar barely minutes into the new session, Lauderdale was caught out. Rashly, he ordered the clerk register to 'break up the dor wher the record lay'. Archbishop Sharp unearthed a printed copy of the disputed act just in time to save the demolition of the offending door and passed it around to quiet the debate. The final election was as Lauderdale had intended: 'If they be amiss blame me, for I wrott the lists and not a man was altered', he informed the king.[43]

It is more than likely that the whole debate as to the election of the articles was a set-up, perhaps a demonstration to Lauderdale of the capacity of the members to bring business to a standstill. It is unlikely that such an important act, the subject of much discussion in 1663, had simply been forgotten by so many, the chancellor included. To the surprise of Lauderdale, the events of the first day revealed that some members were fixed on debating or obstructing almost any measure brought before them. This was to be met by an equal determination on Lauderdale's part to eradicate any such pretence to independence.

The final membership of the articles chosen by Lauderdale could not have been more carefully composed. All of the members had sound royalist credentials and could therefore be expected to approve the pre-prepared legislative programme without too much difficulty. Apart from the young James Douglas, second marquis of Douglas, all of the nobility included on the articles were privy councillors. Of the shire representatives, four were privy councillors and two were collectors of the king's customs. The two remaining members had equally strong crown connections. Sir Alexander Fraser of Dores was physician to the king in exile and Sir John Cochrane of Ochiltree was son of one of the treasury commissioners, William Cochrane, first earl of Dundonald. The burgh representatives were chosen for their previous parliamentary experience, with seven of the eight burgh representatives having served in previous sessions. The new man Sir Andrew Ramsay of Wauchton was the son of a long time ally of Lauderdale, Sir Andrew Ramsay of Abbotshall, provost of Edinburgh, and he joined his father as one of the committee. The duke of Hamilton was included, despite his potential for trouble-making. By giving him this position, Lauderdale hoped not to distance him any further and, surrounded by the commissioner's main supporters, Tweeddale, Kincardine and Argyll, he would be quickly overcome if he attempted to upset the smooth passage of Lauderdale's legislative programme through the articles.[44]

To further secure crown superiority, the practice of allowing free access to the committee's meetings was formally revoked. An order of parliament in May 1662 had inadvertently recognised the right of members who were not actually elected to the articles to be present at its meetings and hear their discussions.[45] This Lauderdale flatly refused to allow, asserting that 'if all members of parliament were allow'd to come into these meetings, they would become tumultuary, and would be too open and . . . unfit for consultation and contriving.'[46] After all, argued the commissioner, was not the whole point of the articles to allow for business to be discussed by a smaller, more manageable body made up of representatives of the whole parliament? Lauderdale's demand was granted and this was a crucial victory. By quashing demands for a wider parliamentary involvement in the election of the articles, he could with some ease ensure that the committee was staffed with loyal supporters. Its meetings and discussions as to the proposed legislation would now also remain secret. The prospects for the controversial union bill and for the supremacy act looked encouraging since it was specifically in the articles that legislation would be changed and amended. Lauderdale believed that his presence in the chamber would check any remaining opposition there.

The answering of the king's letter, and therefore the parliament's response to the union proposal, came up for discussion in the articles on 20 October.[47] The debate was centred on the issue of whether the nomination of commissioners, the quorum and the time and place of the meetings should be left to the king. To place this responsibility in the king's hands would remove the threat of any undesirable members being elected onto the commission, members whom if negotiations became disagreeable may prove to be less compliant than those who would be chosen for their crown support. Lauderdale recognised this fact and pressed for the articles to take their cue from the negotiations in 1604 in which all such particulars were left to the king.[48] After some debate, which was held up by the duke of Hamilton making his now obligatory protest against the whole proposal, a small sub-committee (staffed primarily by the commissioner's close allies) was appointed to draft the parliament's answer.[49] At the next meeting of the articles on 21 October, it was announced that the nomination for commissioners to negotiate a treaty of union was to be left to the king; parliament would, however, reserve the right to veto any decisions they might make.[50]

At the full session of parliament the next day, Lauderdale was given advance warning of the likely reception that would greet the draft reply to the king's letter. Rumours abounded of 'caballing in the hows by som who wer displeased they were not of the articles, lords and others, especially lawyers.'[51] As expected, what caused most concern was the revelation that the commissioners to treat with the English were to be chosen by the king. This undoubtedly negated the main function of parliament in the whole union process, but Lauderdale knew that to allow a free election might threaten the entire scheme. The commissioner refused to back down, but decided not to put forward the draft letter to an immediate vote and risk defeat. Instead, he would allow a free debate to take place, hoping, as Tweeddale later recounted to Moray, that 'the humour might evaporat and he might better know the temper of the hows.'[52]

Firstly, it was argued that the process towards union was moving too fast, that events were progressing apace in Scotland whilst it remained unclear what the parliament of England would do as to the matter. This had been a concern of both Tweeddale and Lauderdale before parliament had been convened, but the commissioner now dismissed such fears, telling the king that such sentiments were due to the 'great paines [that] have been taken to alarum all sort of people' against the union proposal.[53] Robert Dickson, a lawyer representing the burgh of New Galloway, then spoke on the legal and constitutional ramifications of an incorporating union. The fundamental laws, rights and privileges of the kingdom, he argued, were under threat unless parliament had the final say on whether the treaty of union should be allowed to progress or be rejected. The commission granted by James VI in 1604 had preserved these rights, as must the new commission. Dickson was seconded by his fellow lawyers, Sir George Mackenzie of Rosehaugh and by Sir George Gordon of Haddo, representing the shires of Ross and Aberdeen respectively. In a 'long-winded discourse', Rosehaugh declared that any vote on the letter must be delayed to allow time for more debate. The duke of Hamilton, despite his earlier assent in the sub-committee of the articles, likewise urged an immediate adjournment to allow further consultation of the draft reply.[54] Haddo expressed similar concerns and then brought up the valid question of what should happen if the succession of the crown and the Stewart line should fail.[55] At this, Lauderdale could no longer remain silent. Haddo was 'sharply taken up by my lord commissioner and had a sorie reprimand', Tweeddale reported with some satisfaction to Moray.[56] Having listened largely passively to the long debates, Lauderdale consented to the requested delay in proceedings, and ordered that the articles' draft was to be delivered to the keeping of the clerk register, where any member who so wished was free to consult the letter further.[57] This was no defeat for the commissioner. Lauderdale was quite content to allow additional debate on the issue, confident that when it came to the final vote he could depend on the continued loyalty of the majority of members.

Parliament reconvened at 10 o'clock the following day and the debates began afresh (albeit with the same speakers). Sir George Mackenzie of Rosehaugh continued from where he left off, with an hour-long speech that succeeded only in boring those present.[58] Taking his cue from a suggestion first made by Rothes, Hamilton then joined the debate and insisted that if commissioners were to be chosen by the king alone, parliament must possess the right to alter those royal nominees as they saw fit. Haddo made the suggestion that two letters should be sent to the king: one concerning the union in general, another as to the nominations for the commissioners. This, however, was rejected as being impractical. Finally, after two hours of debate, the vote was taken and the original draft from the articles passed with only one objection. Rosehaugh ('in love of singularity as much as solitude', noted Tweeddale) was the lone dissenting voice.[59]

The gathered estates had passed the king's letter by a very comfortable margin, but, to Lauderdale, what the prolonged debates revealed was that many of the members had an exaggerated belief as to the power and privilege of parliament. Rosehaugh had raised a number of important issues when he had stated that if 'union should be a national act . . . all its steps should be nationally concluded.'[60] By this, he meant that parliament should not only choose the commissioners, but should also be consulted on all proposals every step of the way. This was not the role Lauderdale envisaged. Parliament might be the king's 'great council' to whom he turned to for advice, but it was in turn expected to show its loyalty by concurring with the crown's demands.[61] Nevertheless, Rosehaugh, in highlighting the difficulty of balancing loyalty to the crown with the rights of parliament, articulated what was likely to be a widespread opinion, this demonstrated by the long debates concerning parliament's role in the selection of union commissioners.

On 25 October, the articles moved on to consider the scope of the proposed militia act, electing a sub-committee of eight members to compose an initial draft.[62] Since 1668, the privy council had begun to put into effect parliament's earlier act of 1663 that authorised the raising of up to 20,000 footmen and 2,000 horse for the king's service. Given the lack of arms and funds for maintaining such a large number of troops, it was thought more prudent to reduce the number of foot by half. Despite the council's best efforts, progress in raising the regiments was still painfully slow, the commissioners of the militia being hindered by frequent disputes over who was to stump up the cost of sending out fully equipped men.[63] To remedy the situation, parliament was to enact stricter penalties for non-attendance at rendezvous and for non-payment of proportions.

The duke of Hamilton was once again nominated by the commissioner as one of the eight members of the sub-committee, presumably for his previous experience as military commander of his own troop. Yet Lauderdale must have regretted his choice when, at the first meeting of the sub-committee, Hamilton initiated an ill-tempered debate on whether grievances concerning inequalities of proportions should be considered before discussions proceeded any further. Lauderdale's reaction to the duke's proposal was typically over-the-top. Hamilton, he said, was nothing more than 'ane opposser' of the king's service and Charles would be told of the duke's factious behaviour.[64] On 26 October, Lauderdale referred the matter back to the articles to decide whether regulating proportions of horse and foot was part of the remit of the sub-committee. The rest of the articles fell into line. In naming a sub-committee to ratify the council's proceedings in relation to the militia, it was not their meaning that the commissioners should 'meddle' with any grievances relating to the proportions.[65]

A second dispute arose on 27 October when the act drafted by the sub-committee was tabled before the articles as a whole. A clause allowing quartering for deficiency proved so controversial that the act was remitted back to the sub-committee with the instruction that a second copy be brought in replacing quartering with distraining.[66] This was so done and, on 28 October, after lengthy debate, the articles approved the draft containing the quartering penalty. An unknown minority dissented from this decision, the first time in this session than an act did not secure unanimous approval in the articles.[67]

The draft act, complete with disputed clause, was brought into the chamber on 29 October. The substance of the act was approved easily enough in principle, but, in Lauderdale's words, many 'bogled' at the penalty of quartering. Due to the unpopularity of the clause, the act was delivered back to the lords of the articles for amendment and there it was agreed that the rejected draft substituting distraining of the subject's goods for quartering would instead be submitted to the chamber. The act was immediately returned to the gathered estates and passed with only one opposing vote from George Maule, second earl of Panmure.[68]

The resistance to quartering revealed to Lauderdale the extent of the hostility to the billeting of soldiers in the localities. Indeed, the opposition had been so strong as to necessitate the act to be returned to the articles for modification, something that had not been done since before the Restoration. Lauderdale's assertion in a letter to Moray barely two days earlier that in Scotland the king 'can command absolutely' was clearly overstating the extent of the crown's mastery over the estates.[69] If anything, the debates over the militia act demonstrated that parliament, in its role as a check against unrestrained royal authority, was not completely ineffective, nor was parliamentary approval to every act a foregone conclusion.

Protests against the next proposal, an act of supremacy asserting the royal prerogative in ecclesiastical matters, came from usually loyal quarters. The bishops had long been vocal in their opposition towards the indulgence, but it was Sharp's earlier questioning of the legality of the whole policy that still rankled. In July 1669, Moray had drawn up a list of possible contents of an act of supremacy, suggesting amendments to existing legislation to make clear the clergy's subordination to the royal will.[70] Hostility from the bishops to such an act was assured, thus steps were taken to lessen the public fall-out.

Sharp could be easily dealt with, having previously been cowed into submission by vague threats of dismissal, but his fellow archbishop, Alexander Burnet, had never shown any such signs of acquiescence. Burnet's outspoken views on government church policy, given a wider audience by his correspondence with English bishops, had long irritated Lauderdale. Throughout 1669, the archbishop persisted in publicly denouncing the indulgence and was almost successful in persuading a number of his fellow bishops to agree to send a representative directly to the king to complain of the direction of current policy. Matters came to a head at a meeting of the synod of Glasgow in mid-September 1669. A remonstrance was drawn up by the attending clergy that expressly condemned the indulgence and accused the government of a lack of progress towards uniformity of worship and discipline in the church. Burnet seems to have been free of any direct involvement in drafting the protest, but his attendance at the meeting and his silent acceptance of the remonstrance seemed to imply his tacit approval. When informed of events, the king reacted with fury. Opposition to royal policy, whether from presbyterian dissenters or crown appointees, was nothing less than sedition. Burnet was warned to stay away from the forthcoming session of parliament and measures were being taken to effectuate his dismissal.[71]

Burnet's absence from the chamber eliminated one of the major threats to the act. However, Archbishop Sharp now took up the campaign of opposition on behalf of the bishops. Before parliament, he gave a sermon in which he analysed the nature of the royal supremacy over the church, concluding that it was extremely limited. The indulgence, he argued, was a threat to the very independence of the episcopate. Infuriated, Lauderdale promptly ordered Sharp to retract his statements and preach again to the gathered commissioners, this time to the opposite effect.[72]

A draft of the supremacy act, which Moray and Tweeddale had been working on for some months, was presented to the articles on 28 October and a sub-committee of eleven immediately appointed to consider and amend the draft. This done, it was then passed on to Sir Archibald Primrose of Carrington, clerk register, and Sir John Nisbet of Dirleton, lord advocate, for final adjustment.[73] Sharp, as a member of the sub-committee responsible for amending Moray's and Tweeddale's initial draft, had already made clear his opposition at the committee's earlier meetings, although in this he had been obstructed by Hamilton, Tweeddale and Kincardine. Next, Sharp approached Lauderdale in private and assured the bishops' co-operation if a small amendment was made to the wording of the act. To the phrase 'the ordering and disposall of the externall government and policie of the church doth propperlie belong to his majestie' should be added 'as it is settled by law'. Since it was designed to override the existing legislation, such an amendment would have made the act redundant, as Lauderdale knew all too well. Sharp's suggestion was therefore rejected outright.[74] On 2 November, at a full meeting of the articles, Sharp gave a long speech against the act, being careful to couch his opposition in theological terms rather than out of any disloyalty to the king. Yet this too was simply ignored. The act was approved unanimously as it stood, with Sharp himself finally submitting in the face of a complete lack of support for his position amongst his fellow members of the articles.[75]

The king was understandably delighted by the supremacy act. With his full support, Lauderdale put the act before parliament on 16 November.[76] As was the case in the articles, it passed unanimously and without protest. Indeed, vociferous support for the act came from some surprising quarters. The earl of Dumfries, never an ally of Lauderdale, rose to his feet and told the chamber that he was glad that 'now the king was to be mor then a pretender to supremacy and was declared to have better right than Pope or presbiter.' He then imparted to Tweeddale his delight that 'the king had now got in between God and the bishopes.'[77] Enmity towards the bishops was perhaps stronger than the traditional factional divisions that had in the past determined voting patterns.

With the major legislation of the session safely through, attention began to turn back to the issue of union. The arguments over the reply to the king's letter had been largely unexpected, with Lauderdale admitting to Moray 'it may be the worke [is] more difficult then was imagined.'[78] English apathy to the proposal also had to be overcome and the government in Scotland waited anxiously on events south of the border. Charles had decided to leave the naming of the English negotiators to the Commons rather than appoint a commission without election, hoping that this concession would encourage the English to proceed. However, it soon became apparent that union with Scotland was not high on the agenda. The disappointing news from London was that the issue was unlikely to receive any consideration until mid-December.[79]

As parliament could not remain in session until their English counterparts discussed the union proposal, Moray proposed that an act could be passed to allow the king to issue the commission under the great seal. The present session could then be adjourned as soon as all other matters had been dealt with.[80] Without waiting for reaction from Scotland, Charles proceeded to authorise the passage of the act, to the horror of Lauderdale and other key members of the articles. After the hostility displayed at the selection of commissioners, in deference to Scottish sensibilities, Lauderdale had expressly avoided putting a draft of the commission through parliament. That the estates should approve a blank commission, allowing the king to appoint commissioners without further recourse to parliament, would only create further hostility to union. 'No command could be more greevous', wrote Lauderdale, instructing Moray to acquaint the king with the depth of feeling in Scotland. Before anything else could be done, the English must act; whatever was decided there could then be pushed through the Scottish parliament.[81]

Confident that his advice would be taken due to his high standing with Charles, Lauderdale was 'amazed' to receive from court an express command from the king demanding that an act be passed which would allow for commissioners to be named under the great seal.[82] Lauderdale's only comfort was that before the act would be finalised, he was permitted to discuss the matter with other officials to gauge its likely reaction. A meeting of certain members of the articles was therefore arranged for the morning of 8 November. As Lauderdale had expected, the proposal was roundly condemned. The chief objection amongst the committee was that the Scottish parliament had progressed towards union in good faith, expecting the English to do the same. The English parliament's continued refusal to consider the matter was simply an insult to a nation that had suffered so grievously under their trade restrictions for the past nine years. Notwithstanding the loyalty justly owed to the king, it was inappropriate to insist that parliament pass a measure to relinquish its own authority in approving the commission.[83] Despite earlier boasts of his unlimited authority as commissioner, even Lauderdale knew that such an unpopular proposal could not be pushed through an unwilling chamber. In the end, and to the relief of the Scottish administration, the king, expressing surprise at the reaction of the Scots, agreed to drop the idea of a commission under the great seal and await the outcome of the English parliament's debates.[84]

When faced with overwhelming opposition, as with the great seal proposal, Lauderdale was prepared to allow alterations to his pre-planned programme of legislation, albeit reluctantly. He was forced to do so yet again when a number of seemingly innocuous measures proved to be amongst the most controversial of the session. On 15 December, an act for forfeiting the estates of Pentland rising rebels in their absence was brought into the chamber.[85] Lauderdale expected little difficulty in its passage, yet it immediately met with opposition from predictable quarters. First, Sir George Gordon of Haddo spoke 'loosely' against it. He spoke, however, in the 'plurall number we' and Lauderdale soon 'snapt him up and desired to know if he was a single person or spoke in name of a collective bodie.'[86] This silenced Haddo, but Rosehaugh was next to berate the proposal, declaring that by civil law all prosecutions should be heard in the presence of the accused party, it being unlawful for any institution other than parliament to try an absent person. Rosehaugh's concerns were roundly dismissed by Sir John Nisbet, lord advocate, and a number of other lawyers allied to the commissioner. In the end, the official argument won out: the act passed unamended, with only a few dissenting votes amongst the shires and burghs.[87]

The trouble for Lauderdale did not end there. An act for regulating excise and customs duties was the next item brought before the gathered estates. In 1661, to protect Scottish trade, a duty of 40 shillings Scots had been placed on all salt imports; only salt for use in the fishing trade was exempt.[88] Since the loophole had been so heavily exploited, with the majority of imported salt escaping payment, a remedial clause was to be included in the excise act placing a duty on all foreign salt regardless of intended use. Those using it to cure fish could, however, apply for a rebate.[89] There was widespread opposition to the proposals. In the articles, all the burgh members spoke against the act and when it was first presented to the full parliament, it met with such a hostile reception Lauderdale delayed the vote, fearing the act would be thrown out altogether. Burgh commissioners had worked to mobilise opposition, cajoling members of the other estates to join forces and unite against the proposed amendment.[90] When discussions resumed, it was immediately apparent that the burghs had secured widespread support amongst the other estates. Infuriated at the increase of opposition to the controversial clause, Lauderdale interrupted the debate and 'swore that though the parliament stopt the act, yet they should gain nothing by it; for he would, by virtue of his majesty's prerogative, pepper the fishing . . . with impositions.'[91] This assertion only antagonised the act's opponents. Rosehaugh declared that the king had no such right and that the statute of 1663 granting to the king the right to order foreign trade could not be interpreted in this manner.[92] The duke of Hamilton expressed his suspicions that the act was intended only to benefit private individuals, a reference to Lauderdale's ally the earl of Kincardine, who, as a salt producer, stood to gain financially from an increased levy on foreign salt.[93]

The debate had been both lengthy and acrimonious. According to Hamilton, Lauderdale's invectives from the throne had so 'terrified' some members who still had their own private business to conduct before parliament that they voted against their better judgement and personal interests. When the votes were eventually counted, the clerk declared the numbers equal, to the amazement of those who had calculated that a majority had voted against the act. Patrick Lyon, third earl of Kinghorn suspected a miscount and demanded a second vote. The request was refused, Lauderdale challenging Kinghorn to instead pursue the clerk for falsehood. Rothes, in his role as chancellor, gave his casting vote in favour of the act, after an 'apology' to the opposition.[94]

The crown had secured the narrowest of victories against what had been a relatively well-organised opposition. What had begun as an issue of concern only to the burghs had gradually gathered strength so that at the final vote the opposition included members from each estate. However, as Rosehaugh recognised, co-operation between the estates would only go so far. Indeed, it was discernible in the crucial ballot that

> those who were not concerned in their immediate interest, did still vote for the commissioner . . . for those who have salmond, care not how much be imposed upon beef, etc; whereas, when it comes to their share to be concerned, they who have the other commodity do, out of revenge, or at least by the same reason, desert them.[95]

This led to a situation where 'the nobility neglect the burghs; and they again desert the nobility, in what is their concern.' This is undoubtedly a correct description of contemporary parliamentary politics and it was something that had in the past aided the crown, since it was expected that very few issues would unite all three estates in opposition. Lauderdale had not been prepared for the strength of feeling surrounding increases in customs duties, but it proved to be an issue on which members from each estate would unite.

The most important legislation was now safely through and attentions began to turn towards the private business of ratifications. This was the first chance for Lauderdale to reward those who had supported him in the controversial debates, many of whom had already been trusted with positions on committees such as the lords of the articles. For those allied with the commissioner, the rewards could be great. Those granted ratifications on 23 December included the earls of Tweeddale and Atholl, Archbishop Sharp, Sir James Lockhart of Lee, Sir Alexander Fraser of Dores and John Nisbet, lord advocate, all of whom were members of the articles. Reconciliation was offered to Rothes's old military ally William Drummond of Cromlix with a ratification of his lands in Perthshire. It was hoped that the duke of Hamilton would be pacified with the three separate ratifications granted to his family.[96] A ratification in favour of the rehabilitation of Archibald Campbell, ninth earl of Argyll, was also approved, despite protests from a number of individuals who were still owed significant sums of money from the earl's father, the late marquis of Argyll. Indeed, opposition from Argyll's creditors was so vocal that Lauderdale was unwilling to risk a vote. Instead, the commissioner pushed through the act without allowing the gathered estates an opportunity for debate. This was justified, he argued, since it was not the custom of parliament to vote on private ratifications, which were only of concern to the king.[97]

The majority of Middleton's old associates had since been reconciled with the new administration but the business of the billeting affair still rankled the commissioner. Lauderdale was delighted, therefore, with parliament's ratification of a decreet of the court of session re-annexing to the crown the islands of Orkney and Shetland, long dominated by the earls of Morton.[98] The present earl, William Douglas, had been one of Middleton's most important allies and the earl's original disposition of the islands had been approved in parliament, with Middleton's support, in 1662. Confirming Morton's continued allegiance to the disgraced commissioner, he had since married Middleton's eldest daughter.[99] Plans were thus made to deprive Morton of the lucrative income the islands provided and an incident during the Dutch war furnished the government with a convenient pretext. A Dutch vessel had been shipwrecked upon the coast of Orkney with a cargo of gold worth approximately £12,000 sterling. This Morton was foolish enough not to declare, and so, on 23 December, parliament sanctioned the act for the re-annexation of Orkney and Shetland to the crown.[100] This single act caused great loss, if not absolute ruin, to the Morton family, and despite Morton's indiscretion during the Dutch war, many correctly surmised that the true motivation behind the act was Lauderdale's long-standing grudge against Middleton. The whole episode merely served as demonstration of legislation being dictated by the commissioner's personal spite.

This was apparent again in an aborted attempt to silence Sir George Mackenzie of Rosehaugh, a prominent voice of dissent in the debates on union and the excise act. Lauderdale planned to question the election of Rosehaugh in the next session of parliament on the grounds that he held his lands from the bishop of Ross, not the king, and was therefore ineligible for election. Sir Archibald Primrose of Carrington, clerk register, came to Rosehaugh's rescue by persuading Lauderdale that because people were already suspicious of a design to overturn their liberties, his removal would only cause more mistrust. Furthermore, it could be guaranteed that Rosehaugh would 'glory' in his exclusion since it would be believed that the government was unable to execute their intentions if he were allowed to keep his place in parliament.[101] Thus, Rosehaugh won a reprieve, but Lauderdale's conduct revealed an almost megalomaniacal attitude in his role as commissioner to parliament. Growing resentment towards the personal conduct of Lauderdale manifested itself through continued resistance in the chamber to the government's demands.

The majority of the opposition was not directed at the substance and content of the legislation but at the way it was concluded. The previous commissioners, Middleton and Rothes, had at least sought to involve the estates in decision-making, and both had courted parliament in such a way that tended to emphasise its importance. However, from the start of the 1669 session, it was apparent that the new commissioner envisaged a minimal role for parliament, for Lauderdale had come to Scotland with a pre-prepared package of legislation and wanted parliament to simply rubber-stamp it. When he was forced into altering this by overwhelming opposition, as in the case of the militia act, it was done with reluctance and often only after a lengthy diatribe from the throne. Such an attitude aroused some of the usually compliant estates into opposition. Yet it should be noted that at the crucial votes, the controversial legislation was either carried unanimously or with only a few objections. This was because the commissioner could successfully play the different groups, interests and estates against each other. As both Rosehaugh and Hamilton had recognised, the majority would always vote with the commissioner unless specific legislation impinged on their own self-interests.

The act of adjournment of 23 December ordered the next session of parliament to convene on 8 June 1670. In the interval, no new elections for commissioners to the shires and burghs were to be held unless there were vacancies due to death.[102] There was no need to change the membership, for, despite the opposition to a number of acts, Lauderdale was able to carry virtually unchanged all of the measures set out in the instructions he had brought with him at the beginning of the session. 'Never was [a] king soe absolute as you are in poor old Scotland', Lauderdale wrote to Charles after the passage of the supremacy and militia acts, and certainly, the legislation of the 1669 session had achieved everything that both the king and his commissioner had desired.[103] The church and its bishops had been reined in, the appointment of the commissioners for the union negotiations had been left to the king and customs duties had been tightened up. All this was achieved despite the most vocal opposition in parliament since the Restoration.

Lauderdale left a great deal of resentment behind him when he left Scotland in mid-January 1670 to return to court.[104] He had not only offended a number of high profile individuals by refusing to award them positions in his administration, but had alienated those who believed that parliament ought to play a meaningful part in the process of government. By his high-handed attitude,

> the members were rather overaw'd than gain'd to a compliance; for Lauderdale . . . never consulted what was to be done; nor were the members of parliament solicited by him, or his friends, upon any occasion; whereas, on the contrary, he would oftimes vent at his table, that such acts should be past in spight of all opposition.[105]

Rosehaugh's description of proceedings is largely confirmed by Lauderdale's own accounts. He found debate tiresome and certainly believed that he had the right to push through unwelcome legislation by the power of the royal prerogative alone. Yet despite the hostility directed towards Lauderdale for his arbitrary control over proceedings, parliament remained consistently loyal to its king. The next sessions would test this loyalty to the full.

Notes

1 *RPCS*, third series, ii, pp. 334, 361–4.
2 Hamilton and Burnet were joined by the earls of Rothes, Callander, Wemyss, John Scrimgeour, first earl of Dundee and General Dalzell. Lee, 'Government and politics in Scotland, 1661–1681', p. 66; Buckroyd, *Church and State*, pp. 71–3.

3 *RPCS*, third series, ii, pp. 339–41, 347–9; *Lauderdale Papers*, ii, pp. 52–3, 55–9; Lee, 'Government and politics in Scotland, 1661–1681', pp. 66–7.

4 *RPCS*, third series, ii, pp. 438–42.

5 Buckroyd, *Church and State*, p. 72. For Burnet's letters to Sheldon, see *Lauderdale Papers*, ii, appendix A, pp. xlvi–lxi. For Sharp to Lauderdale and his response, see *Lauderdale Papers*, ii, pp. 28–30, 40–1.

6 *Lauderdale Papers*, ii, pp. 59–61 and appendix A, pp. xlix–li; Buckroyd, *Church and State*, p. 73.

7 Lee, 'Government and politics in Scotland, 1661–1681', pp. 120–2.

8 *Lauderdale Papers*, ii, p. 73–4.

9 *Lauderdale Papers*, ii, p. 120.

10 NLS, Yester Mss 7024, f. 121.

11 *Lauderdale Papers*, i, pp. 228–31. Much of Kincardine's correspondence with Moray survives as NLS, Miscellaneous Mss 5049 and 5050.

12 Macinnes, 'Repression and conciliation: The Highland dimension, 1660–1688', pp. 178–80; *Lauderdale Papers*, ii, pp. 98–9.

13 'Letters from John, second earl of Lauderdale to John, second earl of Tweeddale and others', in SHS, H. M. Paton (ed.), *Miscellany of the Scottish History Society*, vi, (Edinburgh, 1939), p. 168.

14 *Lauderdale Papers*, i, p. 279 and ii, appendix A, p. lii.

15 NAS, Hamilton Muniments, GD406/1/8421, 8430; 'Letters from Lauderdale to Tweeddale', in SHS, *Miscellany*, vi, pp. 145–6.

16 'Letters from Lauderdale to Tweeddale', in SHS, *Miscellany*, vi, p. 157; Airy, 'The Lauderdale Mss in the British Museum', p. 434.

17 *Lauderdale Papers*, ii, pp. 21, 111–12; NLS, Yester Mss 7024, ff. 106, 108, 110–11.

18 Buckroyd, *Church and State*, pp. 75–9; G. M. Yould, 'The duke of Lauderdale's religious policy in Scotland, 1668–79: the failure of conciliation and the return to coercion', *Journal of Religious History*, 11 (1980), pp. 252–3.

19 Sharp escaped injury when a shot was fired by James Mitchell, a conventicle preacher, at his coach travelling through Edinburgh, but Andrew Honeyman, bishop of Orkney received a serious wound to his arm. [George Hickes], *Ravillac Redivivus, being a Narrative of the late Tryal of Mr James Mitchell, a Conventicle preacher, who was executed the 18 of January, 1677 for an attempt which he made on the sacred person of the Archbishop of St Andrews* (London, 1678); Sir John Lauder of Fountainhall, *Journals of Sir John Lauder of Fountainhall, with his Observations on Public Affairs and other Memoranda, 1665–1676*, D. Crawford (ed.), (Edinburgh, 1900), pp. 230–1.

20 HMC, *Report on the Laing Manuscripts*, i, p. 372; *Lauderdale Papers*, ii, pp. 189–90; Burnet, *History*, i, p. 509.

21 Hughes, 'Negotiations for a commercial union', pp. 31–2; M. Lee Jr, *The Cabal* (Urbana, 1965), pp. 45–6.
22 NLS, Yester Mss 7023, f. 142; Hughes, 'Negotiations for a commercial union', pp. 35–6; Keith, *Commercial Relations*, pp. 91–2; Lee, *The Cabal*, pp. 46–8. For a complete account of the negotiations between the commissioners for both kingdoms, see NLS, Yester Mss 14492.
23 Lee, *The Cabal*, pp. 49–50.
24 NLS, Yester Mss 14492, f. 34.
25 Lauder of Fountainhall, *Journals of Sir John Lauder of Fountainhall*, pp. 229–30; A. Macinnes, 'Politically reactionary Brits? The promotion of Anglo-Scottish union, 1603–1707', in S. J. Connolly (ed.) *Kingdoms United? Great Britain and Ireland since 1500* (Dublin, 1999), pp. 50–1; Hutton, *Charles II*, p. 263. For an account of the domestic background to the secret treaty of Dover negotiations, see R. Hutton, 'The making of the secret treaty of Dover', *The Historical Journal*, 29 (1986), pp. 297–318.
26 'Letters from Lauderdale to Tweeddale', in SHS, *Miscellany*, vi, p. 174; NLS, Yester Mss 7023, f. 224; NLS, Yule Mss 3136, f. 138; Lee, *The Cabal*, p. 52.
27 NLS, Yester Mss 7001, f. 216.
28 NLS, Yester Mss 7001, f. 220; 'Letters from Lauderdale to Tweeddale', in SHS, *Miscellany*, vi, pp. 213–14.
29 NLS, Yester Mss 7024, f. 166.
30 NAS, Exchequer Papers E9/3; Mackenzie, *Memoirs*, p. 141.
31 Lee, *The Cabal*, p. 53.
32 'Letters from Lauderdale to Tweeddale', in SHS, *Miscellany*, vi, pp. 215–16.
33 NLS, Yester Mss 7023, f. 224.
34 *RPCS*, third series, iii, p. 80; BL, Additional Mss 23132, f. 93.
35 NAS, PA2/29, ff. 1r–3r; *RPS*, 1669/10/1–3; *Lauderdale Papers*, ii, p. 142.
36 NAS, PA2/29, ff. 1r–2r; *RPS*, 1669/10/2.
37 *Lauderdale Papers*, ii, p. 142.
38 NAS, PA2/29, f. 4r; *RPS*, 1669/10/7.
39 NAS, PA7/25/32/8/1–17.
40 NAS, PA2/29, f. 5v; *RPS*, 1669/10/11.
41 NAS, PA2/29, f. 3v; *RPS*, 1669/10/5.
42 *Lauderdale Papers*, ii, p. 142; NLS, Yester Mss 14488, 'Instruction to parliament, 2 August 1669', ff. 79–80. In 1617, the clergy undertook to superintend the election of members to the general assembly, but they failed to procure an obedient membership and James VI's church reforms were delayed.
43 NLS, Yester Mss 7024, f. 182; *Lauderdale Papers*, ii, p. 142. The king had earlier instructed Lauderdale not to undertake any reform of the

committee, presumably because it had served the royal interest so well in the previous parliamentary sessions. 'Letters from Lauderdale to Tweeddale', in SHS, *Miscellany*, vi, p. 221.

44 NAS, PA2/29, f. 4; *RPS*, 1669/10/6; NAS, PA7/22/117/1, p. 226; *RPS*, C1669/10/1; Young (ed.), *Parliaments of Scotland*, i, pp. 127–8, 264 and ii, p. 581.

45 The clause in question stated that 'Nor any persons [shall be] suffered to stay at the articles save members of parliament'. NAS, PA2/28, f. 3v; *RPS*, 1662/5/6. In 1669 and 1681, there were clear indications that some considered the act as giving the whole chamber the right to attend. The intended meaning in 1662, however, was to allow access to the committee only to members of parliament who were *also* members of the articles. The act was amended in 1685 to reflect this. NAS, PA2/32, f. 150v; *RPS*, 1685/4/13.

46 Mackenzie, *Memoirs*, pp. 142–3.

47 For the minutes of the articles concerning their response to the king's letter, see NAS, PA7/22/117/1, p. 226; *RPS*, C1669/10/2–3.

48 'Letters from Lauderdale to Tweeddale', in SHS, *Miscellany*, vi, p. 224. In 1604, James VI sent an already complete commission to Edinburgh for approval but agreed to foot the bill for the commissioners' expenses from his own purse. NAS, PA2/16, ff. 37r–v, 38v–39r; *RPS*, 1604/4/11, 1604/7/5.

49 The sub-committee consisted of the archbishop of St Andrews, the earls of Argyll and Tweeddale, Sir James Lockhart of Lee, Sir Andrew Ramsay of Abbotshall, Sir Archibald Primrose of Carrington, clerk register, and Sir John Nisbet of Dirleton, lord advocate. The duke of Hamilton was also given leave to attend but the other members would again mitigate his influence if he became obstructive. NAS, PA7/22/117/1, p. 226; *RPS*, C1669/10/2.

50 NAS, PA7/22/117/1, p. 226; *RPS*, C1669/10/3; 'Letters from Lauderdale to Tweeddale', in SHS, *Miscellany*, vi, p. 224; *Lauderdale Papers*, ii, pp. 143–4.

51 'Letters from Lauderdale to Tweeddale', in SHS, *Miscellany*, vi, p. 224.

52 'Letters from Lauderdale to Tweeddale', in SHS, *Miscellany*, vi, p. 224.

53 *Lauderdale Papers*, ii, p. 143.

54 Tweeddale attributed Hamilton's bizarre behaviour to his friendship with Rothes: the duke 'is never 24 of a tune and I dare promise nothing of him', he told Moray. The 'factious inclinations and the insinuations of you know who [Rothes] are still soe poerfull with him that he [Rothes] makes him speake his mind whilst himself goes sweetly along.' 'Letters from Lauderdale to Tweeddale', in SHS, *Miscellany*, vi, p. 225; it has been suggested that Rothes was exploiting the less experienced Hamilton for his own ends, Patrick, 'The origins of the opposition to Lauderdale in the Scottish parliament of 1673', p.8. Hamilton does not

mention his own involvement in the debate in his 'Memorandum of some passages in parliament begun October 1669, first session'. NAS, Hamilton Muniments, GD406/2/640/2.

55 Hamilton, whose own family had a place in the succession to the Scottish throne, supported Haddo in this matter and rose to defend him. Union with England might have altered his claim. Mackenzie, *Memoirs*, p. 148.

56 'Letters from Lauderdale to Tweeddale', in SHS, *Miscellany*, vi, p. 224.

57 *Lauderdale Papers*, ii, p. 144.

58 Mackenzie records his speech in his *Memoirs*, pp. 148–55. Tweeddale gives an observer's account in 'Letters from Lauderdale to Tweeddale', in SHS, *Miscellany*, vi, pp. 223–6.

59 'Letters from Lauderdale to Tweeddale', in SHS, *Miscellany*, vi, p. 225.

60 Mackenzie, *Memoirs*, p. 152.

61 Mackenzie, *Memoirs*, p. 153.

62 NAS, PA7/22/117/1, pp. 226–7; *RPS*, C1669/10/4.

63 NAS, PA2/28, ff. 110v–111r; *RPS*, 1663/6/64; *RPCS*, third series, ii, pp. 275, 438–42, 547–8.

64 NAS, Hamilton Muniments, GD406/2/640/2.

65 NAS, PA7/22/117/1, p. 227; *RPS*, C1669/10/5.

66 NAS, PA7/22/117/1, p. 227; *RPS*, C1669/10/6.

67 *Lauderdale Papers*, ii, p. 150.

68 *Lauderdale Papers*, ii, p. 151; Mackenzie, *Memoirs*, pp. 166–7; NAS, PA2/29, ff. 6r–7v; *RPS*, 1669/10/14.

69 *Lauderdale Papers*, ii, p. 151.

70 Buckroyd, *Church and State*, pp. 80–1.

71 NLS, Yester Mss 7001, ff. 230–3; Mackenzie, *Memoirs*, pp. 156–8; Burnet, *History*, i, pp. 510–11; Buckroyd, *Church and State*, pp. 83–5; Jackson, *Restoration Scotland*, pp. 115–16; Yould, 'The duke of Lauderdale's religious policy in Scotland, 1668–79', pp. 254–5. For more on the events surrounding the synod's remonstrance and Burnet's subsequent dismissal, see J. A. Lamb, 'Archbishop Alexander Burnet, 1614–84', *Records of the Scottish Church History Society*, 11 (1955), pp. 138–40.

72 NLS, Yester Mss 7024, f. 185; Mackenzie, *Memoirs*, pp. 159–60; Buckroyd, *Church and State*, p. 82.

73 NAS, PA7/22/117/1–2, pp. 227–8; *RPS*, C1669/10/7; *Lauderdale Papers*, ii, p. 152.

74 *Lauderdale Papers*, ii, pp. 152–3.

75 Sharp's argument was centred on episcopacy being *iure divino*, thus the implication in the act that the king had the authority to change the form of church government was misleading. Buckroyd, *Church and State*, p. 82; NAS, PA7/22/117/2, p. 228; *RPS*, C1669/10/8; NLS, Yester Mss 7024, f. 189; *Lauderdale Papers*, ii, p. 153; Mackenzie, *Memoirs*, pp. 159–60; Burnet, *History*, i, p. 512.

76 NAS, PA2/29, ff. 5v–6r; *RPS*, 1669/10/13.
77 *Lauderdale Papers*, ii, p. 164; NLS, Yester Mss 7024, ff. 192–3.
78 *Lauderdale Papers*, ii, p. 154.
79 Terry, *The Cromwellian Union*, p. 223; *Lauderdale Papers*, ii, pp. 148–9; Lee, *The Cabal*, p. 56.
80 *Lauderdale Papers*, ii, pp. 149–50.
81 *Lauderdale Papers*, ii, pp. 154–5; Lee, *The Cabal*, pp. 56–7.
82 *Lauderdale Papers*, ii, pp. 155–6.
83 *Lauderdale Papers*, ii, pp. 156–8; Lee, *The Cabal*, pp. 57–8.
84 BL, Additional Mss 23132, ff. 150–1.
85 NAS, PA2/29, ff. 13v–14v; *RPS*, 1669/10/30.
86 *Lauderdale Papers*, ii, p. 172; [Sir James Stewart of Goodtrees], *An Accompt of Scotland's grievances by reason of the duke of Lauderdale's ministrie, humbly tendered to his Sacred Majestie* (Edinburgh?, 1672), p. 38.
87 Mackenzie, *Memoirs*, pp. 174–5; *Lauderdale Papers*, ii, p. 173.
88 NAS, PA2/26, ff. 127r–138r; *RPS*, 1661/1/160.
89 NAS, PA2/29, ff. 14v–17r; *RPS*, 1669/10/31.
90 Tweeddale gave Moray an account: 'There was a club mead in the hous, as we fund afterward, for the west country men and north country had bein soe bussie Sunday, Munday and heirsday that many of the nobility and gentry and most of the borrows were fixed against the act', NLS, Yester Mss 7024, f. 192. Lauderdale himself told the king that 'we have been working through great opposition of merchants and almost all the burroughs'. *Lauderdale Papers*, ii, p. 164.
91 NAS, Hamilton Muniments, GD406/2/640/2; Mackenzie, *Memoirs*, p. 170.
92 This was the 'Act asserting his majesties prerogative in the ordering and disposall of trade with forraigners', ratified on 9 October 1663. NAS, PA2/28, ff. 132v–133r; *RPS*, 1663/6/110; Mackenzie, *Memoirs*, p. 170.
93 NAS, Hamilton Muniments, GD406/2/640/2; NLS, Yester Mss 7024, f. 193.
94 *Lauderdale Papers*, ii, p. 173; NAS, Hamilton Muniments, GD406/2/640/2; Mackenzie, *Memoirs*, pp. 170–1.
95 Mackenzie, *Memoirs*, p. 172.
96 NAS, PA2/29, ff. 29v–105v, 108v–109v; *RPS*, 1669/10/60–126, 1669/10/133–4.
97 Charles Seton, second earl of Dunfermline, Gilbert Hay, eleventh earl of Erroll, the earls of Marischal and Kinghorn, Patrick Scougal, bishop of Aberdeen (in name of William Scroggie, bishop of Argyll) and William Anderson of Newtown, commissioner for Glasgow, all formally protested that the ratification should not prejudice the payment of the sums of money due to them by Argyll's father. NAS,

PA2/29, ff. 33r–34v; *RPS*, 1669/10/62–3; Mackenzie, *Memoirs*, pp. 177–9.

98 NAS, PA2/29, ff. 17v–19r; *RPS*, 1669/10/33.

99 NAS, PA2/28, ff. 30r–31r; *RPS*, 1662/5/61; *Scots Peerage*, vi, p. 379.

100 *Lauderdale Papers*, ii, p. 176; Mackenzie, *Memoirs*, pp. 175–6.

101 Mackenzie, *Memoirs*, p. 173.

102 NAS, GA12/05, printed acts of parliament (1670), p. 44; *RPS*, 1669/10/154.

103 *Lauderdale Papers*, ii, p. 164.

104 Lauderdale's last appearance at privy council was on 14 January and he seems to have set out for London soon after this date. *RPCS*, third series, iii, p. 126.

105 Mackenzie, *Memoirs*, pp. 181–2.

Chapter 5

THE GROWTH OF OPPOSITION, 1670–4

❧

Lauderdale left a considerable amount of resentment behind him when he departed Scotland after the first session of parliament in 1669. This was partly due to the manner in which he governed as commissioner. Lauderdale had notoriously little patience when it came to the delicacies of managing the Scottish parliament, preferring instead to play off the different interests and estates against one another. It was a method that had some initial success and, with some ease, he fulfilled all the king's demands in the first two sessions. After the second session, however, the nature of the opposition in parliament changed. Previously the majority had always voted with the commissioner, except when specific legislation impinged on their own self-interests. In subsequent sessions, however, the duke of Hamilton and other disenchanted members of the nobility were able to harness the increasing bitterness that was developing in response to Lauderdale's ministry. With leadership, an organised opposition developed in parliament for the first time since the Restoration.

The second session of the second parliament of Charles II met at Edinburgh on 28 July 1670, having been adjourned twice, first from 8 June to 20 July, and from then to 28 July.[1] A total of 190 attendees are recorded in the rolls taken on the opening day: six members of the clergy, sixty-six nobles, three officers of state, fifty-six commissioners representing thirty-one shires and fifty-nine burgh commissioners representing the same number of burghs.[2] There was no significant drop in attendance, as had been the case between sessions in the previous parliament. Indeed, the membership of 1670 session remained remarkably similar to that of 1669 since no new elections had been held, as per parliament's instruction in the act of adjournment. Only the burghs of Burntisland and Lauder had new representation due to the death of the original commissioner in the interval between sessions.[3]

Lauderdale had arrived in Edinburgh on 25 July, again armed with a comprehensive set of directions from the king laying out the proposed legislation for this session. Contained therein were instructions to pass an act authorising Scottish commissioners to treat with their English counterparts on the issue of union, for legislation to curb the growth of conventicles and details of the penalties to be applied on dissenters who withdrew from the established church.[4] Most of the groundwork had already been done in preparing the acts, although immediately prior to the meeting of parliament Lauderdale ordered the privy council's sub-committee for trying of conventicles to frame a number of suggestions which were then to be passed onto the articles for inclusion in the proposed act for suppressing disorderly religious meetings.[5]

To safeguard the proposed legislation, no new election of the lords of the articles was to be held during the life of the current parliament. Instead, the committee that was selected in the last session (which had already proved itself as overwhelmingly loyal to the crown agenda) was to reconvene with the same members. Following a precedent set by Middleton in 1662, if vacancies did occur due to death or absence, replacements were to be nominated solely by the commissioner, without recourse to parliament. However, the wholesale transfer of the committee's membership from session to session was in itself a new innovation and an unwelcome one at that. On the first day of the session, the duke of Hamilton, privately conversing with the earl of Rothes in the drawing room in Holyrood Palace, queried whether the articles would be newly elected again this session. Interrupted in their discussion by the entry of Lauderdale, Rothes put the question to him, with Hamilton tentatively suggesting that the membership of the committee should again be put to the vote, as had been 'the former practice so farr as I heard'. Lauderdale's reaction to the proposal was typically over the top. In reply to the duke's query, he 'said in pashon ther should be no choise' and that there was to be no further discussion on the matter. Despite the duke of Hamilton's assertion that 'I said it not out of designe of any alteration, but meerly to know his intention, for no wher els I did not so much as move in it in the least', the whole episode simply dragged up the ill-feeling that had been simmering between the two since the last session.[6] It did not bode well for the smooth passage of the forthcoming legislation.

The king's letter was the first matter of business to be dealt with when parliament assembled later that morning. In it, the king declared his intention to pursue the union between Scotland and England and to continue the process that had begun in the previous session.[7] There was even less enthusiasm for the project than there had been in 1669, yet the issue could not simply be dropped. In

March 1670, the English parliament, after some gentle persuasion from the king, had finally given its approval for commissioners to meet with their Scottish counterparts to hammer out some kind of settlement. The English commission, passed under the great seal, was couched in the same vague terms as that previously agreed by the Scots: commissioners were not to be limited by any particular instructions, but they were to agree to nothing that was prejudicial to the laws, liberties or privileges of either kingdom.[8] For discussions to progress to the next stage, all that now remained was for the Scottish parliament to approve the nominees which the crown had chosen on their behalf and to provide a supply to cover the commissioners' expenses.

The act authorising commissioners for union negotiations was ordered to be drawn by the articles on the afternoon of 28 July, approved by the committee on 30 July and brought in to the full parliament that afternoon.[9] There the act met with remarkably little dissent when compared to the long-winded speeches of complaint it first aroused when discussed in the last session. This was despite the fact that Lauderdale refused to reveal the names of the chosen commissioners until after the act was safely passed.[10] Some thought that there should be an immediate debate on the general detail of parliamentary union: for example, it had not yet been resolved if there was to be one or two parliaments or if the laws and privileges of both countries were to be preserved entirely. It was prudent that these issues were discussed before they were predetermined by the king and the union commissioners. Concern was also voiced as to the dominating influence of the English at the negotiations. Not only were they to be held in London (thus the English parliament would have an immediate knowledge of proceedings), but many of the English commissioners were courtiers and therefore had considerable influence with the king. Only Lauderdale could boast of similar connections, but it was doubtful whether he would oppose any unfavourable proposal for which the king was strongly inclined.[11] The purpose of the debate was basically an attempt to secure Scottish interests in advance, but Lauderdale was unwilling to retread old ground. An almost identical discussion along the same lines had taken up two full days of business last session and thus the issue was brushed aside with the promise that parliament would have their say on any finished settlement.[12]

The lack of any vocal opposition towards the union act is somewhat surprising, certainly when considering the hostility the subject first aroused in 1669. Yet what was now apparent to all observers was the lack of enthusiasm with which the whole exercise was being carried out. Lauderdale's assertion to Tweeddale in March 1670 that 'there is no more doubt of a treaty for the union' had already been undermined, first by the lukewarm reception the plan received in England outwith the circle of the king's advisers, and, secondly, by the continued aversion of many of the commissioner's Scottish colleagues.[13] For the king, his secret negotiations with France, culminating in the treaty of Dover, were near completion and an alliance with Louis XIV was a much more attractive means to secure independence from parliament than by pursuing a union in which his control over the Scottish estates could possibly be used to subdue their more intractable English counterparts.[14] It seems highly probable, therefore, that most had already realised that there was little hope in union becoming a reality.

Nevertheless, a motion to raise a supply to fund the union commissioners' expenses engendered a more animated response. The proposition encountered opposition when first discussed in the articles on 1 August, then again when brought into the full parliament a few days later.[15] This was not entirely unexpected, but Lauderdale had attempted to overcome any opposition by asking for a supply that would not only provide for the union commissioners but would also serve as a grant to repair the king's residences in Scotland. By coupling the two unrelated items, it was hoped that those who were simply against the union negotiations would be discouraged from voting against the supply as a whole.

That a supply should be granted was unanimously agreed in the lords of the articles but soon disagreement arose as to the amount. At the committee's meeting on 1 August, Robert Milne of Barnton, provost of Linlithgow, proposed a sum of twelve months' cess, an obviously excessive recommendation and supposedly part of an attempt to 'screw himself into favour' and secure a position on the still to be made public union commission.[16] A grant of ten and then eight months' cess was then suggested by a number of other members, presumably anxious to show their similar devotion for the king. Lauderdale, who had been instructed to secure a supply of three months' cess, interrupted the debate and declared that less than six months would be sufficient. Five months' cess (amounting to £360,000) was the amount finally agreed upon, until the duke of Hamilton intervened. He had been listening with increasing alarm at the amount others on the committee were suggesting. Knowing the poverty and inability of the country, Hamilton rose to argue that it was not in the king's interest to impose such a burden and suggested a more realistic sum might be £240,000. 'I thought I was not out of purpose', the duke recorded in his memorandum of the day's events, 'since it was above what his majestie had desired in his instructions and more then I beleeve will be made use [of] for the ends proposed.' Lauderdale was furious with Hamilton's continued intractability and made a show of noting down the duke's name to later report back to the king. At the vote itself, however, Hamilton was not the only member of the articles to display reservations at the excessive amount to be granted to the union commissioners. Most, if not all, of the bishops (and Hamilton himself) seem to have voted in favour of a supply of only four months' cess (£288,000) and the eventual decision to proceed with a grant of five months was secured by only one vote.[17]

The act was brought in to the full parliament on 3 August. First, Sir George Mackenzie of Rosehaugh called for the names of the union commissioners to finally be made public, since 'much of the quota would depend upon their quality'. His argument centred on the premise that any supply to be granted should be based on the status of the commissioners, 'it being unreasonable that a burgess or baron should get as great an allowance as an earl, or an earl as a duke.' Rosehaugh suggested that the supply should be paid only when the negotiations were over and the Scottish delegation had returned, in much the same way, for example, as commissioners for the shires were reimbursed for their expenses. Parliament would then be able to award a sum based on the outcome of the negotiations. Rosehaugh's contribution to the debate was, however, merely ignored and the act put to the vote. The sum agreed by the articles was approved without much complaint and the method of raising the supply remitted to the next day's session.[18]

The reason why the act was to be voted in two different parts soon became apparent when the actual method of payment was announced to parliament on 4 August. A tax on land was proposed, similar to that voted by the convention of estates in 1667 and equally as unpopular in 1670 as it was then. There were immediate protests from, amongst others, John Kennedy, seventh earl of Cassilis, James Johnstone, first earl of Annandale, the earl of Callander and the duke of Hamilton, and, for once, they were successful in ensuring the act was remitted back to the articles in order to provide for some measure of relief for landowners, on whom the greatest burden fell.[19] On 5 and 8 August, the articles amended the act, inserting a clause giving debtors retention of a tenth part of their annualrents to enable them to pay the cess

imposed, this an attempt to spread the burden of payment by including personal estates in the calculation of the imposition.[20] Some opposition to the additional clause was expected, especially from amongst
the burghs, but the strength of feeling against the amendment when
the draft act was brought before the gathered estates on 9 August was
striking. The clause was thrown out by nearly fifty votes, with opposition coming from almost all quarters. According to Rosehaugh,
although the clause had been instigated for their relief, many landowners also voted against the proposed amendment because they feared a
backlash from their creditors. It was an unexpected blow to Hamilton,
compounded by the commissioner's refusal to amend the final act to
suspend the collection of arrears of cess from the covenanting period
for the duration of the present supply.[21]

In addition to advancing the union proposal, Lauderdale's instructions from the king included specific directions for drafting legislation
to curb the growth of religious dissent, particularly against unauthorised religious gatherings. This had taken on a new sense of urgency
since a particularly large conventicle, attended by perhaps as many as
2,000 people, had taken place at the Hill of Beath in Fife in June 1670,
previously an area undisturbed by such gatherings.[22] The English parliament, sitting a few months before their Scottish counterparts, had
themselves delivered a blow to toleration by passing a second conventicle act, renewing the statute of 1664 which forbade religious
assemblies of more than five people outwith the established church.[23]
For some, however, the English act was not a suitable model for the
Scots to follow. The earl of Kincardine wrote in a letter to Tweeddale
that he found the English punishment of small fines to be 'of ane odde
nature' and doubted that the meagre penalties contained therein
would deter Scottish dissenters.[24] Kincardine need not have worried
about the severity of punishment that was to be meted out to offenders, for the acts presented before parliament comprised the harshest
penalties yet seen.

The notorious 'Act against conventicles', drafted by the committee
appointed to that effect by the privy council, was approved by the articles on 12 August and brought to the full chamber on 13 August.
Under this legislation, holders of indoor conventicles were required to
pay 5,000 merks security for good behaviour or else remove themselves from Scotland. Actual attendance at such a gathering was to be
penalised by fining, the amount rising on a scale of the offender's
income and culpability. The holding of outdoor conventicles, termed
'the rendezvous of rebellion', was to be punishable by the confiscation

of personal property or death, and participation risked fines double the amount stipulated for indoor conventicles.[25] Accompanying this act was a series of legislation punishing irregular baptism, absence from church, assaults on ministers and an act against those who refused to testify against delinquents. Failure to inform the authorities of any conventicle, or to condone them in any way, was to be punishable by fining, imprisonment, banishment to the plantations or, in exceptional cases, death.[26]

Despite the severity of the legislation, it all passed without any real resistance. Only the young earl of Cassilis voted against the conventicle act, conforming, as Lauderdale saw it, to the laudable custom of his father.[27] In a two-hour long debate, Mackenzie of Rosehaugh and Gordon of Haddo had argued spiritedly against the act forcing defendants to testify on oath in criminal proceedings concerning dissenters, arguing that the new law would be tantamount to the powers of an inquisition. Nevertheless, when it came to the final vote, it too passed without objection.[28] On the evening of 13 August, in his chambers at Holyrood Palace, Lauderdale celebrated the passage of the controversial legislation with a large and lavishly catered dinner party.[29]

Collectively, the measures taken against non-conformity represented an attempt to crush any belief that the crown intended a general toleration. However, rather than representing a savage about-turn in policy, the legislation of 1670 can instead be seen as an expedient to deal with a number of political problems first and religious non-conformity second.[30] Active dissent was certainly to be severely punished, principally to serve as a deterrent to the growth of conventicles, but there were a number of other considerations that dictated the need for repression. Prominent among these was the pressing need to simply keep the peace.[31] This was linked to events in England, where the English bishops and the Anglican party in the Commons were in the ascendancy.[32] Lauderdale knew all too well the need to dovetail Scottish policy to that of England to ensure the broadest political support for his ministry. Charles was simply anxious that Scotland remained trouble-free, leaving him to concentrate on matters in his southern kingdom.[33] Stringent action against dissenters also had the effect of extending an olive-branch to the Scottish bishops, much maligned by the granting of an indulgence and then by the act reasserting the royal supremacy in ecclesiastical matters, both pushed through in the face of heavy opposition from the episcopal clergy. Archbishop Burnet had been silenced, with minimal fall-out, but the bishops' continued hostility had been readily apparent in the current session of parliament when they voted against the government's recommended term of supply in the articles. Clearly attempts had to be made to bring them back to the government's side.

That the action against dissenters was not motivated solely by personal spite or malice is given credence by the support given to a proposal of 'accommodation' by Robert Leighton, the new archbishop of Glasgow. Leighton had accepted the post, vacated by Burnet's dismissal, in June 1670 on the condition that he be allowed free reign to put his policies of comprehension for dissenters into practice. Keen to address complaints levelled at the established church, in the winter of 1670–71, Leighton conducted a purge of the orthodox clergy in the west, winning valuable support amongst his parishioners. This followed on from earlier discussions with a number of leading dissenters in August 1670. Thus, whilst parliament was passing unopposed stricter measures against religious non-conformity, Lauderdale and some of the privy council were meeting with indulged ministers to recruit their support for Leighton's initiative.[34] It was a clear message the administration was sending: passive and peaceful dissent would be indulged, active dissent punished.

Indeed, despite the severity of parliament's acts against active nonconformity, more extreme measures had been rejected by the government, again partly due to political implications. The duke of Hamilton had written in June 1670 to Lauderdale suggesting that only a standing army could tackle the problem of dissent in the west, it being so widespread and deep-rooted. With an obvious financial interest in the raising of military forces, Hamilton stood to gain from the suggestion, but such ideas were incompatible with Leighton's new initiative and the duke's suggestion was disregarded. When parliament convened, Hamilton continued to press for a military solution to dissent at the meetings of the privy council's committee appointed for drafting the acts against non-conformity, without success.[35]

Mindful of the problems Hamilton could cause if he was pressed into open opposition to the crown, Lauderdale offered the duke a sweetener to induce his co-operation with the new policy. This took the form of an act passed on 20 August which granted the Hamilton family an indemnity from a debt owed to Patrick Ruthven, first earl of Forth by the duke's father-in-law.[36] Lauderdale had long used the settlement of Hamilton's finances (especially the payment of a debt from Charles I's reign) as a levering tool. However, this measure was little more than a badly disguised bribe and the act did little to calm the duke. In November 1670, Hamilton wrote in a fit of anger to

Lauderdale, furious at being regarded as 'insignificant . . . neglected and misrepresented'. 'I wish to have ground to thinke I might expect friendship from you', he wrote.[37] Lauderdale was understandably disturbed by Hamilton's outburst, yet the commissioner also understood that the duke's 'humour must be cared for . . . to endeavour not to give his grace opportunity to oppose heir [at court] as he did there [in parliament].'[38] However, Lauderdale made no apology for his actions in his reply. Instead, he blamed Hamilton's behaviour in the last session of parliament as the source of his mistrust and warned the duke that he knew well 'how to distinguish betwixt your grace who does express confidence in me and him who is so very diffident of me.'[39] Hamilton heeded the warning and retracted his earlier statement, assuring the commissioner that he meant no offence by his previous letter or by his conduct in parliament.[40] With the large debt to his family still outstanding, he knew better than to alienate the commissioner. Lauderdale himself expressed willingness to let 'bygones be bygones and faire play in time to come'. Relations between the two improved to such an extent that by February 1671, Rothes was able to declare that any misunderstanding was now 'abshulatlie teackin auay'.[41]

Parliament adjourned on 22 August 1670, with a third session appointed for 11 May 1671.[42] By 26 August, many of the Scots nobility and officers of state had left Edinburgh on their journey south to London to attend the union negotiations, which began in earnest on 14 September.[43] Although daily attendance often varied, twenty-five Scottish commissioners attended over the two months of diets, the Scottish membership being made up solely of Lauderdale supporters, a number of bishops and officers of state; the only burgh representative was Sir Andrew Ramsay of Abbotshall, widely recognised as a crown-appointed provost of Edinburgh.[44] Discussions centred on the process of reducing both parliaments into one, a difficult task since both countries had agreed that all laws and privileges should remain intact. Only days into the joint conference, Sir John Nisbet, lord advocate of Scotland, made a 'long and studied speech against any union on any terms'. To negotiate parliament out of existence in this way, he argued, was outright treason. Nisbet's outburst was not a surprise, for, since the conference had begun, he had abstained at every vote and had made it quite clear that if he was allowed to vote as his conscience dictated, he would vote in the negative.[45] Some pointed out that he should have made his feelings known before he gave his assent to the commission, but Nisbet had raised an important point.

Were any of the commissioners willing to vote away the institution from which they acquired their authority?

Faced with such opposition from within his own camp, Lauderdale presented to the Scottish representatives a proposal that smacked merely of desperation. His solution: a small number of Englishmen would sit permanently in the Scottish parliament and, in matters of emergency, the king might call both parliaments together for a joint session at Westminster.[46] The Scottish commissioners, who continued to push for a combined parliament where the entire Scottish estates would be represented along with their English counterparts, never formally adopted this as a valid proposal, but Lauderdale's suggestion brought matters to a complete deadlock. The English refused to accept such a scheme and, on 29 October, Lauderdale informed Tweeddale that the difficulties appeared so great that no further progress could be made at that time. The king eventually called the commissioners together on 14 November and told them that he believed the treaty was not now feasible and adjourned negotiations to an unspecified date in the future.[47]

When the negotiations dissolved without reaching any practical conclusion, the union project that had begun in 1668 was finally abandoned. Like his grandfather before him, Charles II's proposal had never won the support that was necessary for its success. Indeed, the similarities between the events in 1670 and the discussions held by James VI in 1604–7 are striking. English apathy and then downright hostility, especially over any trading concessions to the Scots, had plagued both sets of discussions. It remained that the only kind of union acceptable to the English was one in which Scottish institutions and authority were absorbed into their model. Contrary to this was the Scottish demand that Scotland should never be incorporated or annexed by England, this dominating every aspect of the union question from 1603 to 1707.[48] The Cromwellian occupation, barely a decade earlier, remained fresh in the minds of all Scottish politicians and the events of the 1650s had proved that it was very unlikely that Scottish institutions would survive political union. Thus, opposition to virtually every aspect of the project arose either in Scotland, in England or in both. So the project ended, 'rather to the wonder than dissatisfaction of both nations'.[49]

The planned meeting of parliament in May 1671 was adjourned principally because of the failure of the treaty for union.[50] With no agreement for the estates to ratify, parliament was postponed three times before it eventually reassembled on 12 June 1672 when the outbreak of the third Dutch war necessitated a new grant of taxation.[51] The interval between sessions had witnessed a significant change in the composition of the commissioner's allies, much of it originating from Lauderdale's marriage in February 1672 to Elizabeth Murray, countess of Dysart. Conducted with unseemly haste, barely six weeks after Lauderdale was widowed from his first wife, the match not only alienated the commissioner's chief correspondent at court Sir Robert Moray, but also destroyed his alliance with the earl of Tweeddale.[52] Moray had already experienced a cooling of the friendship in 1668 when he chose his scientific studies in preference to a post in Scotland and his continued support in the union debate for a commission under the great seal had certainly angered Lauderdale. Yet it was Moray's disapproval of the marriage that finally severed relations. Until Moray's death in July 1673, Lauderdale remained hostile towards any attempted rapprochement.

The breach with Tweeddale was more complicated. The earl was not only Lauderdale's closest deputy in Scotland, but, with the marriage of Tweeddale's son to the commissioner's only daughter, Mary, he hoped to further secure his position. If contemporary accounts are to be believed, Lauderdale's new wife was behind a proposal to disinherit Mary so that the Maitland estates could pass to Lauderdale's nephew, who was engaged to marry the countess's daughter. This in itself did not fully sever relations; Tweeddale did little more than protest at the plan, unwilling to sacrifice his career in a vain attempt at securing his son's inheritance.[53] Nevertheless, Lauderdale had become increasingly concerned at the growing power of his deputy and was determined to curtail his influence. Disturbed by his increasing isolation, Rothes, now Tweeddale's only rival, was creative with the truth in his letters to court, magnifying a number of initiatives spearheaded by Tweeddale to make it appear he had higher ambitions. Lauderdale reacted angrily: he had always perceived any such pretensions as a threat to his own standing. When Tweeddale asked for permission to journey south to London, the commissioner answered coolly that he could come if he wished, but that 'he would write for no man'. On arrival at court, Tweeddale was brutally and publicly snubbed by Lauderdale, being refused permission to travel alone to pay his compliments to the countess of Dysart. He returned to Scotland soon after, his political career in ruins. Correspondence between the two earls eventually ceased after October 1671.[54]

Lauderdale's brother, Charles Maitland of Hatton, essentially filled Tweeddale's place, alongside Kincardine, who had earlier been advanced as Moray's replacement. Nothing could have been more insulting to Lauderdale's fallen deputy, for, even before Hatton's elevation to treasurer-depute in late 1670, Tweeddale had expressed criticism of Hatton's management of the mint. Although he had long been guilty of paranoia over the elevation of others, especially those who represented a threat to his own influence, Tweeddale's concerns over Lauderdale's brother were well justified. Already there were suspicions that the currency had been debased whilst Hatton was in charge at the mint. Many contemporaries, his brother included, considered Hatton a liability, motivated solely by greed.[55] By Tweeddale's demotion, Lauderdale had lost a colleague who had governed the many competing interests in Scottish politics with some considerable success. In his place was elevated a man whose self-interest was greater than that which usually consumed the Scottish nobility. The result of all this: Tweeddale's exclusion from policy-making soon bred resentment and he found sympathy for his plight in the duke of Hamilton. It was a potentially formidable combination.

In May 1672, Lauderdale, recently rewarded for his loyal service with a dukedom, received a set of instructions from the king for the forthcoming session of parliament. On his arrival in Scotland, Lauderdale was to call together some eminent persons 'affectionat to our service' to discuss measures for ensuring the peace and security of the kingdom. To place the country on a war footing, the militias should be capable of immediate service, for which necessary impositions may be raised. On the thorny issue of the church and religious dissent, it was left to the commissioner and his advisors whether to enlarge the indulgence or to take further measures against non-conformity.[56]

Parliament reconvened for a third session on 12 June 1672. Recorded in the rolls of the opening day were 179 commissioners: eight members of the clergy, fifty-nine nobles, four officers of state, forty-nine commissioners representing thirty shires and fifty-nine commissioners representing fifty-eight burghs.[57] It was a considerable turnout, the high attendance likely due to the long interval since the last meeting. The 1670 act of adjournment had followed the earlier practice of outlawing new elections except upon the death of the original commissioner, and, due to the lengthy gap between sessions, there were a number of such absences and therefore new members present who all publicly subscribed an oath of fealty before business began.[58] For the same reason, a number of vacancies on the lords of the articles were to be filled, with places also left vacant by the advancement of Hatton to treasurer-depute and Sir James Lockhart of Lee to justice clerk. Following the precedent set by Middleton in the 1662 session, Lauderdale, as commissioner, chose replacement members without recourse to parliament. The new personnel all had impeccable crown credentials: chosen for the clergy, Murdo Mackenzie, bishop of Moray and William Scroggie, bishop of Argyll; for the nobility, the newly elevated William Cochrane, lord Cochrane, now first earl of Dundonald; and for the shires, Sir James Dalrymple of Stair, Sir James Foulis of Colinton and Sir William Lockhart of Lee, the justice clerk's brother.[59]

According to Rosehaugh, Lauderdale's new wife was present at the opening day of the session, with some chairs being placed near the throne in order for the duchess and certain ladies of her train to observe events. It was generally an unwelcome innovation, being a practice not even the queen of the reigning monarch had ever attempted.[60] Yet, despite the disquiet the duchess's attendance seems to have caused, business proceeded as usual. Both the king's letter and Lauderdale's speech itself were uncontroversial and the assertion that the king sought no direct subsidy from this session was greeted warmly. Instead, it was left to parliament to make their own provisions to provide for the security of the country. The king's letter ended with a resolute endorsement of Lauderdale's ministry, praising the 'long and great sufferings he hath endured for ws and the many and great services he hath done to ws'. Were it not for the care with which the king held his parliament of Scotland, it would have been preferable if the duke had stayed at court, where his great skills would be invaluable in dealing with the Dutch crisis.[61] This was a strong recommendation indeed, perhaps intended as a warning to those who were expressing dissatisfaction at Lauderdale's long supremacy over parliament. In many ways, the tone of the letter was similar to those written to parliament during the billeting affair. The king had looked very dimly on those attempts to pull his appointed ministers out from under him, and his current letter left no doubt as to how highly he regarded his commissioner, in spite of the growing animosity towards the duke both in Scotland and in the House of Commons. Parliament's reply to the king made no mention of this. Instead, they congratulated the king for having seen fit to promote their commissioner to a dukedom, assuring the king that Lauderdale's 'usefulnes' in former sessions made his presence necessary for the carrying on of the crown's demands.[62]

The first major legislation of the session was the 'Act for setling the militia', an updated version of the act of 1669, amended by a sub-committee of the articles and introduced to parliament on 25 June. The act ordered all officers and soldiers to subscribe the oath of allegiance and doubled (for the duration of the war) the financial penalties for failure to attend rendezvous and for desertion.[63] This passed without issue, as did an act of 4 September renewing the statute of the last session made against conventicles.[64] A much more controversial matter was the suggestion, first made in the articles by the earl of Atholl (apparently at Lauderdale's insistence), that a subsidy should be levied to provide for the country's own defence during the war, this despite the king's letter and the commissioner's opening speech making no direct mention of a new imposition. Robert Milne of Barnton, commissioner for Linlithgowshire, enthusiastically seconded Atholl's suggestion and suggested a sum totalling twelve months' cess. After some debate, this sum (totalling £864,000) was agreed upon, the amount to be collected in four equal instalments over a period of two years. The proposal proved highly unpopular, even within the articles, and partly to appease the land-owning members of parliament, a clause was inserted that placed part of the burden onto personal estates, allowing debtors to retain one-sixth of their annualrents for one year. A similar proposal made in 1670 had been voted out due to the opposition of the burghs. Thus, to win their support, Lauderdale refused to allow a second amendment which proposed the taxation of financial assets, hoping instead that the burghs would accept the lesser of the two evils.[65] Playing off the different interest groups was a clever move. Both the landowners and the burghs were content that the final act reflected their own recommendations.

It was clearly in the commissioner's advantage to get the subsidy through parliament without too much opposition. However, at the debate prior to the passage of the act of supply on 5 July, Lauderdale's obvious over-reaction to an objection by William Moir, an advocate representing the burgh of Kintore, against the raising of taxation only heightened ill feeling. By the time Moir rose to speak, there had already been a number of lengthy speeches against the use of a cess. Moir was then unwise enough to suggest that commissioners might be allowed some time to consult with their constituents as to the proposed supply (as was the custom in England). According to Rosehaugh, Lauderdale misheard and immediately accused the hapless gentleman of subverting the constitution of the Scottish parliament, an offence for which he should be sent to the bar. Lauderdale's accusation was met with stunned silence until Sir James

Dalrymple of Stair, president of the session, intervened. Accepting Stair's suggestion of imprisonment, Moir was sent to the tolbooth until the commissioner had time to consider his conduct.[66] Although a number of advocates had offered to appear in his defence, on 10 July, the next day parliament sat, Moir chose rather to submit. Brought to the bar and then to his knees before the commissioner, he craved pardon and, suitably chastised, was readmitted to his place. Most were certain that Moir had done nothing wrong and that Lauderdale had acted hastily and in an entirely arbitrary manner. Amongst the lawyers in the house, some feared that the whole episode would serve as an unwelcome precedent, for Moir had been punished in parliament without a vote from the members of that parliament.[67] For many within the chamber, it seemed that Lauderdale was behaving exactly as he pleased, no matter how intolerable such behaviour might be.

More trouble was in store with the passage of an act redefining the privileges of the royal burghs, originating in an action brought in the court of session by the council of Stirling against Falkirk for infringing the royal burghs' trade monopoly. Under an act passed in 1633, only royal burghs could import and export certain commodities.[68] This was now considered an anachronism, detrimental to the economy of the kingdom, and the new legislation put before the articles proposed that burghs of regality and barony would have the right to trade in a number of native raw materials and to import such commodities as were necessary for tillage or building. The obvious benefits to the noble landowners that held these burghs, the earl of Callander and Lauderdale amongst them, did not go unnoticed. It passed easily when it came before the full parliament, the other estates voting with the government, but, although it was never intended as an intentional attack on the royal burghs, the new legislation did little to secure their future support.[69]

A series of measures regulating the justice courts sparked great concern amongst advocates, many of whom were present in parliament representing burgh seats. Lawyers had been protesting since late 1670 against the proposed regulation of the judicatories, with many refusing to swear a new oath restricting the length of court processes and fees they received from their clients. Although some in the articles opposed the new regulations (including Hamilton and Stair, president of the session), the act was sent unchanged into the chamber on 30 August. Here, protests were lodged that the regulations were not one law but a series of laws; as such, they should be voted on separately. Every act was read separately, but in order to secure the passage of controversial clause on clients' fees, they were voted on as one. It was an obvious ploy to ensure that the most controversial aspects of the new legislation were approved. Rosehaugh gave a long and eloquent speech protesting at this 'strange and extraordinary' method, criticising the government for allowing inexperienced noblemen with no experience of legal matters to draw up the new guidelines. It was to no avail, however, and the disputed clauses were pushed through without major difficulty.[70]

There was no deliberate agenda against the burghs. Reducing the cost of employing lawyers and shortening the length of court cases was a popular move. Likewise, the abolition of the privileges of the royal burghs was not intended to threaten their ancient liberties but served instead as a means of opening up trade opportunities in other areas. No matter the good intentions behind the legislation, the burghs perceived the acts as nothing less than a violation of their interests. For Lauderdale, it was these events in this third session that lost him the support of the majority of burgh representatives. This would prove crucial at the next meeting of parliament, when such discontent towards the commissioner was galvanised under the leadership of the duke of Hamilton.

In his role as commissioner to parliament, Lauderdale was behaving in an increasingly arrogant manner, as his treatment of William Moir in the subsidy debate had shown. This was apparent once again in the debates over an abortive proposal to abolish the summer term of the court of session. Although Lauderdale was at first sympathetic to the idea, after further discussion in the articles, the motion was dropped in favour of maintaining the current arrangement. Some were reluctant to let the issue go. Sir Colin Campbell of Aberuchill, burgess for Inveraray, tabled the motion again, this time before full parliament. It was an unwise move to question the commissioner's decision, as those who had felt the full force of his anger in previous sessions could have testified. At Campbell's suggestion, Lauderdale grew 'huffy' and swore that the summer session would never be taken away, 'except his majesty nam'd another commissioner; and none should carry it, except over his belly.'[71] Lauderdale's short temper was rapidly gaining notoriety, but many regarded his behaviour simply as showing contempt for the institution of parliament. Burnet (probably taking his information from a contemporary pamphlet) asserts that the commissioner adjourned parliament for two weeks in order to go on a sightseeing tour with his new wife. The nobility were supposedly

Figure 5.1   *John Maitland, second earl and first duke of Lauderdale (1616–82) by Sir Peter Lely, c.1670s. One of Charles II's leading advisors, Lauderdale was secretary of state for Scotland from 1660 to 1680 and royal commissioner to the Scottish parliament from 1669 to 1680. He is pictured here wearing the resplendent robes of the order of the garter, the most senior English knighthood in age and precedence, which he was granted in June 1672. Arguably the most eminent Scot of his age, it was Lauderdale's position as king's favourite that prompted numerous intrigues against him.*
(In a private Scottish collection.)

'enraged' as Lauderdale attended lavish party after party, amassing a huge bill along the way. Although an interesting anecdote, there is no evidence that this actually happened. Despite this, it seems that Lauderdale's unruly conduct in parliament provided ideal material for inclusion in the propaganda of the opposition.[72]

The session was adjourned on 11 September to June 1673.[73] Again, despite some initial difficulties, it had been another triumphant session for the crown. A generous and voluntary supply had been raised, further laws against religious dissent had been successfully implemented, and, to the dismay of the royal burghs, their monopoly over trade had been abolished. Opposition had been kept to a minimum, even amongst the usual suspects. In November, the duke of Hamilton received a letter from Lauderdale congratulating him on his behaviour for the session and telling him that the king was 'exceedingly satisfied' with his conduct.[74] When Lauderdale set out on his return journey to London, left firmly in control of domestic affairs in Scotland was the commissioner's brother, Hatton.

To the dismay of their opponents, Lauderdale and his allies seemed perfectly secure in their offices. Indeed, despite the loss of influential personnel such as Tweeddale and Moray, the commissioner was actively expanding his influence into a number of other areas. Following Hatton's earlier advancement, in November 1671, Sir Andrew Ramsay of Abbotshall, provost of Edinburgh, Sir Robert Preston of that ilk and Sir Richard Maitland of Pittrichie were all admitted as lords of session, despite having no formal legal experience and in the face of vocal resistance from the advocates.[75] Ramsay of Abbotshall had long been useful to Lauderdale, rapidly rising from the youngest bailie on the council to provost of Edinburgh and continuing in the post for ten successive years. By having the leading vote for the burghs in parliament, his support had often been vital, no more so than at present with stirrings of discontent amongst the burghs. In recognition of his services, Lauderdale prevailed on the king to grant the provost a pension of £200 sterling a year and his lands of Abbotshall and the saltpans of Kirkcaldy were ratified by parliament in 1672.[76] Yet Abbotshall's long stint in charge was the subject of much disquiet within the city council and a motion to supersede him at the annual Michaelmas elections in September 1672 was lost by only two votes. Complaining of a 'tumult' in the town, Abbotshall persuaded representatives of the privy council to investigate the incident. They found no evidence of any wrongdoing, but, to secure his election the following year, Abbotshall received through

Lauderdale a letter from the king accusing James Roughead, clerk of the council, of creating a disturbance at the elections and being chief amongst dissenters on the council. To serve as a warning to others, Roughead was immediately removed from office and Abbotshall again re-elected as provost.[77] He had not long to enjoy his victory: in the next session of parliament, Abbotshall was to be formally accused of corruption and Lauderdale revealed to be behind the provost's long continuance in office. It was to be the beginning of an extraordinary series of events that threatened to oust the commissioner from his indomitable position of power.

The fourth session of the second Restoration parliament began on 12 November 1673. Recorded in the rolls of the opening day were 153 individuals: eight bishops, fifty-four members of the nobility, two officers of state, forty-four commissioners representing twenty-nine shires and forty-five commissioners representing forty-four burghs.[78] Again, this was a very respectable attendance, although there had been a slight drop since the last session. This was to be expected, especially when considering that this parliament was now entering into its fourth session and its fifth year.

The reason parliament had been summoned was to deal with the ever-present problem of religious dissent. Kincardine had written to Lauderdale in September 1673 explaining that the commissioner's presence in Edinburgh was necessary 'to set councell busines in a better condition then they have been of late'.[79] The privy council was in turmoil due to the failure of the second indulgence that had been granted in 1672 and the sudden upsurge in disorder this had brought about. The indulgence granted in 1669 had only been extended to those ministers who were prepared to accept it. However, in 1672, after the second indulgence had been announced, the government drew up its own list of outed ministers and assigned them vacant parishes (mainly in the west), apparently without consultation. The result of this was that around half of those named refused to take up their charge and instead continued to operate outwith the established episcopal church. Indeed, the policy of indulgence seems to have done little to end the spread and growth of conventicles. As indulged ministers took up position in western parishes, their brethren who had refused to subscribe to the government's policy of reconciliation began to move outwith those areas in which they had concentrated activities in the past. As a result, conventicles sprung up in Angus, Perthshire and Linlithgow, parts of the country largely unaffected by conventicling prior to the indulgences.[80]

By the late summer of 1673, the problem of unauthorised religious assemblies had grown so severe that Kincardine believed that it would be 'very hard (at best) to curb them without something be further done by the parliament.' Kincardine's suggestion to Lauderdale that the expense of controlling conventicles ought to be placed on those that were the cause was in fact taken up in the king's instructions issued to the commissioner in October. Lauderdale was instructed to bring in to parliament a motion that would in effect make heritors responsible for any offences committed by their tenants or servants, in much the same way that clan chiefs were held liable for any disorders in the Highlands. Garrisons were to be placed in those areas where heritors refused to provide such security, with the local community providing the total cost of the soldiers' maintenance.[81]

Parliament, however, never got round to authorising this new series of ecclesiastical legislation, for, on the first day of the new session an event occurred which effectively negated Lauderdale's planned legislative programme. From his arrival in Scotland on around 4 November to the day parliament first sat, Lauderdale had been engaged in a series of meetings with the most influential members of parliament and had been hearing disturbing murmurs of complaints, chiefly concerning the series of monopolies that had been granted to a number of individuals in previous years.[82] The 1663 session of parliament had determined that the king might impose as much customs duty on foreign commodities as he pleased and that he may discharge the importation of such goods as he thought fit. Lauderdale had taken full advantage of the ruling, rewarding his loyal allies with lucrative contracts and monopolies. With the importation of salt banned except for use in the fishing industry, Kincardine, granted the sole franchise to farm all Scottish salt, was making huge profits yet supplying what was regarded by many as a vastly inferior product. After the prohibition of the importation of brandy, John Elphinstone, eighth lord Elphinstone, Hatton's son-in-law, was granted the gift of seizures. Much to the chagrin of the people, however, Elphinstone set up, as Rosehaugh saw it, his own 'exchequer', selling import licences and flooding the market with cheap liquor. Sir John Nicolson of that ilk, commissioner for Edinburghshire, benefited too. As a reward for the services of his grandfather, Sir William Dick of Braid, who had lent large sums to the nobility in the 1640s, Nicolson was granted a duty on imported tobacco in recompense of outstanding debts.[83] Tweeddale compared the situation to that of 1667 when Rothes had been in control of the Scottish administration.[84] Yet the corruption that had tarnished Rothes's period in office seemed to be positively trivial when compared to the present situation. Lauderdale, Hatton, Atholl and Kincardine divided eighteen major offices between them, with the commissioner holding eight of them himself.[85] The controversial promotion to the court of session of Ramsay of Abbotshall, the immovable provost of Edinburgh, and Hatton, who had long been suspected of corrupting the coinage as master of the mint, had only angered those individuals such as Hamilton who were languishing in the political wilderness, deprived of major office.

The first business on the opening day of parliament was the reading of the king's letter. In it, the king spoke of the necessary continuation of the war against the Dutch, the confidence that he had in his commissioner and the need for parliament to draw up effective measures against conventicles. Next came Lauderdale's speech, in which the commissioner defended the war and spoke of the crown's determination to protect its bishops.[86] Lauderdale then proposed that the lords of the articles should immediately convene to draw up parliament's answer to the king's letter. At this point, the duke of Hamilton rose and made an extraordinary request: before business proceeded, parliament should first consider the grievances of the country. Twenty more members immediately seconded Hamilton's proposal before the commissioner had a chance to respond.[87] A number of speeches were made on the same lines as Hamilton's until the earl of Dumfries's proposal that a formal committee of grievances should be appointed finally spurred one of Lauderdale's allies into making a response. Kincardine accused those who had supported Hamilton of being disrespectful to the king and of attempting to introduce innovations; parliamentary business could only be introduced through the articles, by no other means, he argued.[88] It seems Hamilton had opened the floodgates, however, and more rose to air their grievances. Sir Francis Scott of Thirlestane, commissioner for Selkirkshire, gave a long speech condemning the war with the Dutch, claiming it was only for the benefit of England and for their trade and plantations, from which Scottish merchants were excluded. He was finally articulating openly the feelings of what so many had complained of over recent years. After this, Sir Patrick Hume of Polwarth, commissioner for Berwickshire, moved that a 'committee might be named [which] he stiled lords of the bills'. Failing the implementation of this, he proposed that the whole house be admitted into the meetings of the lords of the articles so that they could have their input into the reply to the king's letter.[89]

Lauderdale evidently was so taken aback by the whole episode that he sat in stunned silence ('struck as one almost dead', says Burnet) throughout the above exchanges. Writing to his brother the following day, Lauderdale freely admitted that he had been surprised by 'such a spirit as I thoght never to have seen heir'.[90] After hearing the barrage of complaints, Lauderdale declared that he was following established procedure in referring the drafting of the reply to the articles; that there was no intention of surprising parliament, since there would be ample opportunity for the whole chamber to debate the letter at a later date. Yet still the protests continued. The commissioner roundly condemned a compromise proposal supported by Sir James Dalrymple of Stair, president of the session, and first suggested by two advocates, Robert Dickson of New Galloway and William Moir of Kintore, that all members might be admitted to the articles. It seems that Moir's earlier imprisonment in 1672 for factious behaviour had proved no deterrent to voicing such controversial opinions.[91]

The earl of Argyll, in support of the commissioner, argued that all would be able to have their say when the reply had been drafted and was brought into parliament for approval. Tweeddale, in his first explicit act of opposition against his old master, claimed that because most of those that spoke were not members of the articles, it appeared that they had something to offer to the debate, which ought to be represented to the king. Lauderdale, despite his appalling treatment of Tweeddale, must have been amazed at his involvement. Indeed, it seems that Lauderdale temporarily lost his composure and 'answered stormingly' that if 'any such thing were further prest he wold interpose his "No".' In response, Hume of Polwarth moved for an immediate vote on whether it was a free parliament or not, an accusation which Lauderdale demanded was recorded in the official record. Polwarth refused to back down, declaring that he would happily stand by his assertion. He had the full support of the duke of Hamilton, who angrily defended Polwarth when Kincardine, Atholl and Robert Milne of Barnton, commissioner for Linlithgowshire, urged the lord advocate to take action. Parliament could be the only judge in the matter, Hamilton insisted.[92] To bring an end to the stalemate, Lauderdale accepted the earl of Dundonald's motion of an adjournment and parliament was postponed until the following Monday.

Perhaps the most pertinent question is whether the opposition that displayed itself was part of a planned and organised design? Rosehaugh states that a number of commissioners had met the previous night and had resolved that when it came to the answering of the king's letter, they would first urge that their grievances might be considered so that parliament's reply would reflect the predicament of the kingdom.[93] This may be so, but it seems that some sort of strategy had been formulating over a period of some months prior to the sitting of parliament. Numerous policy papers survive amongst Hamilton's own papers which, amongst others, list the grievances that were set out in parliament. It is clear that Hamilton was being recognised as the leader of the opposition and one who was receptive to such material. It is likely that these were used to formulate some kind of concerted address in parliament.[94]

Tweeddale, who in February 1673 had finally given up all hope of reconciliation with Lauderdale, was in frequent correspondence with Hamilton from that period onwards. Yet, it can be argued that Hamilton's opposition was never a certainty until a few months later, for, although the relationship between the two was often strained, Lauderdale was doing everything in his power to secure the duke's future support. He had, without success, been attempting to obtain for Hamilton the order of the garter ('the blew ribban' as Lauderdale calls it).[95] His lack of success was to cost Lauderdale dear since Hamilton felt woefully undervalued. He was conspicuously under-employed and increasingly anxious to be placed in some significant office. Yet the position that was eventually found for him was not by any means his preferred occupation.

What finally forced the duke into opposition was a disastrous miscalculation made by Robert Leighton, archbishop of Glasgow, and supported by Lauderdale. In May 1673, Leighton suggested to the king that a small number of privy councillors, headed by Hamilton, should be commissioned to enforce the laws against religious dissent in the diocese of Glasgow. Lauderdale consented to the archbishop's suggestion and granted the commission. Hamilton, when informed of his new position, greeted the proposal with horror and flatly refused to take any part.[96] Recognising the futility of the fight against conventicles, he believed that it was merely a ploy to ruin him. In this, he was perhaps guilty of over-reaction, but Hamilton knew better than to risk being made the scapegoat for the failure of the indulgence. The situation was not helped by an investigation into the duke's accounts of the 1633 taxation, undertaken by Hatton, which Hamilton feared would be used to 'misrepresent' him at court.[97] In an attempt to appease the duke, Lauderdale eventually secured payment of the final amount owed to him by the crown – a sum in excess of £13,000 sterling.[98] The blatant attempt to buy back the duke's support failed spectacularly: now that he had been financially recompensed in full, Hamilton had nothing to lose by openly opposing Lauderdale.

Perhaps the commissioner had some prior warning of what was to come by events at the convention of burghs held only a few days before the new parliamentary session. James Roughead, the Edinburgh burgess who had been ousted by Ramsay of Abbotshall some months earlier, was elected clerk to the convention, despite the provost's vehement protests. Not one other member of the convention supported Abbotshall and, on his defeat, he stormed out of the chamber. By rights the convention should have broken up, since the provost of Edinburgh, leader of the burghs, was vital to proceedings. Instead, 'without stirring' the burghs chose another to sit in Abbotshall's place. When the convention met again on 13 November, the day after the protests in parliament, they were in a defiant mood. They proceeded with business, ignoring Lauderdale's command to disband:

> After yesterday's sitting in parlament, his grace is come so low that wee are carest with all the humeletie wee could wisch . . . wee know the interest of his majestie and the good of this kingdome so weel that naither his commissioner's fight nor his lawes will make us move in the least to that prejudice of what may be good for both his majestie and this kingdome.[99]

It was extraordinary rhetoric. Lauderdale was facing a potentially formidable body of discontent, greater in number than at any time since the Restoration.

The widespread nature of the opposition was no happy accident and indeed, had taken some months to organise. Both Tweeddale and Hamilton had a wide circle of supporters with whom they kept in close contact. From October 1673, when it was announced that parliament was to meet the following November, Tweeddale's correspondents included Sir Patrick Hume of Polwarth and Sir Archibald Murray of Blackbarony (shire commissioners for Berwick and Peebles respectively). Hamilton claimed to have the support of William Douglas, third earl (later first duke) of Queensberry and the earls of Rothes, Dumfries and Morton amongst the nobility. It is unclear if either Hamilton or Tweeddale had dealings with burgh representatives, but because of the conduct of the convention of burghs, it seems more than likely that they were at least aware, if not involved, in any planned demonstration of opposition. Possibly Sir John Harper of Cambusnethan or Sir George Lockhart of Carnwath, both leading advocates and correspondents with Tweeddale, had been involved in discussions with their colleagues who represented many of the burghs.[100] It was unlikely that they would need much persuasion to join with the opposition, for, after the measures passed in the last session, the commissioner was not short of enemies within the estate. Only the bishops remained overwhelmingly loyal to the crown.

After the dramatic events on the first day of the parliamentary session, the main challenge facing the opposition was how to maintain that momentum. On 13 November, the day following parliament's adjournment, the commissioner called representatives of each estate to a conference to discuss their particular grievances. Somewhat surprisingly, Lauderdale spoke of his willingness to repeal the three monopolies of salt, brandy and tobacco and proposed a new meeting on 15 November to discuss the particulars. Hamilton instead urged that any proposals should be heard in parliament rather than being continued in private discussions. Stalemate was again reached. The meeting broke up without agreement and it is not clear if the meeting planned for 15 November took place.[101]

Abolition of the monopolies was little more than a pretext and when parliament reconvened on 17 November the opposition had come prepared with a number of speeches which set out their true objectives: that the courts of judiciary be purged, the mint be reformed, the acts of the previous session concerning the burghs and the advocates be immediately repealed and all old public debts be discharged.[102] Yet Hamilton and his allies never had the chance to articulate these demands. Lauderdale, after speaking of his willingness to deal with all complaints in an orderly manner, remitted the repeal of the monopolies to the articles and immediately adjourned parliament.[103] Despite Hamilton's immediate complaints, Lauderdale refused to listen to any further debate and left the chamber.

It was not the end of Hamilton's protest, however, since the duke continued to remonstrate against the adjournment when he and some of his supporters met with Lauderdale in a room adjacent to the parliamentary chamber. The earl of Eglinton declared that there were no articles to which the acts could be remitted since they had not yet been formally reconvened. Some said they would refuse to take their seats on the committee, others that they would attempt to enter the proceedings and see who would dare throw them out. Lauderdale calmly replied that he would try those who withdrew from the articles and that he personally would stop any unauthorised personnel from violating proceedings. It seems that the commissioner was unfazed by the opposition's attempts at intimidation. 'I shall never suffer anything to be put to a question to shake the foundation of the articles, or such a thing as may force me to give a negative,' Lauderdale told his brother in a letter of 18 November. What was to prove more serious for the opposition was that the commissioner had the decisive advantage: 'the king hath allowed me by my instruction to adjorne the parliament as I shall thinke convenient, and I will thus use it.'[104]

What was undoubtedly of great concern to Hamilton and Tweeddale, the noble leaders of the opposition, was an order made in the convention of royal burghs on 22 November to send a delegation to the commissioner giving 'their humble and heartie thanks for his cheerfull assistance and great and good progress he has made towards the repairing and redressing' of the monopolies. In a thinly veiled reference to recent events in parliament, the delegation promised that 'nothing shall cool the zeall of the royall burgesses' to the crown. Worryingly for the opposition, this was by no means a minority action. According to the order, the delegation was to consist of the burgesses of Edinburgh, Perth, Dundee, Glasgow, St Andrews, Linlithgow, Culross, Pittenweem, Inveraray, New Galloway and Kinghorn.[105] It is unclear, however, how many actually attended the commissioner since the official record makes no mention of the delegation. But it may have been that now the burghs' principal grievance had been redressed, they were unwilling to continue in opposition.

When parliament next met on 24 November, the earl of Queensberry gave in a complaint against John Paterson, dean of St Giles in Edinburgh, for remarks made in a sermon he had given the previous day. Paterson had denounced the parliamentary opposition for seeking redress of the grievances simply for their own selfish ends, an accusation which would have no doubt delighted Lauderdale who was present in the congregation. The commissioner's only response to Queensberry's motion was to send the complaint to the bishops for their consideration.[106] The following day, the earl of Eglinton submitted another paper, on behalf of the late bailies of Edinburgh, formally accusing Sir Andrew Ramsay of Abbotshall of corruption and demanding his impeachment. The revival of this issue was probably a ploy to win back the burghs' support, made more apparent by the fact that it was members of the nobility who submitted the accusations rather than any burgess.[107] This seems to have caught Lauderdale by surprise and he refused to hear the full paper until the act removing the salt monopoly was ratified. This was agreed, and after the act had been approved without a contrary vote, the matter was returned to.

As the seriousness of the allegations contained in the paper became apparent, there was an attempt by Kincardine, Dalrymple of Stair and Sir Peter Wedderburn of Gosford (commissioner for Haddington and a prominent advocate) to have the proceedings discontinued, arguing that such a complaint must be at first subscribed by the accusers. Rosehaugh suggested that the lord advocate should draw up a formal indictment, but the commissioner refused, stating that he would not apply the king's assent to anything not contained in his instructions. Argyll suggested that the matter should be remitted to the articles and parliament was again adjourned until 1 December.[108]

The opposition regarded Lauderdale's discomfiture over the Abbotshall affair as a small victory and planned to raise the subject again at the next meeting. When parliament next sat, however, on 1 and then 2 December, they were denied the opportunity to do so. Discussion centred on the monopolies, with two acts relating to the importation of brandy and tobacco, and another redressing some difficulties caused by the act of apparel of the last session, being passed before there was another adjournment, this time to 28 January 1674.[109] Two overtures submitted by Hamilton and Dumfries, concerning the appointment of men who lacked legal expertise to the court of session and on abuses in the mint, were received but left undetermined by the adjournment.[110]

Lauderdale wrote to the king on 1 December, telling him of the planned adjournment to January. There had been no less than six adjournments in a period that spanned only three weeks, the sole reason being that the commissioner had found a successful device for stifling debate. As he told the king, 'I have beat doune (not using your authority but with right reason and reasonable adjourneings) all extravagant motions and all manner of vote except to those acts which I moved and caryed on my self.'[111] Hamilton feared that Lauderdale would use the delay to turn the king against them, and so he, Tweeddale, Sir John Harper of Cambusnethan, commissioner for Lanarkshire, and Sir William Drummond of Cromlix, commissioner for Perthshire, resolved to go south to court.[112] The omens were not good, however. Tweeddale's son, John Hay, lord Yester had written to his father on 4 December acquainting him with the outcome of his meeting that day with the king. Upon offering Charles an account of the proceedings of parliament, Yester was informed that the king had 'sufficient accounts already' of all that had passed, that he deplored Tweeddale's involvement in the overture for a committee of grievances and that he regarded his father's actions as an attempt 'to overturne the foundation of the parliament'. His 'greatest resentment' was, however, reserved for the duke of Hamilton, to whom he said he had done considerable kindness and had been rewarded by treachery.[113]

With the other members of the opposition, Hamilton left for London around 8 December. Lauderdale remained in Scotland but immediately sent Kincardine as his agent to court. On his arrival, Kincardine immediately began to familiarise a number of public figures with Lauderdale's version of events. Thus, on 18 December he, along with Hatton, presented to James, duke of York a 'memorandum' which explained all of the proceedings of parliament.[114] Hamilton and his retinue arrived around about the same date and secured a formal meeting with the king on 28 December, at which they presented their case, based mainly on the grievances already submitted to parliament. The king asked if they had put their complaints down in writing: they had not (possibly for fear of being accused of treason), Hamilton answered. Charles then asked whether they had discussed their grievances with their commissioner and again Hamilton admitted that they had not done so. Hamilton was finally given leave to explain the opposition's actions to the duke of York, but he was as uninterested as the king had been. Instead of finding a sympathetic ear, Hamilton and his entourage were forced to listen to a long eulogy from James endorsing the many favours and good service Lauderdale had done for the crown.[115]

Although disappointed with their initial meeting with the king, Hamilton and Tweeddale remained in London, hopeful for another and more favourable audience. It has been suggested that both men were involved in aggravating opposition in England, culminating in an address made in the House of Commons against Lauderdale on 13 January 1674.[116] This was part of a wider hostility in England directed against the continuance of the Dutch war and the French alliance, for which public support had rapidly dropped away after the duke of York's public profession of his Catholic faith. In November 1673, doubting his loyalty, the king had removed from office Anthony Ashley Cooper, first earl of Shaftesbury, lord chancellor. After his dismissal, Shaftesbury remained active in London, a potent force amongst the burgeoning parliamentary opposition, and it was certainly believed by contemporaries (Lauderdale included) that Hamilton and Tweeddale must have met with the earl to discuss a joint strategy.[117] There is no firm evidence of this, but the moves in England to remove Lauderdale must have given the opposition in Scotland fresh hope of success.

Indeed, preparations for a further attack on Lauderdale's ministry at the next session of parliament were well underway. In early January 1674, on behalf of the opposition, Alexander Seton, third earl of Dunfermline had been sent to the burghs of Fife to secure their support, though somewhat disappointingly he was only able to persuade John Geddie of St Nicolas, commissioner of St Andrews, to join them. The earl of Kinghorn was employed in Angus to perform a similar task, although he too was not expected to have much success. The opposition remained optimistic, however, and at a meeting before Christmas had drawn up a number of various strategies, each aimed at recruiting more supporters.[118] 'Our next meeting of parliament will certainly be very full and well convened,' wrote Polwarth to Lord Yester, 'and our strenth will be faire greater than it was the last session.' Envisaging the opposition representative of the kingdom as a whole, Polwarth asserted that 'the hearts of Scotland long and pant after us with the kindness wishes and expressions imaginable, and expect that the interest of this poore and helpless kingdome . . . shall be faithfully represented to his majestie and repared by the medication of his parliament.'[119] Clearly, the parliamentary opposition had ambitions to grow into a body with a broad support over all three estates and were actively intent on pursuing this prior to the next session of parliament.

Lauderdale too was hard at work trying to bolster crown support. In a move directly aimed at appeasing the burghs, he forced Abbotshall into tendering his resignation as provost of Edinburgh and as a lord of session but stopped short of permitting any impeachment attempt.[120] Lauderdale was also behind a number of privy council measures taken to resolve corruption in the mint, issuing a commission to certain members of the council to try the purity of the coin.[121] Whatever success these new endeavours would bring, the commissioner knew he could depend on Charles's continued support. Indeed, the day following the Commons's address, the king wrote a letter of encouragement to Lauderdale assuring him of the 'continuance of my kindnesse to you, which nothing shall alter'.[122] Charles then authorised an adjournment of parliament from 28 January to 3 March, this despite the fact that Lauderdale had never left Scotland.[123] The reason for the delay in the new session was due to the turbulence of English affairs: at no time should there be 'troublesome business' in both kingdoms, warned the king.[124]

There is no detailed official record of what happened at the session held on 3 March – only the minutes of parliament mention that a meeting occurred – but it seems that a riding of parliament of sorts took place as usual, although Lauderdale did not participate, and once the rolls were taken and prayers said, parliament was immediately adjourned to 14 October.[125] The reason that the estates actually met, albeit for such a short and worthless session, was due to fears that if parliament had been simply dissolved by the king without reassembling, the opposition might actually claim victory when none was intended.[126] Again the duke of Hamilton was caught cold by the turn of events and his request that the parliament be allowed to consider the king's letter of November was refused by Lauderdale, who declared that no petition could be received after an adjournment. For the opposition, it was an entirely unexpected and devastating turn of events.[127] Lauderdale had simply denied them a forum in which to express their discontent and there was little they could do in response.

Lauderdale delayed his return to court by a few weeks, to allow English hostility against him to dissipate. He finally arrived to a hero's welcome at Whitehall in April, greeted warmly by both the king and the duke of York. In May, the English privy council declared Lauderdale innocent of all charges brought against him by the Commons and, to further consolidate the commissioner's position, Charles bestowed on him an English earldom, guaranteeing him a seat in the Lords and the legal protection that came with it.[128] The opposition in Scotland remained in anticipation of a new session and Lauderdale knew that the intrigues against him would continue if it were believed that they would have another opportunity to oust him as commissioner. Thus, on 19 May, Charles was persuaded to issue a proclamation formally dissolving parliament.[129]

Partly as a means of pacification, a proclamation had been issued by the privy council in March which discharged the exacting of all bygone maintenance, cess and public impositions, suspending the payment of all annuities until further notice.[130] In the council, however, discord continued as to the sudden dissolution of parliament. Hamilton, Dumfries, Morton, Queensberry, Robert Ker, third earl of Roxburghe, and Drummond of Cromlix all defiantly refused to subscribe to a letter of thanks to the king containing a clause praising Lauderdale for the willingness he had shown in redressing the country's grievances. In response, Lauderdale simply procured another proclamation dissolving the council.[131] When it was reconvened in June, the membership had been thoroughly purged. Only Hamilton, Dumfries and Morton remained, with Tweeddale, Queensberry, Roxburghe, Eglinton, Cassilis, Lord Yester and Drummond of Cromlix all losing their seats.[132] Following his victories in parliament and at court, it was a move that served to underline Lauderdale's complete control over the Scottish administration.

With no parliament in which to voice his discontent and now isolated within the council, Lauderdale hoped that Hamilton would have little opportunity for further mischief. Even if this proved to be wishful thinking, the commissioner knew he possessed a decisive advantage: he alone controlled the flow of information to the monarch. Through his letters sent during parliament's duration, and then by using Kincardine to affirm this version of events at court, Lauderdale was able to persuade the king that opposition to his ministry was all organised from London. Indeed, the Commons' address against Lauderdale's ministry only served as corroboration of this and the disgraced earl of Shaftesbury proved to be an ideal scapegoat. Even the crown's enemies in Holland may have been involved, surmised the commissioner.[133] The fact that the king rarely sought alternative sources of information from Scotland gives some indication both of the significance he placed on events in his northern kingdom and of his implicit trust in his chief Scottish minister.

At no time did Lauderdale admit that his own management of parliament might be the true cause of the opposition. He governed in a different manner than his predecessors, a fact that had been apparent since his first session as commissioner in 1669. As he freely admitted, Lauderdale had little patience, no desire to hear lengthy debates in parliament, or to cultivate the different interest groups. Instead he often exploited these differences, playing one estate off against the other. It was a strategy that achieved initial success. The problems began, however, when the nature of the opposition changed and became widespread, with Hamilton gaining support over all three estates. Moreover, Lauderdale's packing of offices with his allies rewarded a few and disappointed the majority. Indeed, Hamilton may have been won over if he had been found a position in Lauderdale's administration; being snubbed only pushed him further into opposition. The commissioner's appalling treatment of the earl of Tweeddale, who was punished solely for his success in office, was the motive behind his involvement with Hamilton. Thus, disappointed members of the nobility joined with and provided leadership for the other estates who each had their own grievances. Bitterness against the commissioner was the common ground that they shared.

At all times the opposition remained consistently loyal to the crown: the problem for them was that the crown remained similarly loyal to its commissioner. Lauderdale's reliance both on the king's favour and on the crown's prerogative powers were therefore the decisive factors in his triumph over Hamilton's burgeoning opposition party in the winter of 1673–4. This was not without consequence, however. The commissioner's subsequent attempts to rule by brute force alone only inflamed the opposition, so much so that he could risk no more meetings of parliament. Denied a forum in which to express their grievances, Lauderdale hoped that the opposition would largely disband. However, as events over the next four years were to reveal, there were many other public arenas in which the parliamentary opposition could continue to operate.

Notes

1 *RPCS*, third series, iii, pp. 165, 187–8.
2 NAS, PA2/29, ff. 117r–118r; *RPS*, 1670/7/2.
3 In Burntisland, Captain William Ged was elected to replace the deceased David Seaton. In Lauder, Thomas Wood was chosen to replace John Maitland. Young (ed.), *Parliaments of Scotland*, i, pp. 272–3 and ii, pp. 469–70, 630, 740.
4 *Lauderdale Papers*, ii, pp. 184–7.
5 *RPCS*, third series, iii, pp. 197, 203–4.
6 NAS, Hamilton Muniments, GD406/2/640/3, 'Memorandum of some passages past in parliament begune 28 July 1670, second session'.
7 NAS, PA2/29, ff. 119r–v; *RPS*, 1670/7/4.
8 Terry, *The Cromwellian Union*, appendix i, pp. 188–95; Lee, *The Cabal*, pp. 63–4.
9 NAS, PA7/22/117/5, p. 233; *RPS*, C1670/7/1–2; NAS, PA2/29, ff. 119v–120r; *RPS*, 1670/7/5.
10 Mackenzie, *Memoirs*, p. 191. For many, the identities of the commissioners had been the sole subject of discussion in the fortnight prior to parliament. As Sir Archibald Murray of Blackbarony wrote to Tweeddale, it seems that members of the government were also kept in the dark, with the earl of Rothes 'guessing as fast as any, [although he] sayes plainly that he believes he will be left at home'. NLS, Yester Mss 7004, f. 91.
11 Mackenzie, *Memoirs*, pp. 185–6; Lee, *The Cabal*, pp. 64–5.
12 NLS, Watson Mss 595, f. 226.
13 NLS, Yester Mss 7023, f. 235.
14 Lee, *The Cabal*, p. 63; Macinnes, 'Politically reactionary Brits?', p. 51.
15 NAS, PA7/22/117/5, pp. 233–4; *RPS*, C1670/7/3–7; NAS, PA2/29, ff. 120v–121r; *RPS*, 1670/7/7.
16 Mackenzie, *Memoirs*, p. 190.

17 NAS, Hamilton Muniments, GD406/2/640/3; *Lauderdale Papers*, ii, p. 188; Mackenzie, *Memoirs*, p. 191.

18 Mackenzie, *Memoirs*, p. 191.

19 NLS, Yester Mss 7025, f. 20.

20 NAS, PA7/22/117/5, pp. 233–4; *RPS*, C1670/7/5–6.

21 NAS, Hamilton Muniments, GD406/2/640/3; Mackenzie, *Memoirs*, pp. 191–3; BL, Additional Mss 23134, ff. 88, 101.

22 Burnet, *History*, i, pp. 522–3; Buckroyd, *Church and State*, p. 92.

23 Seaward, *Restoration*, p. 52.

24 NLS, Yester Mss 7004, f. 25.

25 NAS, PA7/22/117/5, p. 234; *RPS*, C1670/7/8; NAS, PA2/29, ff. 121v–122v; *RPS*, 1670/7/11.

26 NAS, PA2/29, ff. 120r–124v; *RPS*, 1670/7/6–14.

27 *Lauderdale Papers*, ii, p. 200. This is a reference to the opposition of John Kennedy, sixth earl of Cassilis in the parliamentary session of 1661.

28 NLS, Yester Mss 7025, ff. 19–20; Mackenzie, *Memoirs*, pp. 188–90.

29 Ian MacIvor and Bent Petersen, 'Lauderdale at Holyroodhouse, 1669–70', in David J. Breeze (ed.), *Studies in Scottish Antiquity, presented to Stewart Cruden* (Edinburgh, 1984), p. 263.

30 Lee argues the opposite, stating that the steady growth in the use of troops against dissenters from 1667–72 was indicative of an aggressive, militaristic approach to government and reflective of a wider tendency to use force to implement policy. Lee, 'Government and politics in Scotland, 1661–1681', ch. 4.

31 See Jackson, *Restoration Scotland*, pp. 132–44, which states that the preservation of order was not only the chief priority for the Restoration regime, but one which effectively superseded the traditional rights and liberties of the individual. Even if the royalist administration defended their actions as necessary in response to increasing religious dissent, considerable resistance emerged towards such theories, with varying degrees of success.

32 Seaward, *Restoration*, p. 52; Buckroyd, *Church and State*, p. 93.

33 This, indeed, was the essence of the king's instructions for Lauderdale prior to parliament. *Lauderdale Papers*, ii, p. 184.

34 Burnet, *History*, i, pp. 520–l; *Lauderdale Papers*, ii, p. 200; Yould, 'The duke of Lauderdale's religious policy in Scotland, 1668–79', pp. 257–9. See Buckroyd, *Church and State*, pp. 95–9, for a full account of this initiative.

35 NLS, Yester Mss 7004, f. 115; NAS, Hamilton Muniments, GD406/2/640/3.

36 NAS, PA2/29, ff. 124v–127r; *RPS*, 1670/7/15.

37 NAS, Hamilton Muniments, GD406/1/2702.

38 NLS, Yester Mss 7004, f. 168a.

39 NAS, Hamilton Muniments, GD406/1/8422.

40 NAS, Hamilton Muniments, GD406/1/2704. The draft of Hamilton's reply differs quite significantly from the copy that was actually sent (see *Lauderdale Papers*, ii, pp. 209–10).

41 NAS, Hamilton Muniments, GD406/1/2706; *Lauderdale Papers*, ii, p. 213. Rothes was not completely correct. Hamilton was following Moray's advice, which suggested that Lauderdale, if humoured, 'will really apply himself to serve you'. If not, 'a very small provocation will certainly make him fly quite off the hindges'. Hamilton would only maintain the truce as long as it served his interests. NAS, Hamilton Muniments, GD406/1/6129.

42 NAS, GA12/05, printed acts of parliament (1670), p. 14; *RPS*, 1670/7/70.

43 MacIvor and Petersen, 'Lauderdale at Holyroodhouse, 1669–70', p. 263.

44 For details of both the English and Scottish commissioners, see Terry, *The Cromwellian Union*, appendix i, p. 188. Terry, *The Cromwellian Union*, appendix i, pp. 187–218 and Mackenzie, *Memoirs*, pp. 194–211 have a complete record of proceedings.

45 NLS, Yester Mss 7023, f. 246; Mackenzie, *Memoirs*, pp. 199–200.

46 Mackenzie, *Memoirs*, pp. 207–8.

47 NLS, Yester Mss 7023, f. 246; Mackenzie, *Memoirs*, pp. 210–11. Commercial union was once more mooted in 1674 by the House of Lords but met with little enthusiasm and was not taken any further. Macinnes, 'Politically reactionary Brits?', p. 52.

48 For a near contemporary's view on successive union attempts from Roman times to 1707, see Clerk, *History of the Union of Scotland and England by Sir John Clerk of Penicuik*, D. Douglas (ed.), (Edinburgh, 1993). Clerk, however, largely overlooks the union discussions of the 1660 and 1670s. For another history of union from 1660 to 1707, emphasising the dissimilarities between the two nations, see M. Goldie, 'Divergence and union: Scotland and England, 1660–1707', in B. Bradshaw and J. Morrill (eds), *The British Problem, c.1534–1707* (Basingstoke, 1996), pp. 220–45.

49 Mackenzie, *Memoirs*, p. 211.

50 Lauderdale indicated to Tweeddale in March 1671 that there were no plans for the subsequent meeting. Parliament would not be dissolved, but no date was yet to be decided on for its next assembly. NLS, Yester Mss 7023, f. 266.

51 *RPCS*, third series, iii, pp. 319, 383–4, 496, 524.

52 Contemporaries attributed Lauderdale's increasing belligerent behaviour and conduct to the marriage. 'From this time to the end of his days', wrote Burnet, he 'became quite another sort of man than he had been in all the former parts of his life'. *History*, i, pp. 438–9.

53 NLS, Yule Mss 3134, 'Memorial regarding the differences between the earl of Tweeddale and the duke of Lauderdale', f. 119; Patrick, 'The

origins of the opposition to Lauderdale in the Scottish parliament of 1673', p. 12.

54 Mackenzie, *Memoirs*, p. 212; Burnet, *History*, i, pp. 439–40; NLS, Yester Mss 7023, f. 264; Buckroyd, *Church and State*, p. 103.

55 Burnet, *History*, i, p. 534; Hutton, *Charles II*, p. 310; Buckroyd, *Church and State*, p. 103.

56 *Lauderdale Papers*, ii, pp. 223–4.

57 NAS, PA2/29, ff. 166r–167r; *RPS*, 1672/6/2.

58 NAS, GA12/05, printed acts of parliament (1670), p. 14; *RPS*, 1670/7/70; NAS, PA2/29, f. 167r; *RPS*, 1672/6/3.

59 NAS, PA2/29, f. 167v; *RPS*, 1672/6/4.

60 Mackenzie, *Memoirs*, pp. 219–20.

61 NAS, PA2/29, f. 167v; *RPS*, 1672/6/5; Mackenzie, *Memoirs*, p. 219.

62 NAS, PA2/29, f. 168r; *RPS*, 1672/6/6.

63 NAS, PA3/4, f. 1r; *RPS*, C1672/6/1; NAS, PA2/29, ff. 168v–169r; *RPS*, 1672/6/7a.

64 NAS, PA2/29, ff. 193r–v; *RPS*, 1672/6/51.

65 Mackenzie, *Memoirs*, pp. 228–34; NAS, PA2/29, ff. 171v–172r; *RPS*, 1672/6/11a.

66 NAS, PA2/29, f. 172r; *RPS*, 1672/6/12.

67 NAS, PA2/29, f. 176v; *RPS*, 1672/6/22; Mackenzie, *Memoirs*, pp. 230–1.

68 NAS, PA2/21, ff. 36r–v; *RPS*, 1633/6/39.

69 NAS, PA2/29, ff. 172r–173r; *RPS*, 1672/6/13; Mackenzie, *Memoirs*, pp. 226–7. A second measure of 6 September, the 'Act concerning adjudications', regulating the rights of creditors to the lands of their debtors, was equally unpopular amongst the burghs. NAS, PA2/29, ff. 196v–197v; *RPS*, 1672/6/55.

70 NAS, PA2/29, ff. 186r–193r; *RPS*, 1672/6/50; Mackenzie, *Memoirs*, pp. 234–8.

71 Mackenzie, *Memoirs*, p. 226.

72 Burnet, *History*, i, pp. 600–1; [Stewart of Goodtrees], *An Accompt of Scotland's grievances*, p. 10.

73 NAS, GA12/05, printed acts of parliament (1672), p. 66; *RPS*, 1672/6/160.

74 NAS, Hamilton Muniments, GD406/1/2716.

75 For more on these appointments, see Sir David Dalrymple, *A Catalogue of the Lords of Session, from the Institution of the College of Justice in the year 1532, with Historical Notes* (Edinburgh, 1794).

76 Sir John Lauder of Fountainhall, *Historical Notices of Scotish Affairs, selected from the manuscripts of Sir John Lauder of Fountainhall, Bart., one of the Senators of the College of Justice*, D. Laing (ed.), 2 vols (Edinburgh, 1848), i, pp. 53–8; Mackenzie, *Memoirs*, pp. 246–7; NAS, PA2/29, ff. 234v–236v; *RPS*, 1672/6/96–7.

77 *RPCS*, third series, iii, pp. 605–6; *RPCS*, third series, iv, pp. 4–5, 103–4; Lauder of Fountainhall, *Historical Notices*, i, pp. 53–81.
78 NAS, PA2/30, ff. 43r–44r; *RPS*, 1673/11/2.
79 *Lauderdale Papers*, ii, p. 233.
80 Buckroyd, *Church and State*, pp. 106–7; Cowan, *Scottish Covenanters*, pp. 79–81; *RPCS*, third series, iii, pp. 545–6, 551.
81 *Lauderdale Papers*, ii, pp. 233, 234–6.
82 *Lauderdale Papers*, ii, p. 237.
83 Mackenzie, *Memoirs*, pp. 241–6.
84 NLS, Yester Mss 7025, f. 106.
85 This was one of the key complaints of Stewart of Goodtrees's pamphlet, *An Accompt of Scotland's grievances*. For the full list of the offices each held, see p. 18 of that pamphlet.
86 NAS, PA2/30, ff. 44v–45; *RPS*, 1673/11/4; Burnet, *History*, ii, p. 38.
87 The identities of all twenty are unknown. Of those who can be identified with any certainty are Morton, Cassilis, Robert Ker, third earl of Roxburghe, Alexander Montgomery, eighth earl of Eglinton and William Douglas, third earl of Queensberry. *Lauderdale Papers*, ii, pp. 241–2; Mackenzie, *Memoirs*, p. 256. The group possibly included Charles Erskine, earl of Mar and James Ogilvy, third earl of Findlater. NLS, Yester Mss 7034, ff. 31–2.
88 Mackenzie, *Memoirs*, p. 256
89 *Lauderdale Papers*, ii, pp. 241–2. Such a committee had first been constituted in November 1640 and again in 1661 to deal with private petitions.
90 Burnet, *History*, ii, p. 39; *Lauderdale Papers*, ii, p. 241.
91 NLS, Yester Mss 7034, f. 31.
92 NLS, Yester Mss 7034, ff. 31–2; *Lauderdale Papers*, ii, pp. 241–3; NAS, PA3/4, f. 26r; *RPS*, M1673/11/2.
93 Mackenzie, *Memoirs*, p. 253. In addition, Lauderdale told his brother that he had received information regarding frequent meetings that were held by his opponents at Masterton's tavern. This was the same public house at which the 'Billeting' plot of 1662 had first been devised. *Lauderdale Papers*, ii, p. 245.
94 See NAS, Hamilton Muniments, GD406/2/635/1–6(i–v), 406/2/635/13–14, 406/2/645/16–17 and 406/2/640/4–5.
95 HMC, *The manuscripts of the duke of Hamilton (Eleventh Report, appendix, part vi)* (London, 1887), p. 143.
96 HMC, *The manuscripts of the duke of Hamilton*, pp. 142–8; HMC, *Supplementary report of the manuscripts of the duke of Hamilton (Twenty-First Report)* (London, 1932), pp. 86–7.
97 Mackenzie, *Memoirs*, p. 251; NAS, Hamilton Muniments, GD406/1/2724.
98 HMC, *The manuscripts of the duke of Hamilton*, p. 146.

 99 NLS, Yester Mss 7006, f. 64.

100 NLS, Yester Mss 7006, 7025, 7034, *passim*. Burnet mistakenly asserts that Argyll was part of Hamilton's clique. This was clearly not so, as his conduct on the opening day of the session in support of the commissioner testifies. Burnet, *History*, ii, p. 38.

101 *Lauderdale Papers*, ii, pp. 243–4; NLS, Yester Mss 7006, f. 66.

102 Mackenzie, *Memoirs*, p. 260; NLS, Yester Mss 7006, f. 68; NAS, Hamilton Muniments, GD406/2/640/5.

103 NAS, PA2/30, f. 45r; *RPS*, 1673/11/5.

104 *Lauderdale Papers*, ii, pp. 245–7.

105 NLS, Yester Mss 7034, f. 48.

106 NAS, PA2/30, f. 45r; *RPS*, 1673/11/6; NAS, Hamilton Muniments, GD406/1/2690–1; NLS, Yester Mss 7006, f. 68.

107 For the charges contained therein, see NAS, PA6/21, 'November 25 1673', ff. 1r–2v; *RPS*, A1673/11/1. John Hamilton, second lord Bargany gave in a second copy of the same paper. NLS, Yester Mss 7034, f. 33. This was the first time the English term of 'impeachment' was used in Scotland. See Mackenzie, *Memoirs*, p. 261.

108 NLS, Yester Mss 7034, f. 33; NLS, Yester Mss 14414, no.35.

109 NAS, PA2/30, ff. 46r–v; *RPS*, 1673/11/8–10; *Lauderdale Papers*, iii, p. 4

110 NAS, PA3/4, f. 26v; *RPS*, M1673/11/7; NAS, PA6/21, 'December 2 1673'; *RPS*, A1673/11/2–3.

111 *Lauderdale Papers*, iii, p. 3.

112 HMC, *Report on the Laing Manuscripts*, i, p. 391; NAS, Hamilton Muniments, GD406/1/2772/1.

113 *Lauderdale Papers*, iii, pp. 6–7.

114 *Lauderdale Papers*, iii, pp. 8, 10.

115 Hamilton additionally complained to the duke of York of Lauderdale's long tenure as commissioner and the great charge that the maintenance of this office cost to the kingdom, a sum he calculated at an exorbitant £18,000 sterling a year. *Lauderdale Papers*, iii, pp. 18–20.

116 Airy, Introduction to *Lauderdale Papers*, iii, p. ii; Hutton, *Charles II*, pp. 311, 315–16. The Commons alleged that Lauderdale, 'that foul-mouthed Scot, master of the prerogative office', had treated the English parliament with disdain and contempt. For a pamphlet outlining the English case, see *CSPD, 1673–75*, p. 131.

117 Jones, *Charles II: Royal Politician*, pp. 109–10; Hutton, *Charles II*, pp. 308–9; *Lauderdale Papers*, ii, p. 245 and iii, p. 16.

118 NLS, Yester Mss 7006, ff. 70–2.

119 NLS, Yester Mss 7006, ff. 78–9.

120 *Extracts from the records of the Burgh of Edinburgh, 1665–1680*, M. Wood (ed.), (Edinburgh, 1950), p. 165; Mackenzie, *Memoirs*, p. 262.

121 *RPCS*, third series, iv, pp. 125–6, 131–2.

122 *Lauderdale Papers*, iii, p. 22.

123 *RPCS*, third series, iv, p. 130.

124 *Lauderdale Papers*, iii, p. 23.

125 NAS, PA3/4, f. 27; *RPS*, M1674/3/1; *Lauderdale Papers*, iii, p. 36.

126 *Lauderdale Papers*, iii, p. 29.

127 Mackenzie, *Memoirs*, pp. 264–7; NAS, Hamilton Muniments, GD406/1/2732–3, 406/1/2786.

128 NAS, Hamilton Muniments, GD406/1/2749; Mackenzie, *Memoirs*, p. 266; Hutton, *Charles II*, p. 322.

129 *RPCS*, third series, iv, p. 189.

130 Mackenzie, *Memoirs*, p. 266; *RPCS*, third series, iv, pp. 166–9.

131 *Lauderdale Papers*, iii, pp. 38–40; NLS, Yester Mss 14414, no.37; *RPCS*, third series, iv, pp. 168–9.

132 *RPCS*, third series, iv, pp. 186–9.

133 *Lauderdale Papers*, ii, pp. 237, 241, 245; Paterson, *King Lauderdale*, pp. 208–10.

Chapter 6

THE EMERGENCE OF 'PARTY', 1674–8

Despite his victory over the parliamentary opposition in the 1673–4 sessions of parliament, there were the usual casualties amongst Lauderdale's allies in the months following the commissioner's return to court. Kincardine, like Tweeddale before him, had perhaps been too able and successful as Lauderdale's chief deputy and this bred resentment amongst the commissioner's other associates, specifically Atholl, who seems to have been deeply embroiled in a conspiracy with the duchess of Lauderdale against Kincardine. The seed of suspicion planted in the duke's mind, Kincardine's friendship with Gilbert Burnet, whom Lauderdale believed to be involved with the English opposition in the Commons, took on a different light. Such doubts were all Lauderdale needed and he soon succumbed to paranoia. A small rift rapidly grew into an open rupture and, by the end of 1674, Kincardine had moved into opposition against Lauderdale.[1] It was tremendous news for Hamilton who desperately needed all the support he could muster.

After its purge in 1674, a number of new men were advanced to restore the commissioner's power base on the council. For the first time, two advocates, Sir Thomas Wallace of Craigie and Sir James Foulis of Colinton, were appointed to sit on the council, further bolstering political links with the court of session. To re-establish control in the treasury, Atholl and Argyll were included in a new commission, replacing Tweeddale and the deceased Sir Robert Moray.[2] Notably absent was Hatton, whose influence had begun to subside after the inquiry into his conduct as master of the mint. In England, Lauderdale astutely aligned himself with the new lord treasurer, Sir Thomas Osborne, created first earl of Danby in June 1674. Rising swiftly through the ranks, Danby was soon to become the most powerful politician at court. Thus, despite the efforts of the earl of Shaftesbury, who attempted to represent Hamilton and Tweeddale in a favourable light to Charles, Lauderdale remained comparatively secure. As a bonus, the new personnel who found themselves promoted were almost falling over themselves in gratitude to send messages of their loyalty and support.[3]

The adjournment of parliament in May 1674, however, failed to silence the duke of Lauderdale's critics. Indeed, as one contemporary put it, 'the disease . . . burst forth' in a number of other arenas and 1674 saw a number of crises, which, when combined, left the commissioner in as precarious a position as he had been when Hamilton and his allies challenged the duke's supremacy in parliament.[4] In February 1674, a dispute arose between the lords of session and a number of advocates, stemming from a process between Alexander Seton, earl of Dunfermline and Alexander Livingston, lord Almond (latterly second earl of Callander), for breach of James Livingston, first earl of Callander's matrimonial contract with the countess of Dunfermline. After the lords of session pronounced an interlocutor in favour of Dunfermline on a point of procedure, Almond's advocate, Sir George Lockhart of Carnwath, advised him to appeal to parliament in its capacity as the highest court. It was a move that inadvertently ignited a political storm. Questioning the authority of the session in such a manner was to set a dangerous precedent and Lauderdale, for one, saw it as further evidence of opposition activities.[5] It was not a popular move amongst some lawyers either, with Rosehaugh complaining:

> that by this method the nobility who always govern'd parliaments would thereby too much influence private causes; and that ignorant members of parliament would have an equal vote in the subtilest cases of law with those whose breeding and experience had render'd them fit dispensers of justice.[6]

In referring the matter to them, Carnwath possibly hoped that parliament would be glad to be recognised as the final court of appeal. Lauderdale, however, knew that to allow such a motion to go unchallenged would be a potentially serious threat to royal supremacy. After all, the king chose judges but not members of parliament. Charles wholeheartedly agreed with Lauderdale's concerns and sent a letter north in May 1674 expressing disapproval at Almond's action and stating that he upheld the authority of the session. No action would be taken against those involved if they would repudiate the appeal. At a subsequent inquiry, however, Lord Almond not only owned the appeal but Carnwath and three other advocates, Sir John Cunningham of Lambroughton, Sir George Mackenzie of Rosehaugh and Sir Robert Sinclair of Longformacus, refused to testify upon oath whether they did likewise. Almond's petition, they argued, was merely a lawful protest for remedy of law. When the four lawyers were subsequently debarred as punishment, most of the faculty of advocates joined with them and walked out of the session house in protest.[7] What started out as a relatively minor dispute had rapidly turned into full-scale mutiny.

Long-standing resentment over the earlier forced appointment of unqualified men to their ranks was perhaps a factor as to why so many of the advocates refused to concur with the king's demands. As a contemporary observed, there was now 'so many Maitlands' in the court of session (including two of Lauderdale's own relatives in addition to his other allies) that the packing of the session had been one of the explicit grievances raised by Hamilton in the last session of parliament.[8] The advocates' dispute was closely linked in other ways to the parliamentary opposition, thus the reason for the government's tough stance. Lauderdale was not far off the mark when he surmised that the whole dispute was connected to the opposition's rancour over the adjournment of parliament. At least three of the advocates were affiliated to Hamilton and his allies: Carnwath was a frequent correspondent of Tweeddale while the latter was at London in the winter of 1673–4 and he, along with Lambroughton and Rosehaugh, had advised Hamilton over his legal right to the collection of the 1633 taxation after the prohibition of bygone impositions. Almond, the instigator of the appeal, was married to a cousin of Anne Hamilton, duchess of Hamilton, and his disputant, the earl of Dunfermline, was related to the Maitland family by marriage.[9] It was conclusive enough evidence for Lauderdale. He believed the opposition, buoyed by their success in the last sessions, orchestrated the dispute in order to demonstrate the necessity of parliament.[10]

The advocates' dispute rumbled on through the summer of 1674 without any real indication that it was going to be resolved. However, events at the convention of royal burghs, at the centre of which were supposedly the debarred advocates, brought the issue to the forefront once again. Although the estate as a whole had seemed unwilling to formally join with Hamilton in the last session of parliament, the burghs' blatant disregard of crown demands at the convention held at Edinburgh in August 1674 only convinced both Lauderdale and the king that dissent was spreading.

At the first sitting of the convention, a letter was read from the king that called for a review of current voting qualifications. The convention was directed to consider how their interests had been prejudiced by the recent election of gentlemen and, in some cases, lesser noblemen as their parliamentary representatives. Only residents and those with an economic interest in the burgh were eligible for election, Charles reminded the convention.[11] The probable design of the king's address was to remove certain individuals who had been rebellious in the last sessions of parliament and, in light of the ongoing dispute, was perhaps intended to reduce the instance of advocates representing burgh seats. The convention, however, was less than obliging and an intense debate arose as to the content of their reply. Concerns rested on the implications for the estate's voice in parliament if limitation on elections were agreed. The weakness of some of the current representatives had clearly been shown in the parliamentary debate redefining the ancient privileges between royal burghs and burghs of regality and barony in July 1672; able men were therefore needed to fight the burghs' corner. In the convention's reply to the king, the majority of commissioners sanctioned the elections of non-residents since 'they might be upon other accompts serviceable to thair interest'. Non-residents were especially devoted to the king's service, they argued, and had always been recognised as lawful commissioners 'notwithstanding of any acts formerly made'. The true cause of the decay of the royal burghs was due to the debilitating effects of the recent legislation that had destroyed their ancient privileges rather than the election of unqualified commissioners, the letter continued. For the speedy redress of the present situation, a new session of parliament must be summoned as soon as possible to take these issues into further consideration. Sir Patrick Thriepland of Fingask, provost of Perth, James Currie, provost of Edinburgh, the commissioners for Haddington, Banff and the two commissioners for Edinburgh were the few who refused to subscribe the defiant letter.[12]

The debarred advocates certainly took advantage of existing discontent amongst the burghs to inflame the situation. According to Rosehaugh, it was he that drew up the first draft of the convention's reply to the king. It was then passed on to Carnwath and his colleague Walter Pringle, who altered Rosehaugh's 'dutiful letter' into 'a most unpolisht and indiscreet paper'. This may partly have been due to personal spite, since Rosehaugh had mostly lost the support of his fellow advocates after he had shown signs of hesitation about their walkout.[13] Essentially, however, the whole affair was a reaction to the legislation passed against the burghs in the last sessions of parliament, the letter being intended as little more than a display that their privileges could not be so easily removed. The advocates, currently at a deadlock in their own dispute, had seized the opportunity of making their voices heard once more and had capitalised on the ill-feeling against the government in the burghs. They had provided the leadership that was lacking when the convention had challenged Lauderdale previously in 1673.

The burghs, however, also had genuine grievances that they wished to have rectified. As they made clear in their controversial letter to the king, they traced their decline in prosperity back to the passage of the act redefining royal burgh privileges in July 1672. Without a doubt, the granting of importation and retailing rights of particular goods to burghs of regality and barony, manufacturing companies and private persons destroyed the old monopoly under which the royal burghs had flourished and was the cause of constant complaint amongst the burgesses. Compounded by a general economic recession in trade due to the third Dutch war, the situation had become so desperate for some burghs that they attempted to resign their status, leading to a situation where the convention of royal burghs now had difficulties in maintaining the existing numbers. Kilrenny and Anstruther Wester waged a battle for almost twenty years to escape from the roll of royal burghs on the grounds of poverty. Cromarty made similar appeals and was the only burgh that succeeded, but the convention continued to pursue payment of arrears some nine years after it had resigned its status.[14] Under such harsh circumstances, it was possibly only a matter of time before the burghs made such a prominent display of their antagonism towards current policy.

The convention's show of defiance was nevertheless short lived. In January 1675, under increasing pressure from the crown, the next meeting of the convention passed an act disowning the letter sent to the king.[15] There was no question that they would fail to back down since the convention had been thoroughly purged since the last meeting. Of the twenty-three who had signed the contemptuous letter to the king, only two remained. The new commissioners, hoping that the king would not 'impute the failings of a few to the whole bodie of your royall burrows', declared the letter the work of some 'tourbulent' persons who had infiltrated the convention.[16] A new act enforcing the limitation on elections was passed at a meeting of the convention the following July. As the king had requested, the selection of non-residents as commissioners was prohibited as a practice destructive to the interest of the burghs and detrimental to their position as 'a third distinct estate of the kingdom'.[17]

The events at the convention in 1674 convinced the government that the burghs could prove a serious problem unless more care was taken over the representatives that were elected. Excluding non-residents from standing for parliaments or conventions was only the first step; in the major towns, at least, a campaign of direct interference in elections was to begin. Thus, in Edinburgh, the council election of 1674–5 was disallowed simply because it had been held on the wrong day. This enabled James Currie, one of the few members of the convention of burghs to dissent from their letter to the king, to continue as provost for another year, much to the displeasure of certain other burgesses. Robert Baird, dean of guild, refused to acknowledge Currie's authority and amassed a large opposition party who waited anxiously for an opportunity to cause trouble. An occasion arose in July 1675 when Hatton agreed to a new election if the council's support could be counted upon in the convention of burghs. As part of the agreement, the council would agree to take the 'advice' of the king's ministers when choosing candidates for a new election.[18] James Roughead (who had stood for election against Sir Andrew Ramsay of Abbotshall in 1673 but had since transferred his allegiances) had been authorised to propose his father-in-law Francis Kinloch of Gilmerton as provost. Baird and his party, however, had the numerical advantage; they refused to support Kinloch and proceeded to a new election, ignoring the terms set out by Hatton. In response, the king simply expelled Baird and eleven others from office for being 'factious'. They were joined by Robert Petrie of Portlethen, provost of Aberdeen, William Anderson of Newtown, provost of Glasgow, and Andrew Ainslie of Blackhill, provost of Jedburgh, who were all fined and debarred from office following a privy council investigation into their involvement in the drafting of the convention of burgh's insolent letter to the king.[19]

A similar fate would meet those who refused to back down in the continuing advocates' quarrel. Anxious to bring an end to the long and drawn out dispute, the government set a deadline of 28 January 1675 for those willing to return. Rather than submit, however, most of the advocates subscribed a number of petitions addressed to the privy council and court of session reasserting their grievances. Again the negotiations reached stalemate, which was only broken by Carnwath's and Lambroughton's journey to court. They had hoped to gain an audience with the king to acquaint him personally with their case but their very presence in London at a time when the Commons were preparing another address against Lauderdale was too dangerous a threat. This finally hastened a settlement and Carnwath and Lambroughton successfully secured an end to the legal process against them.[20]

The majority of the other advocates stayed resolute in their opposition until the end of the year when they too finally submitted. No one was able to claim victory. Rumours abounded that Lauderdale, fearful of the advocates joining up with his enemies at court, had simply given in to stop the dispute escalating further. The advocates meanwhile had been damaged by the defection of one of their most significant members, Sir George Mackenzie of Rosehaugh, to the government's side.[21] Worryingly for Lauderdale, what the advocates' dispute and events in the convention of royal burghs clearly showed was that far from being quietened by the adjournment of parliament in 1674, opposition, especially to government interference in the various national institutions, had only grown stronger.

This was further demonstrated by the actions of once close allies. The earl of Kincardine had predictably not taken Lauderdale's earlier snubs lightly and, by the end of 1675, had moved into an overt alliance with members of the parliamentary opposition. Yet he still stubbornly held onto a number of influential positions, chiefly as a privy councillor, a fact which Lauderdale was keen to rectify. An ideal opportunity arose when the council undertook an investigation into a scuffle that followed the arrest of James Kirkton, a suspected conventicle preacher, by Captain William Carstairs. On hearing of his brother-in-law's capture, Robert Baillie of Jerviswood forcibly rescued Kirkton from Carstairs's custody. For this, Jerviswood was cited to appear before the council, where investigations revealed the warrant for Kirkton's arrest was antedated and that Carstairs had acted unlawfully. In an angry debate lasting three hours, Hamilton, Kincardine, Morton, Dumfries and Dundonald defended Jerviswood's conduct. The majority of the council, however, found him guilty of resisting a lawful arrest and Jerviswood was subsequently fined and imprisoned. Hatton immediately drafted a report to the king complaining that Kincardine, Hamilton and their allies persistently retarded the king's service and promoted the interests of fanatics. On 12 July 1676, Charles sent notice to Hatton to remove Kincardine, Hamilton and the other three dissenters from the council.[22]

In order to complete the purge of all remaining opposition influence from the council, Lauderdale prevailed on the king to declare that all officers of state were to renounce their right to hold office for life and were to continue in their current position only at his majesty's pleasure. Rosehaugh claims that the measure was directed against the earl of Rothes, but it was in all probability part of a wider attack on the commissioner's enemies since it ended the need to reconstitute the privy council in the future.[23] It was soon used to oust Sir John Nisbet of Dirleton as lord advocate, principally because he was suspected of being a sympathiser with presbyterians. On 4 September 1677, Mackenzie of Rosehaugh was elevated to the post, ushering in a regime noted for its severity against religious non-conformity. Since the advocates' dispute, Rosehaugh had become increasingly distant from his fellow lawyers and although he had once been a fervent opponent of the government, he forged a new alliance with the royalist administration. The uncompromising policies he now pursued would see the new lord advocate being branded for posterity with the sobriquet 'Bluidy Mackenzie'.[24]

The hardening of attitudes to religious dissent had actually begun in the summer of 1674 when it became clear that the previous indulgences were proving unsuccessful. As Sharp had persuasively argued to Lauderdale, given the failure of past experiments of toleration, there was no reason to suppose that any future leniency would have any positive effect. Thus, faced with the increasing spread of conventicles, the privy council instituted a new series of measures aimed at rooting out the ringleaders. Landlords were obliged to procure a bond from their servants and tenants promising not to attend any illegal religious gatherings. In burghs, local magistrates were made liable for conventicles held within their boundaries. A commission was given to Sharp authorising him to use standing forces and militia to put the policy into force. Further measures were taken in 1675 when the use of the army to garrison certain areas of the countryside began.[25] It was all intended to demonstrate the government's increased readiness to use force to crush the long-standing problem of dissent. An unwelcome spin-off was that it could also be interpreted as further testimony of an arbitrary misuse of power, providing ample ammunition for Hamilton and his allies.

The new measures coincided with the arrest and subsequent prosecution of James Mitchell, would-be assassin of Sharp, who had finally been captured in February 1674. The authorities intended his case to be a show trial to act as a warning to dissenters; instead, it became an all too public display of contradictory government policy. When Mitchell was arrested, the privy council had promised that his life would be spared if he made a full confession. However, by the time Mitchell's trial eventually took place in January 1678, to conform to the new hard-line policy, the council rescinded on their earlier promise and Mitchell was asked to renew his confession, this time without any possibility that he would not be condemned to death. Although subject to the most brutal forms of torture his captors on the Bass Rock could devise, Mitchell steadfastly refused to acknowledge his guilt. At trial, Lauderdale, Rothes, Sharp and Hatton testified that no promise of life had been made to the defendant, yet when the council registers were mistakenly read out in court, all were publicly shown to have committed perjury. The trial was hurriedly completed and Mitchell put to death but already tarnished reputations had taken further damage.[26]

Lauderdale, accompanied by his wife, was on a rare visit to Scotland in 1677 when Mitchell's case got underway. Previously (and with some reluctance) he had only journeyed north in his capacity as commissioner to attend sessions of parliament, but on this occasion he had come to deal with a personal matter: the marriage of two of the duchess's daughters. To cement ties with Lauderdale's allies, the eldest, Elizabeth, was contracted to Archibald Campbell, lord Lorne, afterwards first duke of Argyll, and the youngest, Catherine, to James Stewart, lord Doune, eldest son of Alexander Stewart, fifth earl of Moray.[27] The marriage celebrations, however, were overshadowed by the seemingly intractable problem of religious dissent, which had increased to unprecedented proportions. The stringent measures previously enacted by the privy council had been worthless at best and Lauderdale hit upon an idea that would, he thought, deal with the dissenters once and for all. Exaggerating the risk of rebellion in the western shires, Lauderdale was given leave by the king to enact what later became known as the 'Highland Host', an army of some 8,000 men recruited predominantly, but not exclusively, from the Highland clans and sent to quarter upon the west. As an added bonus, by quartering troops on the duke's lands and tenants, Lauderdale could also use his Highland forces to wreak personal revenge on Hamilton, destroying religious non-conformity and his key opponent in one fell swoop.[28]

The Host was nothing more than a huge disaster for the government. From January 1678 until April, when the troops were sent home, the soldiers ran riot, plundering and molesting the western shires without restraint. Hamilton was furious at his own personal loss and he, accompanied by Roxburghe, Charles Hamilton, fifth earl of Haddington, and William Cochrane, first lord Cochrane, journeyed to court in late March to make their complaints to the king himself. On their arrival, somewhat surprisingly, Hamilton and his allies encountered Atholl and James Drummond, fourth earl of Perth, two of the Highland lords whose dependants had taken part in the invasion of the west. For both men, the Host marked the end of their alliance with the commissioner. Perth had taken part in Lauderdale's scheme with little enthusiasm and so his defection was not a great surprise. For Atholl, however, the failure of the Host (and the lack of material benefits he had expected as reward for his involvement) was the final straw in a long series of recent disappointments that had soured relations with Lauderdale. They both found ample sympathy for their plight in Hamilton.[29]

Despite the unexpected bonus of welcome additional support for their case, Hamilton and his allies met with a sadly familiar situation on their arrival in London. At first the king refused to meet with the opposition, remitting their concerns to a contingent of his cabinet. Within a few weeks, however, Charles relented, first admitting Atholl and Perth and then, at a later date, Hamilton, Cochrane and their legal advisors. At their crucial audience with the king, Hamilton presented a carefully considered case outlining the illegality of free quartering and appealed for parliament to be called to judge the complaints. Charles, however, remained steadfast in support of his commissioner, indeed, going so far as to associate Hamilton and his associates directly with the religious troubles, later telling Lauderdale's ally Sir James Foulis of Colinton that 'they intende and indeavord nothing mor then the subversion off the government off the church . . . and the alteration off the constitution off the parliament, especiallie off the articles.'[30] Facing such entrenched opinion, it was an impossible task trying to persuade the king of the validity of their complaints.

It was while Hamilton and his allies were at court in May 1678 that Lauderdale, still resident in Scotland, ordered elections for a convention of estates. Summoned solely to provide money for raising additional troops to tackle dissent and prohibited from discussing any other matter, a convention rather than a meeting of parliament prevented the opposition from launching an attack on government policy as they had done in the last meeting of the estates. Rumours of a forthcoming session had been rife since 1677 when there seemed to be increased government interference in the annual Michaelmas elections. The opposition suspected that Lauderdale's arrival in Scotland was precisely because a meeting of parliament was imminent and when the elections were held, Hamilton ordered his allies to make a special effort in areas where they had influence.[31] There had been few years since the adjournment of parliament that there had not been great contest over candidates in local elections. In 1676, for example, the opposition tried unsuccessfully to prevent Sir James Dalrymple of Stair, president of the session, from being returned for Wigtownshire. Hamilton and Queensberry were also both active in the election contests of Dumfries-shire and had sympathisers in Ayrshire who were 'doing what they could to make friends to gett themselves chosen . . . at the next head count.'[32] Those representing the commissioner's interest were equally busy. In 1677, Hatton, accompanied by his son, had travelled to Fife 'to use their interest for the electtors' but could only secure one additional vote and 'were treated by the gentlemen with very little respect.'[33]

Elections in those shires without current representation and in all the royal burghs were held on 7 June 1678, with Hamilton and his allies still either at court or on their journey homeward. This was part of a determined strategy for securing a compliant membership, with Lauderdale realising that there could be no repeat of the events of the 1673–4 sessions since, politically, he was in an even more precarious position. Burnet tells of how the election writs were purposefully sent out whilst the opposition were still in London 'knowing nothing of the design' and 'these being returnable in three weeks . . . before they could get home all the elections were over.'[34] Twenty days' warning was required for conventions of estates, although the growing approximation of conventions to parliaments produced an impression, even upon members of the privy council in 1678, that the period of notice should be forty days, as was the case with full parliaments.[35] Indeed, despite their earlier suspicions of an imminent meeting of the estates, Hamilton and his allies seem to have been caught out by the speed at which elections were called and had little time to organise their supporters. Many key men remained in London and were hurriedly sent northwards when the news of the convention became public.[36]

The opposition were well aware of attempts to keep them from influencing elections to the convention. As he related to the duchess of Hamilton, Queensberry had been given previous notice that no radical 'will be suffert to elect or bee elected members of this convention, but how legall this can be done I know not.' He raised a good point: how could the government legally exclude opposition (but otherwise valid) candidates? In fact, an earlier act of the privy council from June 1674 commanding all servants and tenants to subscribe a bond against attending conventicles proved to be the ideal measure. Many of the opposition's supporters in the localities had refused to obey the council's directive and were thus declared incapable of holding positions of public trust, leading Hamilton to complain that 'the design is to keep us as criminalls that wee may not be admitted to the convention of estats.'[37]

On behalf of the government, special efforts were being undertaken to secure the key seats that were under the influence of the opposition nobility. Thus, Queensberry was not surprised to find 'oposition against me in the election of this shyr [Dumfries]', although he assured Hamilton that he was actively 'doing what is possible to render it ineffectual'.[38] The duchess of Hamilton wrote to her husband on 15 June giving an account of the Haddingtonshire election. 'Many letters' had been written and 'many imployed to solisite' the electorate on behalf of the government. On the day of the election itself, John Hamilton, first lord Belhaven took 'severall of the gentlemen aside and spoke to them for such tuos being chosen as my lord commissioner had delivered.' Not to be outdone, Hamilton's son, James Hamilton, earl of Arran, also made appeals to the several gentlemen, hoping thereby to secure their vote for the opposition candidates.[39] There was 'great heat and contention' in sundry other elections, according to Fountainhall, and 'much briguing [intrigue] to mould them to the duc of Lauderdale's stamp.'[40] Offers were made also to members of the opposition nobility to induce a change in loyalty. The earl of Perth was 'mightly courted and great friendships promised him', but Hamilton was relieved that this did not 'prevail to make him change his former principles or friends'. Alexander Young, bishop of Edinburgh paid a visit to Hamilton to try and arrange reconciliation between him and Lauderdale prior to the convention, but, like his allies, Hamilton refused all inducements.[41]

As is apparent from the extent of their activities, the opposition had clearly taken on some form of structure and their recent involvement in local politics can certainly be regarded as something akin to a fledgling general election campaign. Regular meetings had been held, mainly amongst the noble members, since the beginning of the year and planned at these meetings was active involvement in the elections of primarily Lowland shires, such as Stirling, Linlithgow, Renfrew, Dunbarton, Ayr and Dumfries. With Lauderdale resident in Scotland from late summer 1677 onwards, Hamilton and his supporters were, however, forced to conduct their business with increasing secrecy. Prior to his arrival, they had met in Edinburgh (before the council's purge, possibly using these meetings as a cover), but this, Hamilton told his colleagues, was now impossible. Lauderdale's presence severely restricted the opposition's business prior to the convention, which was only further disrupted by the journey of Hamilton himself to court.[42] However, as extant correspondence indicates, there were plenty of other less conspicuous allies industriously at work in a number of localities.

Despite the secrecy with which the opposition operated, Lauderdale had been receiving reasonably accurate reports about their activities. The sophistication of their structure also drew attention, with Alexander Stewart, earl of Moray being amongst the first to describing the parliamentary opposition as the 'Party'.[43] The connotations of this term are critical. Labelling Hamilton's supporters as an actual political movement, a Scottish equivalent of the developing Whig and Tory political parties that were forming in response to the exclusion crisis in England, indicated just how seriously the threat to Lauderdale's supremacy was being regarded.

The commissioner's instructions for the convention, issued by the king on 13 June, left no doubt that any opposition was to be thoroughly purged. His first task after the calling of the rolls was to 'name a committee to consider of elections of shires and burroughs', presumably to oust those Party candidates who, despite best efforts, had successfully been elected to the convention. Thus, on 13 June, only six days after the elections were held and even before the results could possibly have been known in Whitehall, the government were planning precautionary measures against a possible repeat of dissent in the parliamentary chamber. This strategy was not to remain secret for long, however, with the duchess of Hamilton writing to her husband on 15 June telling him of the rumours that 'befor the convention sit down ther will be a comatie apointed to conseder of the elections wher ther is doubell commissioners chosen and to admit only of such as pleases them.'[44]

Six days prior to the full meeting of the estates, a convention of royal burghs assembled in Edinburgh. On 20 June, a representative group of burgesses were sent to pay their respects to Lauderdale at his lodgings in Holyrood Palace. There, the delegates endured a lengthy lecture from the commissioner representing to them the several favours conferred on the burghs by monarchs past and present, with Lauderdale concluding by instructing the burghs to demonstrate their loyalty to the king in the forthcoming convention. The address received a polite but lukewarm response. Hamilton arrived in Edinburgh on 24 June and met with the commissioner the same day, passing some pleasantries on the weather and the state of the highways. A more meaningful exchange occurred in a later meeting with the archbishop of St Andrews and the bishops of Edinburgh and Galloway, where Hamilton denounced the short period of notice given prior to elections for the convention, especially when many of the nobility were absent from the kingdom. The duke also expressed disquiet about the 'many prelimitations [that] were used at the elections' and alleged that the 'lieges' had been 'menaced and frighted' by the bond to be subscribed against conventicles. Such issues, he hoped, would be taken into consideration by the convention itself.[45]

In the 1673 session of parliament, Lauderdale had been surprised by the widespread and organised nature of the opposition; they had obviously been meeting outwith the parliamentary chamber to decide on tactics, as they had been recently. For the forthcoming convention, Lauderdale was instructed to remind the gathered estates that in pursuance of two acts of 1661, it was 'illegal to convene and determine any matters of state before or during convention.' Any members found guilty were to be tried under the full force of the law. If discord still arose, specifically if 'any lords or others shall . . . appear in opposition to our service, so as the design for which wee have called the convention may thereby be in any hazard of being frustrated', Lauderdale was authorised to adjourn the convention until further notice.[46] It was an extraordinary set of instructions. The king had given his commissioner the authority to quibble any commission, eject any members he saw fit and adjourn the meeting if there was a repeat of the disturbances of the last sessions.

The convention of estates assembled in Edinburgh on 26 June 1678. The rolls of the opening day record an attendance of 180, consisting of ten bishops, fifty-five nobles, four officers of state, fifty-one commissioners representing thirty-one shires and sixty commissioners representing fifty-nine burghs.[47] The membership, as planned, had been carefully purged of many of the opponents that had attended the last session of parliament in 1673. There were eleven new shire representatives and the membership of the burghs had been massively altered since the last session, with the enforced limitations on burgh elections after the 1674 convention of burghs providing the perfect excuse to exclude those prone to 'factious' behaviour. Thirty-one new burgesses were recorded in the rolls, 51 per cent of the estate's representation as a whole. Significantly for Hamilton, certain key members of the opposition nobility decided not to attend the convention. Kincardine remained in London, much to the fury of others in the Party, and Atholl, their most recent convert, also stayed away. Their reluctance can be explained by fears of incurring yet further displeasure from the king, possibly even actual punishment in the form of fining or confinement. Prior to his own journey north, Hamilton himself was extremely nervous about returning, fearing imprisonment for his past defiance.[48]

After prayers by the archdean of St Andrews, the rolls taken and the oaths subscribed, Lauderdale produced from his pocket a list of names that he announced were his nominations for a committee to consider debatable elections. Halfway through reading out the list, he was interrupted by the duke of Hamilton who voiced suspicions that this way of procedure was very unusual and that there could be no nomination of a committee without prior consultation with the estates. In the past, he argued, this had only been granted at their desire and there had been no formal motion in the convention to remit nominations to the commissioner. In any case, before a committee be chosen, it seemed proper to consider if debatable elections might first be discussed by the convention as a whole; if it was decided by a majority to refer these to a committee, only those whose commissions who were themselves unchallenged could possibly be allowed to sit on the committee. Hamilton, seconded by the earl of Dumfries and Sir Alexander Bruce of Broomhall, expressed reservations that not only were some of those included in Lauderdale's list incapable of sitting in the convention but were perhaps also ineligible for holding any position of public trust.[49] This initial exchange set the pattern for whole session: it was to be a battle over membership, played out over the decisions of the committee for debatable elections.

Lauderdale attempted to assure Hamilton that the committee he named would only have the power to report and would produce before the convention all relevant evidence to authenticate their decisions. Long speeches in support of the commissioner were then made by Hatton, Sir Thomas Wallace of Craigie, justice clerk, and Sir James Dalrymple of Stair, president of the session, arguing that the naming of committees was the commissioner's privilege. 'It is a strange thing to see this controverted', declared Mackenzie of Rosehaugh, 'for, if his majestie were here in person, who would deny him the privilege?'[50] Hamilton listened patiently but remained unconvinced by the legal arguments. Seeing that the committee only had the power to report, why go to the lengths of setting one up, he argued. It would only mean that all the particulars regarding each election would have to be first considered in the committee and again in the full convention. He claimed that in previous sessions, namely in 1661, disputed elections were dealt with in full parliament. After arguments refuting this, the records were brought out, consulted and Hamilton found to be correct. The production of the parliamentary record for 1661 brought about an extraordinary set of exchanges between the two opposing groups. The earl of Argyll retorted that the Restoration parliament was a 'lame parliament', it being summoned while the country was still under commonwealth rule and it following no particular historical procedure since matters of state were still in turmoil. Archbishop Sharp agreed that it was a weak and defective session because there had been no members of the clergy present. It was a dangerous route to take and Hamilton seized upon their statements. Were not Argyll and Sharp's remarks seditious? To question the parliament wherein 'his majesties rights and prerogatives were more inlarged and fully cleared than at any time before or after' was surely to set a dangerous consequence, argued Hamilton. He was seconded again by Broomhall, one of Kincardine's kinsmen, who added that a committee ought not to be named until the estates had decided which elections were to be examined. That right alone belonged to the convention.[51]

Despite the arguments of Hamilton and others, without a vote, Lauderdale insisted that his initial list of nominations be accepted. The official record states that the convention did 'humbly desyre' the lord commissioner to appoint a committee, although it is clear that the suggestion originated with Lauderdale himself. Thus, it set a precedent that the naming of committees was a privilege belonging to the monarch or commissioner and only granted to parliaments or conventions out of favour or respect. This crucial meeting was, by implication, not one of these occasions.[52]

After all the effort to exclude them from partaking in the elections to the convention, there was little doubt that Hamilton and his allies would also be omitted from the committee for determining double commissions. Lauderdale's list of nominations was made up of six bishops, thirteen nobles, eleven shire and nine burgh commissioners. Amongst those entrusted with settling the electoral disputes were two of Lauderdale's own relatives, Richard Maitland of Gogar and John Drummond of Lundin (related by marriage to the Maitland family), Francis Kinloch of Gilmerton, provost of Edinburgh, a crown sponsored candidate at the 1675 Edinburgh council election, and Sir James Foulis of Colinton, a frequent correspondent and close ally of the commissioner. Amongst Hamilton's associates only the earl of Morton was included. The nomination of the committee now complete, the convention adjourned to 28 June to allow the consideration of the elections.[53]

Because of their debates taking longer than initially expected, the first submission from the committee for debatable elections was not produced before the full convention until 29 June. On being given notice that the committee had completed its deliberations, the duke of Hamilton stated that he wished to declare a number of other objections to several shire and burgh commissions before the committee's report was read. There had already been attempts to submit these to the committee some days previously but any submissions not approved by the convention had been refused. Hamilton also objected to what he perceived as an unauthorised extension to the remit of the committee, since it had not only considered elections with double returns but also those commissions in which there had been questions over voter eligibility, such as in the shires of Selkirk, Sutherland and Kirkcudbright and in the burghs of New Galloway, Culross and Lanark. Until any outstanding cases be considered, Hamilton argued, the report should be held back. There was further dispute over the eligibility of convention members, with Charles Erskine, fifth earl of Mar, alleging that William Erskine, second earl of Buchan, was incapable of taking his seat as he was still a minor. Buchan was only allowed to remain after he gave his 'word of honour' that he was above the age of twenty-one.[54] The Party supporters then made various attempts to use the debatable elections to their advantage. Both the earls of Dumfries and Perth voiced their opinion that it would be an 'absurditie' if those commissioners whose elections were in dispute should be able to vote prior to their case being determined. If this had carried, over a quarter of the shire and burgh representation would have been disbarred from voting, thereby increasing opposition influence.[55]

Despite Hamilton's complaints, the report from the committee of debatable elections was read in its entirety. The elections for New Galloway and Culross were remitted to the convention of royal burghs for their consideration. Next, the election of the shire of Selkirk was considered, the principal complaint being that James Murray of Philiphaugh, as sheriff and convenor, had given only two hours' warning of the election. This was true, the committee found, but as the majority of freeholders were present at the election, it was concluded that the commission could stand. Hamilton, seconded by many others, immediately protested, claiming that the committee had the remit only to advise and not determine the outcome of each dispute. The papers and evidence for each respective case should therefore be made available to the chamber; the members could then assess each individual election and come to their own conclusions. This was rejected as being likely to delay the supply for which the convention had been summoned. James Ogilvy, second earl of Airlie, David Wemyss, second earl of Wemyss, Charles Gordon, first earl of Aboyne, and Alexander Falconer, lord Falconer of Halkerton, all urged an immediate vote on the committee's decision, according to Nisbet's account of proceedings being 'much scandalised at the retarding of the king's service'. Hamilton, Perth, Dumfries, Queensberry, Tweeddale and others of the Party proclaimed it impossible to vote in a business of which they know 'nothing of the grounds'. Despite frequent outbursts from Lauderdale, who 'diverse times thundered with great passion from the throne against what was desired', it was at last conceded that the convention could hear in more detail the particulars of each election.[56]

Lauderdale had previously attempted to reach a settlement with the Party leaders, calling Hamilton, Queensberry, Perth, Robert Carnegie, second earl of Southesk, and Drummond of Cromlix to a private conference prior to the day's business. At this meeting, the commissioner urged Hamilton not to press a public debate of the elections in the convention in order not to delay the grant of taxation. In hope that an accommodation might be reached, Lauderdale delayed the start of the session to 4 o'clock, but none was agreed.[57] If contemporary reports of a private meeting between Hamilton and Lauderdale are correct, it represented a significant concession on the part of the commissioner. Only once before (after the unprecedented revolt against him in the parliamentary session of 1673) had he thought it necessary to seek private bargains with the opposition. Although there was no doubt that the government had a large numerical superiority in the convention and that the supply was likely to pass unimpeded, it revealed that Lauderdale was all too aware of the damage inflicted to his personal reputation by Hamilton's constant questioning.

In light of the vote allowing the particulars of each election contest to be fully discussed, the convention resumed consideration of the election of Selkirkshire. The crown's superiority in numbers proved to be the decisive factor, with the report of the committee recommending that the election should stand being approved by approximately fifty or sixty votes. This figure gives some idea of the strength of both the crown interest and the opposition party within the chamber. Fountainhall, an apparent observer of events, estimated that in general the 'most that syded with Duke Hamilton ware about thirty-nine in number and about 100 went with the commissioner.'[58] A second source gives a slightly more generous estimate in Hamilton's favour, stating that in the actual voting 'the commissioner comes at least two thirds part clear.'[59] Thirty to thirty-five is probably a more accurate estimate of the core of the Party and this was a significant number given the lengths to which the crown had interfered in elections. Approved crown candidates were themselves conspicuous, with Lauderdale's every action being enthusiastically 'seconded by a great many others whose constant course it was in such turns to call incessantly for a vote as if they had been sett there for no other purpose.'[60]

The convention proceeded to analyse disputed elections in the shires of Cromarty, Perth, Kirkcudbright and Berwick. The election in Cromartyshire was endorsed without lengthy debate, as was that of Perthshire after a short dispute about whether the seat had actually been vacant at the Michaelmas elections. The election of Richard Murray of Broughton for Kirkcudbrightshire was queried because there was a decreet of infamy against him by the court of session. However, he had since obtained the king's remission and even Hamilton's allies were unwilling to question this too forcibly. As a result, Broughton's election was confirmed.[61] In Berwickshire, there had been fierce competition between the opposition and government candidates. Sir Patrick Hume of Polwarth, one of Hamilton's most explicit allies in the previous session of parliament, had collected around twenty votes in comparison to Sir Roger Hogg of Harcarse's thirty-nine. However, of these thirty-nine, Polwarth argued, twenty-five were ineligible to vote.[62] Harcarse was an eminent lawyer and Polwarth made an unusual request for his advocate to speak for him, admitting that he felt not qualified to defend himself. This was flatly refused, despite protests, since to have allowed complex legal argument to decide the outcome of electoral disputes may have extended the convention by weeks. Rosehaugh and others stated that it was not the convention's role to study the eligibility of electors: if they did, 'all the barrons of Scotland shall be forced to bring in their charters and evidents to Edinburgh' and the convention 'shall never fall to their business'. Indeed, the debate had already begun to tire Lauderdale and he often interrupted proceedings urging a vote, finally crying out with indignation: 'When shall we show our zeall for his majesties service? When shall we fall to the work for which we met?' After a ballot, Polwarth's election was declared void and the convention adjourned to 1 July.[63]

When the rolls were called at the next session, it became evident that some commissioners had been omitted. Lauderdale announced that the members for the shire of Sutherland, the burghs of New Galloway, Lanark and several others who remain unidentified had been excluded from taking any further part in proceedings until their elections had been considered. Bruce of Broomhall, his own election still to be discussed, complained that this was contrary to the decision made at the last session, which allowed those commissioners whose elections were in dispute to vote in the convention until their cases had been reviewed. Lauderdale was reluctantly forced to acknowledge the validity of Broomhall's complaint and the absent members ordered to be called in the rolls at the next voting.[64]

The election of George Dickson of Bughtrig for the burgh of New Galloway was next to be declared null in light of the recent limitations placed on burgh elections, with Dickson freely admitting that he was not a merchant or resident of the burgh and indeed that he considered himself to belong to the estate of gentry or lesser nobility.[65] Thereafter, the election of Thomas Stoddart for the burgh of Lanark was approved, this conforming in all respects to the acts of the conventions of burghs.[66] A second report was then brought in from the committee which contained objections against a slew of shire and burgh elections. Hamilton and his allies had clearly been busy. In total, out of the thirty-one shires that were represented in the convention, there were complaints made against the representatives of twenty-two of them.[67] The burghs fared slightly better: out of the fifty-nine in attendance at the meeting, objections were handed in against thirteen of them.[68] Although there were complaints against elections in almost all parts of the country, by far the majority of disputes were centred in the central lowlands and the south-west, the duke of Hamilton's main area of influence, and the borders, the stronghold of both Queensberry and Tweeddale. The Party had been more successful in electing candidates in shires than in burghs, partly because shire elections had always been under the influence of local nobility. Burgh seats were more difficult to secure, one possible reason being that town councils had been thoroughly purged after the dispute in the convention of royal burghs in 1675 and were thus most probably staffed with loyal government supporters. The recently enforced restrictions on elections only being open to resident trafficking merchants further limited opportunities for interference.

In addition to the reading of the committee's general report, the minutes of their last meeting, containing details of the particular objections against numerous elections, were read out to the gathered estates. This seems to have been done in error, with Sir Thomas Murray of Glendoick, clerk register, on realising his mistake, initially refusing to continue reciting the minutes. After vociferous protests from Hamilton, Perth, Dumfries and others, Lauderdale eventually yielded on the condition that the minutes were read only for information purposes and were not to be considered as part of the report. The reason for this reluctance was soon made clear when the paper was read out. Referring to an unspecified complaint submitted by Hamilton himself, the committee's opinion was that this was 'a calumnious objection' and that he and others who had submitted similar protests 'were obstructers and retarders of his majesties service'. Hamilton was furious, angrily defending his conduct and demanding that the minutes be formally considered by the convention in order to clear his name. Broomhall declared that it was 'nonsence to offer that general report if notwithstanding of it the consideration of the particulars were reserved.' Even Rothes as chancellor admitted that it was highly unsatisfactory for the convention not to consider the particular details of each election prior to a vote. Interrupting attempts to resume debating the particulars of the elections of the burghs of Linlithgow, Tain and Queensferry, Lauderdale called for an immediate vote on the contents of the general report, instructing the estates to ignore what was contained in the minutes of the committee's meetings. The report as it stood was approved by a majority, but Hamilton, alleging 'that he was highly injured by several expressions' contained within the minutes, made a request for an extract of the committee's proceedings. This Lauderdale flatly refused, again stating that the minutes of the committee were not actually part of the report. Hamilton formally took instruments in protest, throwing his instrument money angrily down on the clerk's table and proclaiming that although he had little hope of getting an extract, he was 'glad he had famous witnesses' to confirm this slander.[69]

In an attempt to bring to an end the protracted discussions over elections, the commissioner addressed the chamber, telling the gathered estates that several objections had been given in without any corresponding evidence and this had seriously impeded the business of the convention. Thus, it had been decided that, except in cases of double returns, no objection could now be handed in that had not first been made at the time of the election. It was clearly an attempt to prevent the opposition from using the process of electoral disputes as a means of further stalling the supply.[70]

Figure 6.1   *William Douglas, third duke of Hamilton (1634–94) by Sir Godfrey Kneller, c.1682–4. The noble leader of the opposition group and fledgling political party that formed during the 1670s in response to the autocratic parliamentary management of the duke of Lauderdale. Deprived of significant office throughout much of the Restoration period due to his conflict with Lauderdale, he eventually found favour and position under James, duke of York, being awarded the order of the garter in 1682 (which he is pictured here wearing) and commissioner to the treasury in 1685.*
(On loan to the Scottish National Portrait Gallery from Lennoxlove House, Haddington.)

When the convention reconvened at the next day's session on 2 July, there was an additional surprise for the opposition. Polwarth, whose election had earlier been declared null, had been arrested in his night-clothes in a midnight raid on his lodgings for some unspecified 'factious' behaviour. The warrant for his arrest, issued at Whitehall on 27 June, alleged that he had 'been of late very much endeavouring to create disturbances in some of the king's affairs.'[71] The authorities made a very public search of all his papers, 'thinking to make it appear that he has been tampering and keeping correspondence with some members of the House of Commons.'[72] Polwarth's fate was a none-too-subtle reminder to other members of the Party of the power that Lauderdale still possessed. At the start of the day's session, the commissioner rebuked the gathered estates for believing the many 'malitious and scurrelous reports' alleging that to the act of supply a clause would be added ratifying the invasion of the south-west by the Host. This was manifestly false, Lauderdale reassured the chamber, and, in any case, could only be done by a parliament.[73]

The convention next resumed consideration of the remaining double elections, with Ayrshire the first to be discussed. The election of the Party candidates Sir John Cochrane of Cowdoun and Sir John Cunningham of Lambroughton, despite having almost three times the amount of signatures as its rival, was found null simply because the election clerk had not signed it.[74] The votes in the election of Stirlingshire were declared equal after the signatures of numerous electors were disallowed. Hamilton complained that this was contrary to the decision made regarding the Berwickshire election on 29 June when the convention had agreed that it was not viable to investigate individual electors. To this, he seemingly received no answer and the convention confirmed Sir John Stirling of Keir and James Seaton of Touch as commissioners.[75] In the election of Renfrewshire, the committee decided that Sir John Shaw of Greenock and Sir John Maxwell of Nether Pollok should be preferred over the competing commission. However, after George Ross, eleventh lord Ross, complained that Pollok had refused the bond against conventicles, he too was excluded.[76]

The last remaining disputed election was considered in the convention on 3 July. In the case of Dunbartonshire, the committee's opinion was that the commission to Sir Patrick Houston of that ilk and William Hamilton of Orbiston should stand. Alexander Stewart, fourth lord Blantyre, protested that this commission lacked the electoral clerk's signature and therefore, considering the decision made the day before in the case of Ayrshire, the election should also be disallowed. If they proceeded differently, Blantyre argued, the convention would 'destroy this day what they had built the day befor.' These objections were disregarded, the committee's decision approved and the commissioners called into the chamber. When they failed to appear, it was announced that the two gentlemen had already left for home, believing the convention's decision in the Ayrshire election had determined their fate. Lauderdale suspected differently, asserting that Houston and Orbiston had left Edinburgh because they were 'disaffected' and had refused to sign the necessary oaths for sitting in parliament.[77]

The settling of the electoral disputes had just taken over a week, not what the crown intended at the outset of the meeting. A committee had been instituted precisely to avoid the kind of lengthy arguments that had taken place and was supposed to save time by dealing with the particulars of each disputed election in private. Hamilton and his allies managed to debate each case in turn, and, although this made little difference to the outcome of the disputes, by making the committee explain its often contrary decisions, it demonstrated to the gathered estates that it was political considerations that determined elections, not matter of historical precedence, law or even a majority of votes. The discussions had been a huge embarrassment for Lauderdale and thus a major victory for the parliamentary opposition.

The estates met for a short session on 4 July, when the king's letter requesting a grant of taxation (to be raised by means of a cess) was read. Lauderdale and Rothes both gave speeches urging the convention to put behind them past disputes concerning elections and instead to give ample testimony of their zeal for the king's service by granting a generous supply without further disagreement. A committee was nominated to consider the quota and proportion of the supply, the commissioner decreeing that the membership should be the same as the committee for debatable elections, with the additions of Robert Dook and Robert Watson for the burghs of Ayr and Dumbarton respectively. As a sop to the opposition, it was expressly declared that the committee only had the power to advise and that any members of the convention, after the report of the committee had been submitted, would be free to 'argue and object as to any particulars that shall be offered by the committie in relation either as to the proportion of the supplie or the maner of raising of the same.' The convention then adjourned for a period of three days to enable the committee to begin its deliberations.[78]

The estates reconvened on 8 July fully expecting to hear the report of the committee for supply. This was delayed, however, by yet further disagreements over elections. Hamilton interrupted the calling of the rolls by questioning the inclusion of William Blair of that ilk as commissioner for Ayrshire, since the committee had not yet reported on the legality of his election. Dalrymple of Stair (who himself had been elected to the seat but had chosen instead to honour his commission to Wigtownshire), immediately defended Blair's inclusion, contending that it would be wrong to exclude him because the shire would have no representation. It was not a particularly convincing argument. Broomhall made the valid point that by ejecting other commissioners for deficiencies in their elections (in Dunbartonshire, for example), those shires were also now without representation. Lauderdale intervened, determined not to waste any more time retreading old ground.[79] All business regarding the elections was now over, he declared. Blair's inclusion in the roll was put to the vote and he was admitted by 140 votes to thirty.[80]

The report from the committee of supply was at last brought forth before the estates. If the commissioner had thought that opposition would be centred solely on elections, he was to be immediately proved wrong. Barely had the reading of the report begun when Hamilton intervened and demanded what use the government had for the money that was to be raised, a total of £1,800,000 to be collected five months of the year for a period of five years. The sum had been calculated to meet the necessary costs of raising troops to suppress conventicles in the west and for defending the county in the event of invasion, Rothes answered. Hamilton's reply was that he did not doubt the calculation, only that he thought the sum too great for the country to bear. If the commissioner would allow an adjournment to enable further discussion on the committee's report, it was likely that a far easier means of imposing the burden could be found, which he thought was the king's intention in his letter to the convention. Lauderdale's response was typically abrupt. Refusing to authorise any further delay in the supply, he declared that none could speak for the king except himself. It had been decided that a regiment of foot, three troops of horse and three troops of dragoons were the absolute minimum necessary for the security of the kingdom and nothing less than £360,000 a year could maintain these troops. After further debate, a vote was held on whether £72,000 a month for twenty-five months should be the supply. It passed easily enough, with only the earl of Haddington, James Fletcher of Saltoun, Adam Cockburn of Ormiston (both for

Haddingtonshire), Robert Gordon of Gordonstoun (Sutherlandshire) and John Anderson of the burgh of Dunfermline voting against the sum.[81]

The convention met again on 9 July for another short session to discuss a number of amendments to the draft supply act. A proposal to renew the burden upon annualrents was bitterly opposed and the clause was rejected by eleven votes, all the burghs, without exception, voting against it.[82] A final draft of the act of supply was produced before the convention on 10 July. After being read in its entirety, a number of concerns were raised by two of the members that had voted against the specific enactment of £72,000 a month as the amount of supply. One particular clause of the act declared that all existing commissioners of excise were automatically to be appointed as commissioners for uplifting the cess, yet Fletcher of Saltoun and Cockburn of Ormiston, despite being excise commissioners for Haddingtonshire, had both been omitted from the act. Their exclusion, Lauderdale declared, was because he would allow no man to have any hand in regulating that supply which they had voted against. This prompted an immediate flood of protest. Hamilton claimed that the commissioners were not against the supply in principal, only against the quota being five months per annum when they believed four was sufficient. For that reason, it was surely improper and excessive to put such 'a note of infamy upon any gentilman'.[83]

Hamilton had his own objections to the list of commissioners, questioning why in almost every shire were sheriffs and their deputies nominated as convenors of the cess except in the sheriffdoms of Lanark, Ayr, Renfrew, Peebles, Selkirk, Perth, Forfar and Dumfries where he and some others were sheriffs. He was assured that there was no design: in sound shires, sheriffs had been given the office; in others, the lord commissioner had nominated others 'without any prejudicial intent'. Hamilton was incensed with Lauderdale's reply, stating that he took his omission from the act as a 'mark of disgrace'. To so publicly deprive Hamilton of his only remaining office was a tactless move and, with continued assertions of his loyalty to the crown, the duke, supported by the earl of Southesk, demanded that an immediate vote be held to decide whether all shires should have their sheriffs as convenors.[84] After some quarrelling over the exact wording, it was finally resolved that the question should be whether the convention approved the convenors as nominated by the committee of supply. All except twenty-seven voted in favour of the list as it stood.[85]

After instructing Rothes, as chancellor, to remove his name from the list of cess commissioners for the sheriffdom of Lanark, since if he was 'not permitted to serve the king in the same capacitie with others of the lyke office he would keep non of their meetings to his ane disparagement', Hamilton stormed out of the chamber. He was closely followed by the earl of Southesk, Alexander Gordon, fifth viscount of Kenmure, John Hamilton, second lord Bargany, Cockburn of Ormiston, Cromwell Lockhart of Lee and Sir Robert Hamilton of Silvertonhill (both commissioners for Lanarkshire). The earls of Tweeddale, Roxburghe, Haddington and Fletcher of Saltoun had left prior to the vote and did not return. The full act of supply was then presented before the remainder of the convention and only James Ramsay, bishop of Dunblane, and the earl of Dumfries (who both 'approved what related to the king but not the other circumstances') voted against its enactment.[86]

Lauderdale's allies revelled in Hamilton's walkout, deriding the Party's impotency in a number of letters sent south to court. As one correspondent wrote, despite the attempts of Hamilton and his supporters to oppose every measure that was brought before the chamber, it was strikingly obvious 'how little ther opposition signified' since 'they can neither hinder nor stop any thing in this convention.'[87] This was true: the crown's superiority in numbers did prevent the Party from successfully challenging the many disputed elections or from thwarting the act of supply. This, however, was never their aim. Instead, by winning smaller battles, such as by forcing the committee of debatable elections to disclose the reasons behind its decisions, Hamilton and his allies were purposefully pursuing an agenda by which Lauderdale's own method of governing was brought in to focus. When the often contradictory nature of the reasoning behind the settlement of electoral disputes was revealed, it was ample demonstration of the arbitrariness of those presently in command. By constantly challenging Lauderdale's authority as commissioner in this way, the Party were making an overtly public statement: in Scotland, Lauderdale did not possess the absolute control that he liked to boast of.

The one remaining item to be considered before the convention's adjournment was the reply to the king's letter. The draft presented to the convention on 10 July, penned by Mackenzie of Rosehaugh and John Paterson, bishop of Galloway, attempted to make light of the difficulties of recent weeks, informing the king that although there were regrettably some disaffected subjects in his kingdom, there was no danger of rebellion. In a thinly veiled sneer at Hamilton and his supporters' impotence, the letter went on to assure the king that in the actual convention the interest of those disaffected subjects appeared to be very small. The remainder of the letter was as much intended for an English audience as a Scottish one, containing a fulsome panegyric of Lauderdale's abilities as commissioner and finally concluding with a comparison some contemporaries regarded as blasphemous: 'Your majestie, who uses alwayes to lessen our greatest guilt and to highten the value of our meanest endeavours . . . a king who, like God (from whom alone our kings deryve their power), never uses his power but to do good.'[88] With the majority of the Party absent, it was left to the earl of Perth to make the lone complaint to the letter. After stating that he was as dutiful as any of the king's subjects and that he 'took no reflection to himself of what was in that letter', he declared that in reference to Lauderdale's tenure as commissioner, he would 'applaud nothing of his procedur'. The commissioner merely replied that it was too late to discuss the letter and adjourned the convention to the following day. At this session on 11 July, the letter was twice read and, without a vote, subscribed with a general assent.[89] The convention of estates then formally dissolved.

Lauderdale celebrated the end of the convention in style by entertaining the estates with 'a most splendid dinner'.[90] Fountainhall was one contemporary forced to admit that Lauderdale had reason to be triumphal, of the opinion that the commissioner 'had recovered any thing he lost in the parliament 1673.' He had similar praise, however, for the commissioner's opponents:

> Duke Hamilton went away from the penult meeting in a passion; yet it cannot be denied but the duke of Hamilton all alongs behaved himselfe very weell and showed much acutenesse and readines of wit in his reasonings, and very prudently did tak the advantage to retort his adversaries' arguments against themselfes.[91]

Although they did not have the numbers of supporters necessary to mount a serious challenge to measures such as the grant of taxation, the Party successfully managed to discredit Lauderdale. This proved as damaging as any defeat over the passage of an act. Few would have agreed with the assertions made in the convention's reply to the king's letter that Lauderdale had managed the convention with justice and equity.

Actively expressing any form of opposition could be considered an achievement in itself, considering the unprecedented management that had been taken over the membership to the convention.

However, Hamilton was not able to take advantage of the other estates' grievances as he had done in 1673. The majority of the burghs remained unwaveringly loyal since they had learnt to their cost in the convention of royal burghs how unwise it was to oppose the crown. Only a few opposition shire members had been elected in the face of widespread governmental interference in elections. Hamilton simply did not have the breadth of support he had enjoyed in the last session of parliament.

Ultimately, Lauderdale was victorious because he had the continued backing of the king, this a vital endorsement not just for maintaining current office but for the fundamentals it represented. In parliaments, the commissioner personally embodied the crown. It made no difference, therefore, that many resented Lauderdale's long tenure and found his autocratic methods of stifling debate offensive: this in itself was not enough to persuade the majority to join forces against him. It was likewise inconceivable that Hamilton and his allies would follow the example of religious dissenters and actively resist the government. They were not, in this sense, revolutionaries. Throughout, the parliamentary opposition remained consistently loyal to their king. It was common hatred of Lauderdale and his methods of government that united them.

After his return to London in August 1678, the commissioner did not seem quite as unassailable as he had been previously. There were the beginnings of a number of worrying cracks in his relationship with the king, with Lauderdale being instructed by Charles that Hamilton and his allies must be treated better in future, indicating that some of the Party's many complaints had at last struck home.[92] English hostility against Lauderdale's ministry only intensified, increasing to new heights at the outbreak of armed rebellion in Scotland in 1679.[93] It was with the arrival of James, duke of York, in Scotland in 1680 that Lauderdale was finally cast into the political wilderness. Nevertheless, as future events were to demonstrate, the opposition's grievances were not to be resolved simply by the removal of one deeply unpopular minister. Beneath this often personal battle between two dukes lay a debate about the limitations of royal authority and the role of parliament. It was surely hoped that the duke of York, Lauderdale's successor as commissioner, would govern in a more inclusionary manner. However, by the end of the next parliamentary session of 1681, it was clear that Lauderdale and his much-maligned style of leadership had not been vanquished, only replaced.

Notes

1 Mackenzie, *Memoirs*, p. 315; Burnet, *History*, ii, pp. 58–9.

2 *RPCS*, third series, iv, pp. 186–9; NAS, Exchequer Papers E6/2, p. 181; Lee, 'Government and politics in Scotland, 1661–1681', p. 80.

3 *RPCS*, third series, iv, pp. vi–viii; Hutton, *Charles II*, pp. 322–3.

4 NLS, Miscellaneous Mss 9375, 'Complaints against the duke of Lauderdale, December 1674', f. 7.

5 Mackenzie, *Memoirs*, p. 268; Burnet, *History*, ii, pp. 55–6; *RPCS*, third series, iv, pp. 631–3; NLS, Miscellaneous Mss 9375, ff. 7–10.

6 Mackenzie, *Memoirs*, p. 268

7 Lang, *Sir George Mackenzie*, pp. 114–15; Mackenzie, *Memoirs*, pp. 276–7; *RPCS*, third series, iv, pp. 283–4. For the relevant submissions in the dispute, see *RPCS*, third series, iv, pp. 630–45 and Mackenzie, *Memoirs*, pp. 280–308.

8 NLS, Miscellaneous Mss 9375, f. 22.

9 NLS, Mss Yester 7006, ff. 115, 121, 137; *Scots Peerage*, ii, p. 363, iii, p. 372 and iv, p. 380; Lee, 'Government and politics in Scotland, 1661–1681', pp. 242–3. For more on the Lockhart of Carnwath family and their involvement in Scottish public life throughout the seventeenth and early eighteenth centuries, see D. Szechni, 'Constructing a Jacobite: the social and intellectual origins of George Lockhart of Carnwath', *The Historical Journal*, 40 (1997), pp. 979–82.

10 BL, Additional Mss 23126, f. 173.

11 *Records of the Convention of the Royal Burghs of Scotland*, iii, (1615–76), pp. 639–40.

12 NAS, Biel Muniments, GD6/994, 'Copy of sederunt of the convention of royal burghs concerning their insolent letter to the king and observations thereon by Sir John Nisbet, king's advocate', f. 2; NAS, Hamilton Papers, GD406/2/M1/225, 'Reasons why the burghs should not be restricted in the election of their commissioners to parliament and convention of estates'; NAS, Hamilton Papers, GD406/1/2758; *Records of the Convention of the Royal Burghs of Scotland*, iii, (1615–76), pp. 640–2; Rait, *Parliaments of Scotland*, pp. 296–7.

13 Mackenzie, *Memoirs*, pp. 275–6, 278; NAS, Hamilton Papers, GD406/1/5974; NLS, Watson Mss 597, f. 265; *Lauderdale Papers*, iii, pp. 65–6.

14 Rait, *Parliaments of Scotland*, pp. 259–61.

15 *Records of the Convention of the Royal Burghs of Scotland*, iii, (1615–76), pp. 644–5. Despite submitting, the convention continued to protest against the loss of their privileges, the next motion after their apology being for a memorial to be despatched to Lauderdale acquainting him of the 'heavie burdeens the borrowes lyes under' because of the 'continued tradeing in burghs of barronie and regalitie'.

16 *Records of the Convention of the Royal Burghs of Scotland*, iii, (1615–76), pp. 643–4. Even with a purged membership, there was still opposition to the restricting of elections, with the commissioners for Ayr, Dumbarton, Edinburgh and two others not identified 'debated strongly' against the submission to the king's demands. If passed, they argued, it would 'cutt off [or] at least render this state insignificant in parliament in regard most of the burghs in the kingdome either are not able to maintain a commissioner or have not a man capable of that trust.' Nevertheless, it was believed prudent that an apology should be offered. NAS, Hamilton Papers, GD406/1/2827.

17 *Records of the Convention of the Royal Burghs of Scotland*, iii, (1615–76), p. 649.

18 Mackenzie, *Memoirs*, pp. 310–11.

19 Mackenzie, *Memoirs*, pp. 310–11; *RPCS*, third series, iv, pp. 367, 469–71, 475. The opposition expressed delight when it became apparent that the sentence against the three provosts was only carried by one vote, despite the fact neither Hamilton nor Morton were in attendance at council on the day the verdict was passed. NAS, Hamilton Papers, GD406/1/2843.

20 NAS, Hamilton Papers, GD406/1/5905; *RPCS*, third series, iv, pp. 350–6; Mackenzie, *Memoirs*, p. 309; Burnet, *History*, ii, pp. 56, 73–5; Lee, 'Government and politics in Scotland, 1661–1681', p. 255.

21 Mackenzie, *Memoirs*, pp. 308–10.

22 Burnet, *History*, ii, pp. 113–15; Wodrow, *Sufferings of the Church of Scotland*, ii, pp. 327–30; Mackenzie, *Memoirs*, pp. 317–18; *Lauderdale Papers*, iii, pp. 83–5; *RPCS*, third series, v, pp. 6–9. Lauderdale wrote triumphantly to Sharp trumpeting the 'effectual purge' of the council. 'Thirty-four letters written to James Sharp by the duke and duchess of Lauderdale', in SHS, *Miscellany of the Scottish History Society* (Edinburgh, 1893), i, p. 274.

23 Mackenzie, *Memoirs*, pp. 325–6.

24 Burnet, *History*, ii, p. 138. See D. Allan, *Philosophy and Politics in later Stuart Scotland: Neo-Stoicism, Culture and Ideology in an age of crisis, 1540–1690* (East Linton, 2000), pp. 190–200, for a study into the philosophical reasons behind Mackenzie's shift in allegiances.

25 NLS, Papers of Charles Kirkpatrick Sharpe, Mss 2512, f. 159; Buckroyd, *Church and State*, pp. 114–17; *RPCS*, third series, iv, pp. 186–91, 197–200.

26 *RPCS*, third series, iv, pp. 135, 152–3, 500–1; Burnet, *History*, ii, pp. 138–40; Mackenzie, *Memoirs*, pp. 327–9; Lauder of Fountainhall, *Historical Notices*, i, pp. 183–6; Buckroyd, *Church and State*, pp. 118, 127.

27 Burnet, *History*, ii, p. 136; *Scots Peerage*, i, p. 370 and vi, p. 323.

28 Burnet, *History*, ii, pp. 144–5; *Lauderdale Papers*, iii, p. 89; Buckroyd, *Church and State*, pp. 124–8; J. R. Elder, *The Highland Host of 1678*

(Glasgow, 1914). A third of the army was actually drawn from regular forces and Lowland militia. Macinnes, 'Repression and conciliation: the Highland dimension, 1660–1688', pp. 185–6.

29 *Lauderdale Papers*, iii, pp. 107–9; Lee, 'Government and politics in Scotland, 1661–1681', pp. 263–7. The earl of Cassilis, branded a rebel for his failure to comply with the government, went separately. He denounced the free quartering as contrary to law and set in motion a debate on the legality of the government's proceedings. NLS, Yester Mss 7008, f. 101.

30 Lee, 'Government and politics in Scotland, 1661–1681', pp. 267–9; *Lauderdale Papers*, iii, pp. 114–16, 149–50.

31 Drumlanrig Castle, 'Transcripts of Queensberry letters', no.13 and no.35.

32 *RPCS*, third series, v, pp. 459–61; HMC, *The manuscripts of his grace the duke of Buccleuch and Queensberry, preserved at Drumlanrig Castle (Fifteenth Report, appendix, part viii)* (London, 1897–1903), i, p. 217; Drumlanrig Castle, 'Transcripts of Queensberry letters', no.18.

33 W. Fraser (ed.), *The Stirlings of Keir and their Family Papers* (Edinburgh, 1858), pp. 513–14.

34 Burnet, *History*, ii, p. 149.

35 Sir John Lauder of Fountainhall, *Historical Observes of Memorable Occurrents in Church and State, from October 1680 to April 1686, by Sir John Lauder of Fountainhall*, D. Laing and A. Urquhart (eds) (Edinburgh, 1840), p. 264; Rait, *Parliaments of Scotland*, pp. 157–8.

36 'The envoy of . . . our own shire [Lanarkshire] and the gentlemen of Linlithgow shire that is heer, we are hasting them home', wrote Hamilton to his wife in late May 1678. NAS, Hamilton Papers, GD406/1/8095.

37 NAS, Hamilton Papers, GD406/1/2965, GD406/1/8095. For the text of the bond, see *RPCS*, third series, iv, pp. 197–200.

38 NAS, Hamilton Papers, GD406/1/2965.

39 NAS, Hamilton Papers, GD406/1/8678.

40 Lauder of Fountainhall, *Historical Observes*, p. 265.

41 Drumlanrig Castle, 'Transcripts of Queensberry letters', no.19.

42 Drumlanrig Castle, 'Transcripts of Queensberry letters', no.19 and no.36.

43 See *Lauderdale Papers*, iii, pp. 127, 149, 151. Although writing some years later, the term 'Party' is also consistently used by Mackenzie of Rosehaugh throughout his *Memoirs* to refer to the parliamentary opposition centred on the leadership of Hamilton.

44 BL, Additional Mss 23242, 'Instructions to Lauderdale for the convention of estates', f. 64; NAS, Hamilton Papers, GD406/1/8678.

45 *Records of the Convention of the Royal Burghs of Scotland*, iv (1677–1711), pp. 8–11; *CSPD, 1678*, pp. 234, 243.

46 BL, Additional Mss 23242, f. 64. The two acts cited were the 'Act for his majesties prerogative in makeing of lawis' and the 'Act anent conventions and publict meitings', both of which prohibited external discussion on matters of state without crown approval. NAS, PA2/26, ff. 11, 13–14; *RPS*, 1661/1/17, 1661/1/23.

47 NAS, PA8/1, ff. 175v–176v; *RPS*, 1678/6/3. Given the frequent occurrence of disputed elections in the convention, attendance figures culled from the opening day's roll need to be treated with considerable caution. It is clear, for example, that Sir Patrick Houston of that ilk and William Hamilton of Orbiston, commissioners for Dunbartonshire, were present at least for the first few days of the convention, although, expecting their election to be disallowed, they were reported to have left for home by 3 July. The entry for Dunbartonshire is left blank in the parliamentary register. See NAS, Biel Muniments, 'The calling and proceedings of the convention of estates holden at Edinburgh, the 26 Junii 1678, by the duke of Lauderdale, his majesties commissioner', GD6/1108, f. 35.

48 NAS, Hamilton Papers, GD406/1/8095–6. To assuage opposition concerns, in early June the king gave orders that no opposition noblemen were to be troubled for their arms or horses on their return, nor were any to be imprisoned or fined for their past actions. *Lauderdale Papers*, iii, p. 153.

49 NAS, Biel Muniments, GD6/1108, ff. 10–11; *RPS*, A1678/6/6; *Lauderdale Papers*, iii, pp. 155–6.

50 *CSPD, 1678*, 'A true account of what passed in the convention', p. 249.

51 NAS, Biel Muniments, GD6/1108, ff. 11–12; *RPS*, A1678/6/6; *Lauderdale Papers*, iii, pp. 157–8. For the procedure regarding disputed elections in 1661, see NAS, PA3/3, ff. 2r–v; *RPS*, M1661/1/4.

52 NAS, Biel Muniments, GD6/1108, f. 12; *RPS*, A1678/6/6; NAS, PA8/1, f. 177r; *RPS*, 1678/6/6; Rait, *Parliaments of Scotland*, p. 84.

53 NAS, PA8/1, f. 177r; *RPS*, 1678/6/6–7. Gogar was the eldest son of Lauderdale's brother, Charles Maitland of Hatton. As part of Lauderdale's campaign to cement links with his allies, Gogar married Anne, daughter of Archibald Campbell, ninth earl of Argyll, while the convention was sitting. Young (ed.), *Parliaments of Scotland*, i, p. 204 and ii, p. 467.

54 NAS, Biel Muniments, GD6/1108, ff. 14–15; *RPS*, A1678/6/9. On 8 July, Mar produced papers confirming his earlier belief that the earl of Buchan was under-age, being three months short of his majority. This was disregarded, however, and Buchan allowed to remain. NAS, Biel Muniments, GD6/1108, f. 37; *RPS*, A1678/6/15.

55 NAS, PA7/22/141, pp. 290–1; *RPS*, M1678/6/5; NAS, Biel Muniments, GD6/1108, ff. 14–15; *RPS*, A1678/6/9.

56 NAS, Biel Muniments, GD6/1108, ff. 15–16; *RPS*, A1678/6/9; *CSPD, 1678*, pp. 257–8. The committee's report on the Selkirkshire election can be found at NAS, PA7/22/126, p. 249; *RPS*, C1678/6/1.

57 *CSPD, 1678*, pp. 257–8.

58 Lauder of Fountainhall, *Historical Observes*, pp. 270–1.
59 *CSPD, 1678*, p. 259.
60 NAS, Biel Muniments, GD6/1108, f. 17; *RPS*, A1678/6/9.
61 NAS, Biel Muniments, GD6/1108, ff. 17–21; *RPS*, A1678/6/9; Lauder of Fountainhall, *Historical Observes*, pp. 272–4. See also the committee's report into the three cases, NAS, PA7/22/126, pp. 249–50; *RPS*, C1678/6/1.
62 NAS, Biel Muniments, GD6/1108, ff. 21–3; *RPS*, A1678/6/9; Lauder of Fountainhall, *Historical Observes*, pp. 274–5. In 1675–6, Polwarth had been declared incapable of public trust and imprisoned for a time. The minutes taken at the election are extant and protests as to the eligibility of voters were aired at that time. See NAS, PA7/10/43, 'Minutes of a meeting of the freeholders of the sheriffdom of Berwick for electing a commissioner to the convention, June 1678'.
63 NAS, Biel Muniments, GD6/1108, ff. 21–2; *RPS*, A1678/6/9; Lauder of Fountainhall, *Historical Observes*, p. 275.
64 NAS, Biel Muniments, GD6/1108, f. 24; *RPS*, A1678/6/10.
65 NAS, PA8/1, f. 178v; *RPS*, 1678/6/11. It was relatively uncommon for a baron to stand for a burgh seat. Much more prevalent were cases of members of the lesser nobility being elected as shire commissioners and this was not prohibited by either the 1661 or 1681 acts regulating shire elections. However, in 1678, in circumstances that have not been recorded, the lord advocate made a ruling that a nobleman's eldest son and heir, although he may possess forty shillings of land in a shire, could not be elected 'because he is of the estate of the nobility and not of the small barons, and one man cannot be of two estates.' It is likely that the adjudication was part of the electoral management for the convention. Lauder of Fountainhall, *Historical Observes*, pp. 277–8; Rait, *Parliaments of Scotland*, p. 288.
66 NAS, PA8/1, f. 178v; *RPS*, 1678/6/11.
67 The shires were Edinburgh, Berwick, Selkirk, Dumfries, Wigtown, Ayr, Dunbarton, Bute, Renfrew, Stirling, Linlithgow, Perth, Inverness, Cromarty, Argyll, Banff, Kirkcudbright, Sutherland, Caithness, Elgin, Clackmannan and Ross. Nisbet also mentions an illegal election in the shire of Orkney, although it is not clear whether this was investigated. NAS, Biel Muniments, GD6/1108, f. 5; *RPS*, A1678/6/3.
68 The burghs were Edinburgh, Linlithgow, Glasgow, Lanark, Tain, Culross, Banff, Rothesay, Rutherglen, North Berwick, Lochmaben and Queensferry. The case of George Dickson of Bughtrig for New Galloway was also disputed and declared null. In addition, Nisbet records that the elections in the burghs of Aberdeen, St Andrews, Inverness, Whithorn, Cullen and Fortrose were all in violation of the limitations placed on burgh elections but were not queried in the convention. NAS, Biel Muniments, GD6/1108, f. 5; *RPS*, A1678/6/3.

69 NAS, Biel Muniments, GD6/1108, ff. 27–31; *RPS*, A1678/6/10; NAS, PA7/22/141, pp. 291–2; *RPS*, M1678/6/6–7; *CSPD, 1678*, p. 269.

70 NAS, PA8/1, ff. 178v–179r; *RPS*, 1678/6/12.

71 NAS, Biel Muniments, GD6/1108, f. 32; *RPS*, A1678/6/11; *CSPD, 1678*, p. 254.

72 *CSPD, 1678*, p. 270.

73 NAS, Biel Muniments, GD6/1108, f. 32; *RPS*, A1678/6/11.

74 NAS, PA7/22/126, p. 251 and PA7/22/130–1, pp. 260–1; *RPS*, C1678/6/4; NAS, Biel Muniments, GD6/1108, ff. 32–3; *RPS*, A1678/6/11; Lauder of Fountainhall, *Historical Observes*, p. 277; *CSPD, 1678*, p. 252. Cowdoun was kinsman of the earl of Dundonald and Lambroughton had been prominent in the advocates' dispute.

75 NAS, Biel Muniments, GD6/1108, f. 34; *RPS*, A1678/6/11. Keir and Touch were both related to Sir Archibald Stirling of Garden, the prominent royalist and parliamentary representative of Linlithgowshire in the early 1660s. Young (ed.), *Parliaments of Scotland*, ii, pp. 629–30, 681.

76 NAS, PA7/22/126, p. 251; *RPS*, C1678/6/4; NAS, Biel Muniments, GD6/1108, f. 35; *RPS*, A1678/6/11.

77 NAS, Biel Muniments, GD6/1108, ff. 34–5; *RPS*, A1678/6/12; *CSPD, 1678*, p. 274.

78 NAS, PA8/1, f. 180v; *RPS*, 1678/6/16.

79 NAS, Biel Muniments, GD6/1108, f. 37; *RPS*, A1678/6/15.

80 BL, Additional Mss 23242, f. 75. This is one of the few precise voting figures from the convention that exists and gives what is probably an accurate indication of the strength of the Party, albeit their number would certainly have been depleted after numerous elections had been disallowed.

81 NAS, Biel Muniments, GD6/1108, ff. 40–1; *RPS*, A1678/6/15.

82 NAS, Biel Muniments, GD6/1108, f. 42; *RPS*, A1678/6/16; Rait, *Parliaments of Scotland*, p. 501. The burghs had met the same day, prior to the meeting of the convention, and agreed 'unanimously as one man . . . to doe all that is in their pouer to oppose the said retention as being the true interest of the burrows sua to doe.' *Records of the Convention of the Royal Burghs of Scotland*, iv (1677–1711), p. 11.

83 NAS, Biel Muniments, GD6/1108, ff. 42–3; *RPS*, A1678/6/17.

84 NAS, PA7/22/137, pp. 282–3; *RPS*, M1678/6/14; NAS, Fea of Clestrain collection, GD31/121; BL, Additional Mss 23242, f. 79; *CSPD, 1678*, pp. 284–5.

85 BL, Additional Mss 23242, f. 79.

86 NAS, Biel Muniments, GD6/1108, ff. 43–5; *RPS*, A1678/6/17; BL, Additional Mss 23242, f. 79.

87 BL, Additional Mss 23242, f. 74.

88 NAS, PA8/1, ff. 190r–191r; *RPS*, 1678/6/24; Rait, *Parliaments of Scotland*, pp. 84–5. Rait believes that the language of the convention's

letter 'represents the most complete domination obtained by the crown over the estates'. This is inaccurate. Lauderdale was using the letter to proclaim his own victory over Hamilton, intending to silence his many English enemies at court; it was not a considered treatise on the nature of kingship.

89 NAS, Biel Muniments, GD6/1108, ff. 45–6; *RPS*, A1678/6/18.
90 BL, Additional Mss 23242, f. 80.
91 Lauder of Fountainhall, *Historical Observes*, p. 279.
92 Charles's letter to Lauderdale, desiring him to treat Hamilton and his allies with 'all civility', is quoted in full in W. B. Gardner, 'The later years of John Maitland, second earl and first duke of Lauderdale', *The Journal of Modern History*, 20 (1948), p. 121. Lauderdale was allegedly so distraught by the command, he left instructions to his wife to wrap the letter in lead and have it hung round his neck and buried with him. This appears to have been done after the duke's death in 1682.
93 In May 1679, the Commons approved another address instructing Charles to remove Lauderdale 'from his presence and councils', alleging that in Scotland the commissioner had 'brought in arbitrary power'. For more on this attack on Lauderdale, see Harris, *Restoration*, pp. 169–70.

Chapter 7

A NEW BEGINNING? JAMES, DUKE OF YORK IN SCOTLAND, 1679–85

࿇

The formal adjournment of the convention of estates on 11 July 1678 did not see an end to Party activities to oust Lauderdale from office. Although, as one contemporary noted, in the days following the adjournment 'both parties seem asleep, one having perfected his seven days' work, the other through the grief of his disappointment', it was widely believed that this was not the end of the political conflict, that 'in a short time both interests will awake and try the other's strength in further contests.'[1] Observers did not have long to wait. When Lauderdale left Edinburgh on 15 July for a short spell at his country retreat at Lethington, near Haddington, prior to proceeding to court, Hamilton returned to the city, most probably for meetings with his supporters. By 23 July, Hamilton departed for London to seek an audience with the king.[2]

In Scotland, the commissioner still seemed unshakeable. It was noted that all judicatories 'are absolutely at duke of Lauderdale's beck, that in judgement a dog cannot move his tongue against him . . . he is able to effectuate anything he pleases and every day his hands wax more and more strong.' To sustain this superiority, great care was to be taken that no 'presbyterado creep into the government.' Thus, in December 1678, a number of council officials in Edinburgh were ousted from their positions because of their refusal to subscribe the declaration.[3] Some members of the opposition were beginning to despair of ever regaining a position of authority. In January 1679, Tweeddale, one of Hamilton's most prominent supporters, attempted a reconciliation with Lauderdale, writing in a begging letter to the commissioner, 'If yow please to call to mind . . . what yow self has som times said (let bygones be bygones), your grace shall finds non more willing and ready to serve you than I.'[4] Tweeddale's attempt at rapprochement was soundly rebuffed, but the attempted defection of one of the Party's key figures indicated that some may have lacked the desire to persist in opposition.

It was events in England that eventually threatened Lauderdale's dominance. Implicated in the Popish Plot, the earl of Danby had been impeached in December 1678 by the Commons, despite attempts by Charles to save him. Lauderdale was left dangerously isolated and when attacked first on 25 March 1679 by Shaftesbury in the House of Lords and then on 8 May in the Commons, he could not expect the same degree of support from the king as in former times. The Catholic menace was directly associated with political absolutism, best represented by the France of Louis XIV, but there was a far more immediate target in the English opposition's sights. Shaftesbury's address made blatant references to Lauderdale's Scottish policies: in England, popery was to have brought in slavery; in Scotland, slavery went before and popery was to follow. The Highland Host had merely confirmed long-held suspicions that a standing army was ready and likely to invade England, possibly at the behest of a Catholic monarch.[5] It was looking entirely probable that Charles would be forced to sacrifice his Scottish minister.

The familiar problem of religious dissent north of the border made Lauderdale's position even less secure. The departure of the commissioner from Scotland in the summer of 1678 had been the catalyst for an increase in conventicles and religious unrest, with scuffles between troops and dissenters at a large conventicle at Lesmahagow in March 1679 beginning an escalation of violence that culminated on 3 May in the brutal murder of Archbishop James Sharp by a band of renegade conventiclers. Such an event called for immediate retaliation and was thus used by the privy council as justification for extreme measures of suppression. By all accounts, it was a case of too little too late. Government forces met with an embarrassing defeat at Drumclog in early June and the council were forced to admit that the Scottish army was unable to control an uprising. English troops under the command of James Scott, duke of Monmouth, the king's illegitimate son, were thus sent north and the rebels defeated at the battle of Bothwell Brig on 22 June.[6] The disorder in Scotland provided ideal ammunition for Shaftesbury and an opportunity for the Party to gain the upper hand. Opposition on both sides of the border was more confident than ever of achieving the outcome they had so long desired, compiling a list of candidates suitable to replace Lauderdale and his associates once they had been removed from power.[7]

Hamilton's journey south in the late summer of 1678 was not in vain, for, unlike his visit in 1674, this time he received a more favourable reception, particularly from English sympathisers. The

*Figure 7.1   Archbishop James Sharp (1618–79) by Sir Peter Lely. During the interregnum Sharp was regarded as the leader of the more moderate and loyal wing of the kirk. Following the restoration of Charles II in 1660, Sharp was appointed king's chaplain and in 1661 consecrated archbishop of St Andrews. Considered a traitor for his acceptation of episcopacy, he was detested by presbyterians. He survived one assassination attempt in 1668 but was ambushed on Magus Muir near St Andrews on 3 May 1679, dragged from his carriage and murdered in front of his daughter by a group of radical dissenters.
(In a private Scottish collection.)*

king, however, was less welcoming and Hamilton was consistently refused an audience with either Charles or James, duke of York. As a result, Hamilton and his allies remained in London into the following year, the streets of the English capital awash with numerous discontented Scotsmen. As the fall-out over the Popish Plot claimed more victims and Lauderdale became directly implicated via the attacks of the English opposition, the king could no longer ignore Scottish complaints, and in July 1679, Charles agreed to a formal conference at Windsor. Hamilton, Atholl and various supporters, accompanied by their legal advisors, stated their case, arguing that for a number of years the administration of public affairs had been both contrary to law and had infringed the rights and liberties of the nation's subjects. Accused by Lauderdale of unlawfully questioning the crown's prerogative powers in the last meeting of the estates, Hamilton vigorously defended his actions, declaring that he had only wanted to see the convention conform to the laws and practices of the kingdom. He warned that 'his majesty's government was destroyed and not supported by illegalities . . . [which] left a stain and a blot on the government.' The disorders in the kingdom could be directly imputed to Lauderdale's mismanagement of government, Hamilton argued, but there remained enough loyal subjects to ensure that peace would be restored if only the king would dismiss his failing ministers.[8] A robust defence of the commissioner's conduct by Mackenzie of Rosehaugh temporarily saved Lauderdale from dismissal, with the lord advocate successfully persuading the king that whatever was alleged against him the commissioner had at all times acted within the limits of law and the crown's prerogative powers.[9]

The grievances expressed by Hamilton at the Windsor conference were the basis for a number of pamphlets published throughout 1679. *Some particular matters of fact relating to the administration of affairs in Scotland under the duke of Lauderdale* specifically singled out the corruption that had flourished under Lauderdale's rule: the manipulation of the magistracy of Edinburgh, the illegal imprisonment of innocent subjects and the bribery that had become endemic in Scottish society. Lauderdale made active attempts to suppress its distribution.[10] Another tract entitled *Some farther matter of fact relating to the administration of affairs in Scotland under the duke of Lauderdale* had a decidedly English partiality, suggesting that it was written to mobilise opposition south of the border. Although this pamphlet touched on Scottish matters such as the Highland Host and corruption, it also addressed specifically English concerns: Lauderdale's popish tendencies, his contempt for the Commons and his subservience to France.[11]

Despite the apparent success of Rosehaugh's bullish defence of the commissioner's conduct, Hamilton and his supporters left the Windsor conference believing that Lauderdale's time was truly up. It seems likely that they had been given private assurances that Charles's longest standing Scottish minister was to be forced into retirement at some point in the near future.[12] The current priority, however, was to ensure that the uneasy peace which had broken out in Scotland after Bothwell Brig be secured and maintained. Under the supervision of Monmouth, a series of initiatives aimed at displaying a more conciliatory attitude towards dissenters was put into motion. A declaration of indulgence was proclaimed on 4 July 1679, authorising the practice of house conventicles outwith the major cities, this being followed by an indemnity for the rebels involved at Bothwell Brig. On 13 August, at a special meeting of the privy council, a letter from the king was read which extended the indemnity to all past offenders that had been convicted of ecclesiastical offences.[13] It seems unlikely that Lauderdale was behind such an obvious reversal of a policy he had so championed and that decisions were now being made that bypassed the most senior Scottish minister. Hamilton was elated with the turn of events, writing to Queensberry in July that Lauderdale's dismissal was now just a formality and surely just the first of what he hoped was a comprehensive purge of the royalist administration in Scotland. In October, Lauderdale's demotion was finally achieved when the duke of York was sent in his place to oversee the administration in Edinburgh.[14]

Sent north largely to escape the exclusion crisis unfolding in the English parliament, James arrived in Scotland to an enthusiastic reception from a country that had so long been deprived of royalty in its midst. It was not long, however, before the problem of his religion also raised difficulties north of the border. On 6 November 1679, a πnumber of privy councillors (including Rothes, Hatton and Mackenzie of Rosehaugh) wrote to Lauderdale questioning whether the Catholic duke could take his seat on the council without first taking the oath of allegiance (containing a declaration against popery). The councillors' considered advice was that it would be impossible for the king to dispense with the oath by letter because, as a statute, it was a 'parliamentarie contract betwixt king and people'. To simply ignore the oath and allow the duke to take his place would have its own difficulties since it would bring into question the very validity of bonds of allegiance to the crown.[15] In response to the council's query, Lauderdale wrote to James advising him that if he refused to subscribe the oath, he should not take his seat. The duke of York merely replied that he had sat on the Scots section of the English privy council without taking any oaths and strongly disagreed with Lauderdale's advice that he should not take his rightful place on the Scottish council; to do so would only encourage his enemies. James instructed the lord advocate to draw up a way round this mere technicality, and, having first secured the king's permission, he joined the other members of the privy council on 4 December without taking the oath.[16]

James paid little attention to Lauderdale's other prophecies of doom concerning the factional divisions in Scotland. From December 1679 to February 1680, for the first short period of his attendance at the council, James made several attempts at reconciliation. Although Hamilton remained aloof, sulking because many of his rivals were still in favour, the earls of Perth, Atholl and Queensberry were newly re-appointed as members of the privy council and in regular attendance at sessions from December onwards. The earl of Dundonald, absent throughout much of 1679, also began to attend frequently once more. The indulgence proclaimed by Monmouth after Bothwell Brig had been for the most part successful and James was careful to ensure that the council should use such moderation as would be conducive to the peace of the kingdom. Although the suspension of widespread religious persecution was but a short one, James's first period of office gave initial hope that the absolutism of Lauderdale's administration was over.[17]

In many ways the personnel that governed Scotland under the duke of York remained remarkably similar to those who held office under Lauderdale, with James making up 'a mongrell party of his owne in Scotland, partly composed of Lauderdale's friends and of other new ones whom York assumed.'[18] The appointment of Atholl, Queensberry and others to the council was a significant step, however, indicating that James embraced a variety of opinions and that the council's recent role as simply a clique of Lauderdale's yes-men was at an end. In May 1680, Rothes was created a duke, rewarded with a massive pension and given the important task of controlling council policy. Many doubted whether he could stay sober long enough to fulfil his responsibility. Joining Rothes were the earls of Argyll, Moray and Hamilton's ablest ally, the earl of Queensberry, who had no qualms about grasping every opportunity of advancement. Some members of the parliamentary opposition were simply unwilling to play the same role as they had against Lauderdale. In February 1680, Kincardine became dangerously sick, prompting another begging letter from Tweeddale to Lauderdale asking for possible advancement. He was again more than willing to discard his opposition politics for a return to office.[19] In October 1680, a more significant position became vacant when Lauderdale finally resigned the post of secretary. In latter months the duke had suffered from failing health, which impeded his involvement in political life, but it was no secret that systematically he was being removed from all positions of power. His last public act was a defiant one: voting for the condemnation of the Catholic earl of Stafford. This lost him the support of the duke of York who, as Fountainhall records, 'broke his power . . . all he could'.[20] The earl of Moray, a close friend, was appointed secretary of state in his place. Lauderdale approved of the choice, writing in a letter to Thomas Wallace of Craigie, clerk register, 'you may be sure my mind is, God be thanked, very much at ease.'[21]

In August 1679, Alexander Burnet had been advanced to the see of St Andrews as Sharp's replacement. A staunch advocate of the policies of persecution that were now supposed to be at an end, Burnet's appointment, along with a gradual shift in council policy against toleration, began a whole new cycle of religious repression for which James voiced his full support. There was little evidence of an increase in dissenting activity. Indeed, apart from the continued activities of the Cameronians, a small sect of radical presbyterians, widespread field conventicling had ceased and most localities were quiet. Instead it seems that the policies of moderation were abandoned purely because James was intent on scoring political points in England. Monmouth, the favoured candidate for the throne amongst the English opposition, had been the chief architect of the indulgence, and so, by overruling his rival, James was making an overtly political statement.[22] More significantly for those in Scotland, another opportunity to finally settle the church had been allowed to slip away.

Despite the duke of York's supposed animosity towards Lauderdale, it was he whom he turned to for advice when appointed king's commissioner to parliament for the forthcoming meeting of the estates on 28 July 1681. York was interested in mainly procedural matters, for example, the drafting of the private instructions that would be sent to the king prior to the meeting and the method for choosing another president of parliament (Rothes, finally succumbing to years of excessive drinking, was seriously ill and not expected

to attend).[23] Lauderdale's reply defended excessive government interference in parliamentary politics, instructing James that prior to the
session the elections for shires and burghs must be 'secured' and 'all
the methods laid doune and a scheme drawen.' This was vital to
secure the governmental interest and enabled the commissioner to
'give more than a guess' about the success of proposed legislation,
although Lauderdale admitted that from his own experience it was
'impossible to forsee every particular [that] may be offered.'[24] The
appointment of the duke of York as commissioner caused some initial
confusion, it being suggested that James should take on the title of
prorex or viceroy as it was 'more august for his eminency then that
of commissioner.' Mindful of attempts to promote a more democratic means of government, the proposal was quietly laid aside over
concerns that where a commissioner was tied to instructions, a
viceroy had no limitations at all.[25]

The duke of York's instructions to parliament, issued at Windsor
on 4 July, dealt with a number of wide-ranging and familiar issues.
New legislation was to be brought in to suppress 'fanatical schism', to
secure the offices and liberties of the bishops and to prevent assassi-
nations, the holding of conventicles and the outbreak of rebellion. For
enforcing these measures, the current act of supply was to be extended
to fund additional standing forces. The principal means of calling a
meeting of the estates, however, was to legislate for the hereditary succession of the crown. As commissioner, James was instructed to ensure
that the royal prerogative was vigorously asserted and 'the just rights
of the crown and monarch in its natural, due and legal course of
descent may be owned by a clear and positive law, so that none may
call the same in question.'[26] Such a pre-emptive move would hopefully
head off the kind of crisis that was gripping England.

The elections for parliament were not as closely contested as in previous years, possibly because some of the opposition were unwilling
to continue in that position. After the convention of estates in 1678,
the annual Michaelmas election had been postponed, so 'the whole
shires of the kingdom [were] represented by the men they most abhor
and the persons they entrust with their commission affronted and
turned out of doors.'[27] New elections were, however, held for the
forthcoming session of parliament, and, allowing for the usual fluctuations due to death and ill health, many of those elected to the previous meeting of the estates were replaced. In the rolls of parliament
taken on the opening day of the session, 194 are recorded: twelve
bishops, sixty-one members of the nobility, four officers of state,

fifty-seven commissioners representing thirty-three shires and sixty burgesses representing fifty-nine burghs. Once again, the burgh membership seems to have been thoroughly purged. Of the sixty commissioners present, forty-three of those elected had no previous experience of serving in parliament. It is likely that this was the result of the continuing clampdown on the eligibility of candidates (prior to the meeting of parliament, James was instructed to remind the burghs of the restrictions on their elections). Perhaps, however, the noticeable lack of experienced representatives confirmed the burghs' argument that if no non-residents were permitted to serve on their behalf, many burghs would be forced to send unqualified men in their place. The shire membership seems to have escaped a widespread purge, although twenty-four out of a total membership of fifty-seven had never previously served in parliament.[28]

Despite Lauderdale's political demise, only a small number of Hamilton's staunchest allies from the convention of estates in 1678 attended parliament. Amongst those successfully elected was Sir John Cunningham of Lambroughton for Ayrshire, who had cemented his links to Hamilton by journeying to London with the duke and Sir George Lockhart of Carnwath (himself newly elected for Lanarkshire under his additional designation 'of Braidwood') to present charges against Lauderdale in 1679. Andrew Ainslie of Blackhill, provost of Jedburgh, banned from public office in 1675 for his involvement in drafting the dissident letter to the king from the convention of royal burghs, and Andrew Fletcher of Saltoun, soon forced to flee to Holland due to his opposition to the current administration, were both also present. Hamilton's other main supporters amongst the elected estates, Sir Patrick Hume of Polwarth, imprisoned for factious behaviour during the convention in 1678, and Sir Alexander Bruce of Broomhall, who vociferously heckled Lauderdale at every turn in the previous meeting of the estates, did not compromise their oppositional stance by attending.[29]

Despite an albeit small body of opposition candidates present in parliament, from the outset Hamilton declared that he was unwilling to provide the same leadership as he had formerly. As Burnet records, having 'been in a storm of seven years' continuance by his opposing of duke Lauderdale', Hamilton refused to 'engage in a new one with a stronger party unless he was sure of the majority, and they were far from pretending to be able to bring matters near an equality.'[30] It remained to be seen whether, without adequate leadership, those opposition candidates who had been successfully elected to parliament could mount any successful challenge to the crown's legislative programme or, indeed, whether they would have any cause to do so.

The session formally opened in Edinburgh on 28 July 1681 with the traditional riding of parliament. The format had changed somewhat at the instructions of the duke of York and this occasioned a large number of protests from nobles who were determined not to lose precedence.[31] On arriving at parliament hall, the estates encountered another innovation: a number of seats at the end of the row where the burghs sat were kept free for Mary of Modena, duchess of Albany and York, Anne, her step-daughter, and a number of their ladies-in-waiting. They sat only for the first day of the session. Unsurprisingly, in the presence of the heir to the throne, there was no repeat of the complaints that had accompanied the equivalent attendance of the duchess of Lauderdale in 1672.[32] Next, the duke of York's commission was read, the rolls taken and the oaths subscribed by all present except the commissioner.[33] The marquis of Atholl was then appointed president of parliament in the absence of the chancellor. As had been predicted, Rothes's earlier illness had been life-threatening and he died of jaundice, the result of years of heavy drinking, at Holyrood the day before parliament met.[34]

The king's letter to parliament was read, which identified the succession of the throne and the peace of the church as matters that were to be legislated for in this session.[35] The lords of the articles were then elected by the procedure set out in 1663, the difference in membership of this key committee from previous sessions providing the greatest evidence of the change in commissioner. Hamilton, Queensberry, Perth and Dumfries were amongst the noble members and, for the shires, Lockhart of Carnwath and Sir George Gordon of Haddo gained admittance.[36] Only Hamilton had been permitted to sit on the committee under Lauderdale, thus ensuring that the opposition party had little influence in the drafting of legislation. Although still vastly outnumbered by crown supporters, the appointment of these Party members to the articles was a significant step, signifying the end of their political isolation that had bred much of their discontent.

When parliament met for a second day on 1 August, the act of 1662 for ordering the house was revived. Lauderdale had informally enforced this in the convention of estates of 1678 to deal with a large numbers of interlopers who, entering to hear the results of the controverted elections, mingled with the elected members in the chamber. The act specifically ordained that only those who were officially members of parliament could attend debates.[37] The draft of parliament's reply to the king's letter was next brought in to the chamber, where Sir John Cochrane of Ochiltree, commissioner for Ayrshire, tabled a motion for a delay until all the disputed elections had been dealt with and the full membership present. This was not seconded and so refused.[38] Sir John Cunningham of Lambroughton was the first to raise the issue of religion. He argued that, considering the great significance of the king's request for legislation to protect the Protestant religion, there should be more time for members to fully consider the tenor of parliament's reply. The duke of Hamilton, Rosehaugh, Carnwath and Sir George Mackenzie of Tarbat all insisted that there was nothing in the answer that would anticipate parliament's subsequent discussion. The letter was put to the vote and passed with only two negatives, that of Lambroughton and William Anstruther of that ilk, one of the shire commissioners for Fife.[39]

Hamilton and his allies, despite their earlier election to the articles, were all absent from the committee for disputed elections that had been selected on the first day of the session. This was now set up as a matter of course to deal with the increasing amount of electoral petitions. Unlike the articles, there was no formal election of members, and, following the example of Lauderdale in 1678, the commissioner simply nominated twelve commissioners, three from each estate, who were to debate and report on each individual case. At first, only a few commissions were under discussion, but the committee received further complaints of other suspect elections throughout the first few days of parliament. Mackenzie of Rosehaugh objected in the articles on 30 July to William Riddell, commissioner for Rutherglen, alleging that he was an accessory to the rebellion at Bothwell Brig. Riddell was immediately seized, accused of treason and imprisoned, although he was soon set at liberty. He was, however, suspended from voting and does not appear in the sederunt of parliament.[40]

On 5 August, the committee's reports concerning the burghs of North Berwick, Selkirk and Inverkeithing, along with that of Peeblesshire, were presented to the full parliament.[41] In the case of North Berwick, George Suittie of Balgonie's election was disallowed because it had been held at 6 o'clock in the morning, with the burgesses receiving only thirty minutes' notice of the impending ballot. Balgonie's election was also in contravention of the restrictions on burgh elections, he being selected as commissioner despite the fact he was neither a resident nor a trafficking merchant, although he had formally been appointed a burgess some hours after the election was held.[42] When these particulars were read out, a lengthy debate ensued about the restrictions on burgh commissioners. Lord Bargany questioned the committee's decision; the situation was similar, he argued, to that of a nobleman created a noble during the course of parliament: he may sit in parliament notwithstanding he was not a nobleman before parliament was proclaimed. Others joined Bargany in rejecting the committee's judgement and vigorously defended Balgonie's election, possibly because the other candidate for the seat was Charles Maitland, a kinsman of the duke of Lauderdale.[43]

Hamilton, seconded by Lockhart of Carnwath, asked for a general review of the 1675 act made in the convention of royal burghs concerning their elections, claiming that it was too restrictive. Cunningham of Lambroughton asserted that the ancient custom of burghs electing either one of their own or a suitably qualified 'country gentilman' had force of law by itself.[44] This angered Mackenzie of Rosehaugh, who loudly declared that 'he saw seditious Bothuel Bridge faces sitting as members of parliament.' This caused much displeasure amongst the burghs. To quiet the resulting uproar, Rosehaugh was forced to revise his statement: what he had intended to say was that if the burghs had liberty to choose whom they pleased to represent them, 'factious and disloyal persons might prevail to get themselves elected.' As for those present he suspected of complicity in the recent rebellion, he hoped that because they had sworn the oath of allegiance and declaration of public trust, they would conduct themselves as such.[45]

As in the convention of estates in 1678, discussion of disputed elections began a lengthy debate as to the particular restrictions on those who could elect and be elected. To bring this to an end, Sir John Bell of Hamilton Ferme, provost of Glasgow, moved for the act of convention of burghs setting out limitations on elections to be ratified. Hamilton suggested a different vote: should non-residents be eligible for election to parliament as burgh commissioners. The proposal was rejected by fifty-two votes. Next, the decision of the committee concerning North Berwick was taken into consideration and Charles Maitland approved as commissioner by a majority of only fourteen. The election of Sir Patrick Murray of Pitdunnes for Selkirk was rejected in light of this judgment, since he too was not a resident merchant in the burgh. That of John Dempster of Pitliver for Inverkeithing was confirmed in respect he was provost of the town and traded in victual and timber within the burgh's boundaries.[46]

On 6 August, debates concerning elections further delayed proceedings. Following an earlier allegation made against him by the lord advocate, William Anstruther of that ilk submitted evidence showing that he was over the age of twenty-one and therefore eligible for election. After asking for the committee's decision in the election of North Berwick to be again read, Cochrane of Ochiltree next complained that Sir James Dick of Priestfield, provost of Edinburgh, was banned from trading, being a collector of the king's customs, and should therefore be refused his seat. Mackenzie of Rosehaugh dismissed the suggestion, stating that this would be taking the meaning of the act restricting burgh elections to the extreme. Without a vote, Priestfield was admitted. The elections of the burghs of Lochmaben and Annan were also quarrelled and remitted to the articles for consideration, although the outcomes of both contests are not recorded.[47]

Legal questions raised by a number of disputed shire elections necessitated a new statute modifying the existing franchise later in the session. All of the five shire election contests investigated by the committee – Haddington, Linlithgow, Berwick, Peebles and Stirling – centred on the eligibility of electors, and, to avoid future delay in subsequent meetings of the estates, the new act of 17 September set out clearly voting qualifications.[48] Those who possessed forty shillings land of old extent from the king retained their ancient right to vote, but the act also extended the franchise to those freeholders who were 'infeft in property or superiority and in possession of a fourty shilling land of old extent.' Thus, legally, even though the freeholder transferred his land to another and did not collect any profits or revenue, provided he still retained the superiority, he remained tenant of the crown and eligible to vote in elections. The rights of the forty shilling freeholder were further secured by an additional clause. Since old extent had ceased to be a basis of taxation and thus increasingly redundant as a method of proving voter qualification, an alternative figure of £400 of valued rent (the annual value of land as determined by the assessment for public taxation) was deemed to be the new standard for eligibility. A number of debateable points concerning the position of debtors, mortgage holders and life-renters were also resolved by the act.[49]

Although the total electorate is difficult to ascertain (surviving records often give a one-sided view, the only figures available being signatories to the successful commission)[50], it is likely that the new statute greatly extended the shire franchise. In Aberdeenshire, twenty-one voters signed the shire's 1680 commission (for the parliament of the following year), this rising to twenty-four in 1685. There was a similar increase in Fifeshire, from thirty-three in 1681 to forty-three in 1685. After 1681 (until the act was rescinded in 1690), all eligible voters were required to subscribe the Test, this normally done at the election itself. Signatories to surviving Test acts therefore provide a more accurate picture of the total electorate. In Aberdeenshire, fifty-eight signed the Test on the day the election was held for the shire's representative to the 1685 session; in Fife, the comparable figure was seventy-three.[51] Paradoxically, the implementation of the Test act had a detrimental effect on the electorate in certain other shires, especially in the radical south. In Dumfries-shire, eighteen individuals sub-scribed the shire's commission to the 1681 parliament; for the session of 1685, this had fallen to eleven, the same number who additionally signed the Test on the same day. It was a similar story in Lanarkshire: those subscribing their representative's commission fell from twenty-two in 1681 to seven in 1685; the Test was subscribed on the same day by only nine.[52]

The importance of the extension to the franchise was not, however, immediately recognised. John Paterson, bishop of Edinburgh, com-menting on the controverted election of Haddingtonshire, suggested that, in the royal interest, parliament might 'verie lawfullie praefer one who was inferior in votes . . . to hold out a Shaftsburie.'[53] Such a statement only revealed that the increase of the shire electorate was not driven by democratic considerations, nor was there to be any less-ening of government interference in local elections. Indeed, although there was not the same public demonstration of election tampering as there had been at the 1678 convention, there was still widespread manipulation of the elected estates, occasionally with menacing undertones. Fountainhall records an incident during the 1681 session in which a shire elector who had voted against 'the duke and the court faction' in the election of Fife was brought to prosecution on a spuri-ous charge of being absent from the king's host at Bothwell Brig. Drummond of Cromlix, commissioner for Perthshire and long-time Hamilton ally, was likewise threatened with prosecution for claiming he had forty shillings of land held from the crown when investigations revealed this was doubtful. When Cromlix accused the committee of disputed elections of 'open injustice', a charge of defamation was added to the indictment.[54] The crown also looked retrospectively for motives to punish those who opposed the royal will. After voting against the government on a number of occasions in 1681, soon after parliament had risen, William Cunningham of Brownhill, provost of Ayr, was prosecuted for assigning billets to a covenanting force three years previously. Despite protesting that he did so to prevent the town being pillaged, he was not only imprisoned and fined by the privy council but remitted to the court of session on a criminal charge.[55] Continued government interference in local elections, combined with the subsequent passage of the Test act, only placed further restrictions on those eligible to elect and be elected.

On 13 August, an act asserting the right of succession to the crown of Scotland was considered by the gathered estates. The recent attempts in England to have an exclusion bill passed by the Commons had revealed just how necessary it was for James to be certain of his position in Scotland and parliament now declared any attempt to alter the lineal succession to the throne an act of rebellion. Although on the surface the succession act made sense, James being the undoubted heir to the throne, it explicitly stated that neither religion nor statute could alter the hereditary descent of the crown. Despite this, the act passed unanimously, without much discussion, although there were unsuccessful efforts to delay the act to allow for further consultation. James's presence in the chamber likely had an intimidating effect on any would-be opponents.[56] Much more controversial was the draft of an act for securing the Protestant religion, which was presented to the estates on the same day. Cunningham of Lambroughton protested that the chamber was not full, a number of disputed elections still being under consideration, thus any discussion should be delayed until the majority of members were present. This, however, was rejected. After concerns that the act did not specifically mention existing legislation against papists, nor did it ordain the same to be put into execution, the draft was amended to include a clause ratifying all previous acts against popery. The amended act was passed by a comfortable margin of 100.[57]

The first draft of an act of supply was presented to parliament on 15 August. The act extended the grant of cess raised by the convention of estates in 1678 (which was due to expire in 1683) for another five years at the same rate of £360,000 per annum. The duke of Hamilton urged the retention of annualrents to help spread the burden and additionally suggested that it may also be appropriate to place 'reek-money' on every chimney. Both would fall disproportionably on the burghs, however, and proved unpopular, although it was agreed that some measure of relief for heritors could be considered. When the draft was read to the chamber, Hamilton, Cunningham of Lambroughton and some other unidentified members moved for a delay until the remaining elections were discussed and 'religione farder secured', likely fearing that parliament would be immediately adjourned when the subsidy was through. A vote to delay was defeated by fifty-nine votes, but the inclusion of a proposed relief clause required the act to be returned to the articles for amendment.[58] After submissions from the commissioners of burghs, the articles rejected all proposals to renew the burden on annualrents, agreeing instead to an additional clause allowing heritors to tax their vassals, feuars, tenants and others whose incomes were not derived from land in the same manner as granted by the convention of estates of 1667. The amended act was returned to the chamber on 20 August and touched with the sceptre.[59]

On 19 August, an early draft of an act for securing the peace of the country, allowing heritors to fine or evict tenants who attended conventicles, was debated. Cunningham of Lambroughton asked that, seeing as it was a particular concern of the shires, arrangements might be made to allow their commissioners time to study the draft in detail. This was permitted, but Lambroughton's second request for parliament to next consider further acts for securing the Protestant religion was dismissed with the promise that an act was planned for later in the session.[60] Now aware that the articles were currently considering such legislation, Cochrane of Ochiltree attempted to influence their discussions, submitting to the committee on 22 August two 'Overtures for securing the Protestant religion'. The first suggested that to the oath of coronation should be appended a clause stating that the monarch would not consent to any alteration of the Protestant religion, nor 'tolerate priests, Jesuits nor trafficking papists to abide in this region or . . . suffer any papist to be in any publick trust, power or office.' The second paper recommended that all those in positions of public trust should not only subscribe the oath of allegiance but also swear to adhere to the 1567 confession of faith. Ochiltree's suggestions were passed on to the bishops for consideration.[61]

The articles' discussions culminated on 27 August in a draft act to secure religion, obliging all office holders to subscribe a test oath to uphold Protestantism as defined in the 1567 confession of faith (as per Ochiltree's suggestion) and the royal supremacy in all temporal and spiritual matters. It was an extraordinary piece of legislation, blatantly self-contradictory and internally inconsistent. Prior to parliament, James had consented to an act guaranteeing the Protestant religion but planned to frame this in the vaguest possible terms. The act presented to the estates, however, was anything but. The reference to the confession of faith was included apparently at Sir James Dalrymple of Stair's suggestion and, according to Burnet, on the presumption that this would be refused. The confession of faith, the cornerstone of the Scottish reformation, explicitly endorsed lawful resistance to the crown if an alteration in religion was forced on an unwilling population, permitting a conditional obedience to the civil magistrate, whereas the traditional oath of allegiance, also part of the act, vowed unconditional adherence. As such, the confession contradicted the 1669 act of supremacy which the Test act was supposed to confirm. Only a few within the chamber seem to have realised the illogicality of the oath, with Burnet alleging that 'scarce any in the whole parliament had ever read' the confession of faith, 'none of the bishops had, as appeared afterwards'. Indeed, when Hamilton asked for the act to be returned to the articles where it could be modified into two separate statutes, one concerning Protestantism and one for papists, Rosehaugh declared that the bishops had already given their approval to the act as it stood.[62]

The draft Test act was laid open for consultation before being returned to the chamber on 29 August. When the debate resumed, John Hamilton, second lord Belhaven, publicly noted the discrepancies within the proposed act, describing it as a 'very good act for securing our religion from one another' but not suitable for securing 'our Protestant religion against a popish or phanticall successor to the croun'. James Ogilvy, second earl of Airlie, and some others argued vociferously that Belhaven be committed to prison. The young lord was given leave to explain his statement, but largely repeated what he had said formerly. A large majority voted in favour of his immediate imprisonment in Edinburgh Castle and Rosehaugh, in his capacity of lord advocate, declared there were grounds for an indictment of treason against him.[63]

The fate of Belhaven may have silenced some members, but others continued to voice their discontent. Only minutes after Belhaven had been removed from the chamber, Ludovic Grant of Freuchie, commissioner for Elgin and Forres-shire, voted against the Test act, incurring the wrath of James himself.[64] Sir Alexander Seton of Pitmedden, commissioner for Aberdeenshire, asked for clarification that the Test did not sanction unalterable episcopal government, contradicting the 1567 confession of faith. Robert Gordon of Gordonstoun, commissioner for the shire of Sutherland, vehemently opposed the very use of penal laws in matters of religion on the grounds that 'conscience cannot be forced and that those severe sanctions and penalties operated nothing, save to render men hypocrites', probably a view that was paradoxically shared by the Catholic duke of York.[65] The earl of

Argyll was the most prominent dissenter, attempting in the articles to add a clause to the draft Test sanctioning 'all acts against popery'. In the chamber, Argyll argued that the provision excepting the monarch's family from subscribing the Test should be withdrawn since there should be 'no gap left open for the royal family to differ in religion.'[66]

The Test, similar to the declaration of public trust and oath of allegiance, was a mandatory requirement for the exercise of public office. Fountainhall records that one of the main designs of the act was 'to get elections of commissioners in shires and burrows so packed as none should vote but those who took this Test.' Together with the recently enforced restrictions on burgh elections, the implementation of the Test would ensure that in elections to future parliaments only those whom 'the court pleases to recommend in most shires and burrows' would be able to participate.[67] Indeed, the Test had widespread repercussions in the localities. Large numbers of public officials throughout Scotland refused to subscribe the new oath, with Ayr being left with no council when all the burgesses resigned rather than submit.[68] In almost every burgh, there were a number who refused the Test and resigned their offices. The result was a general dislocation of municipal business that constantly called for the intervention of the privy council.[69]

A more significant casualty was Sir James Dalrymple of Stair, president of the court of session. Deprived of his commissions for court and council on his refusal to take the Test, he subsequently found exile in Holland after being driven from retirement at his Ayrshire estate by threats made to his personal safety.[70] The duke of Hamilton was amongst five noblemen who also refused to subscribe the oath because of misgivings over its wording, as did the duke of Monmouth, arguing that although he was a privy councillor he was not resident in Scotland and therefore the law did not apply.[71] Hamilton and the three other nobles eventually conceded in July 1682 on the brink of losing their offices. The last to hold out was Argyll and the sentence of treason and forfeiture laid against him for his refusal is perhaps one of the better known events of the Restoration. On 3 November 1681, when Argyll took the Test in front of the privy council, the earl made a statement asserting that the Test was self-contradictory and he took it only in so far as it was consistent with itself and the Protestant religion. It was only after the council had risen that James and the other councillors realised the significance of Argyll's codicil. The following day, on being asked to explain himself,

Argyll repeated his statement, this time submitting his reasons in writing. As a result, the earl soon found himself imprisoned in Edinburgh Castle, indicted for lease-making, perjury and treason. Argyll maintained throughout his subsequent trial that he had committed no act of political disloyalty; rather that he was being prosecuted for 'the sense of words misconstrued to the greatest height and stretched to imaginary inclinations, quite contrary to my scope and design.'[72] Escaping the sentence of death pronounced against him by fleeing to Holland, Argyll remained in exile until 1685, when he returned with a small expeditionary force in an unsuccessful attempt to foment rebellion against King James.[73]

The severity of punishment meted out to Argyll for what was merely a verbal attempt to resolve a dilemma of conscience was greeted with horror in both Scotland and England and only confirmed fears of James's supposed absolutist tendencies.[74] Despite this, it did not discourage others from similarly refusing the oath. Many conformist ministers refused the Test because of theological objections against the attached confession of faith, and for the same reason no Catholic could hope to benefit. In November 1681, the council was forced to issue an explanatory act declaring that the Test was only meant to imply adhesion to the Protestant religion as opposed to popery and fanaticism.[75] The self-contradictory nature of the act was, however, apparent for all to see. The council's response was to declare that the confession of faith, despite its symbolic status, was an imperfect act, passed in the infancy of the reformation. It was not enough to convince up to eighty ministers who resigned their offices rather than take the Test.[76]

Within the parliamentary chamber itself, in addition to those protests already mentioned directed towards the content of the Test act, there were also complaints from a number of the estates that acts, including the Test, were being put to the vote far too quickly, so that members had little time to consider them in detail. Limiting the period available for consultation – when draft acts were 'laid upon the table' – was an obvious ploy by the government to minimise debate. The regular procedure of acts being laid open (possibly in the chamber where the register and his clerks sat) was not common practice until the 1690s, although it seems likely that a similar mechanism was instituted at the Restoration. The parliament of 1681 is the first session for which firm evidence exists for draft legislation being made publicly available for a certain period of time to enable non-members of the articles to study the particulars of acts. The most significant statutes advertised in this way were the acts ratifying laws in favour of the Protestant religion, for securing the peace of the country, for religion and the Test and for the election of shire commissioners.[77]

Contemporary complaints of attempts to stifle debate were directed primarily against the articles and by the means in which those acts brought in from the committee were presented to the rest of the estates for approval rather than amendment. With the opening of the committee to Hamilton and other Party members, however, the articles clearly encompassed a variety of opinion not seen under Lauderdale's administration and, as per its original function, the committee operated adeptly as a means of preparing and amending legislation. A total of twelve sub-committees were instituted by the articles to discuss all major acts and a number of minor proposals ranging from the mending of highways and bridges to trade and sumptuary laws. Throughout the session, acts in various stages of formulation were remitted to particular interest groups for comment, such as the act for religion and the Test to the bishops and the act of supply to the burghs. In certain cases, amendments were made as a result of this extended consultation, with the burghs successfully obstructing the proposed retention of annualrents in the act of supply and the articles altering the final draft to reflect this.[78] Such efficiency of operation continued into the next parliamentary session of 1685–6, where a more inclusive committee, representing factions within the chamber, not only successfully modified acts but acted as a restraint on limitless royal authority, defeating James's unpopular plans for religious toleration for Catholics.[79]

In 1681, the articles operated perhaps too efficiently, excluding the majority of estates from the decision-making process. In addition to restrictions on the length of time acts were made available for public consultation, there were conspicuous attempts to suppress debate outwith meetings of the committee. On 29 August, prior to the vote for the act's approval, Cochrane of Ochiltree gave in a paper against the Test but this was disregarded because supplications could only be submitted through the articles.[80] However, on 10 August, as Fountainhall recounts, Lord Bargany presented a petition in plain parliament, 'so that it is not absolutely necessar to goe first to the articles'.[81] Although Bargany's petition dealt with a private matter (it concerning a spurious complaint made against him for complicity with the rebels at Bothwell Brig) and, being read, was then remitted to the articles, it challenged the generally accepted rule that nothing could be tabled in parliament without first going through the committee.

Fountainhall believed that this was a 'late novation, destructive of the liberty and power of the parliament'. This view was shared within the chamber itself, with Lockhart of Carnwath declaring in a speech that 'the articles rejecting a bill ought not to have such a negative as to preclude the parliament from calling for it, if they please, and considering it.' Indeed, the act reviving the lords of the articles in 1661 explicitly stated that if the articles refused a measure, the proposer was free to 'present the same to his majesties commissioner and the estates of parliament'; the later statute of 1663 modifying the constitution of the articles did not explicitly disallow this. The resulting debate was, however, 'stifled' because of 'his royall hynesse shewing his dislike of it'.[82]

On the day the Test act was brought into the main chamber, several members (including two peers) made a request to attend meetings of the articles, observe their discussions and peruse certain acts still at the planning stage. Although this was not immediately refused, the clerk register agreeing to study the records and ascertain the former custom, a decision was continually delayed until parliament was adjourned.[83] By reviving the 1662 act for ordering the house, the government had unwittingly renewed the clause ('Nor any persons suffered to stay at the articles save members of parliament') that recognised the right of members to be present at the articles in an observational role only.[84] The act of 1662 was not an express invitation for members to attend the committee's meetings, but contemporaries obviously regarded the ambiguous wording as being open to various interpretations, with some considering the act as giving the whole chamber the right to attend. In 1669, Lauderdale had ended the short-lived practice in order to thwart opposition against the union proposal with England, but it was never prohibited by statute. The intended meaning in 1662 was to allow access to the committee only to members of parliament who were also members of the articles. In 1685, an additional clause was added to the act clarifying the matter: 'That by a posterior order of the house in the yeares 1668 and 1669, none is admitted to sit or be present with the articles but the members of the articles and clerks.'[85]

Dexterous management of parliamentary time further frustrated attempts by members to question decisions already made by the articles. In addition to complaints that draft acts were not made available for adequate consultation, there were concerns that the committee's reports were being deliberately held back or suddenly introduced without warning into the chamber. Thus, on some days when the articles had met in the morning, the estates were kept waiting until mid-afternoon or later to scrutinise their report. On the day the Test act was passed, the report was not brought in until 6 o'clock in the evening. As Fountainhall records, 'by surprise affairs and acts were brought in upon the parliament, past in the articles that morning, and very seldom delayed but put to a vote that same dyet.' Members had no 'leisure to prepare themselves for arguing, nor to deliberate, combine or take joynt measures.'[86] Burnet noted that:

> there was not much time given to consider things, for the duke [of York], finding that he was master of a clear majority, drove on everything fast, and put bills on a very short debate to the vote, which went always as he had a mind to it.[87]

Legislation was hurriedly rushed through, albeit with the consent of a majority. Nevertheless, there was a widespread feeling that parliament's right of consultation was being disregarded and discontented voices were beginning to make themselves heard. As his predecessor had done before him, by taking the complicity of the gathered estates for granted, James was treading dangerous ground.

In parliament on 6 September, Lord Belhaven was given leave to apologise to the chamber for his earlier criticisms of the Test act and, on his knees at the bar, he sought pardon for 'the rash and unadvised expressions uttered by him'. Suitably chastised, he was readmitted to his place.[88] Cromwell Lockhart of Lee, commissioner for Lanarkshire, very nearly joined Belhaven as prisoner in Edinburgh Castle after being involved in a disturbance within the house. During the acrimonious debates over the Test, Lee attempted to either leave or enter the chamber and was prevented from doing so by the macer. After a heated exchange, the two men came to blows, drawing the attention of the commissioner. Striking an officer in the house while parliament was in session was strictly prohibited by an act of 1593, and Lee, who according to Fountainhall had already 'offended' the duke of York by his voting, only escaped immediate punishment by paying the exorbitant sum of £1,000 sterling as security to the injured party.[89]

Tempers were obviously running high inside the chamber and a number of minor proposals proved unexpectedly controversial. An act discharging the summer session of the courts of justiciary attracted criticism because the lord advocate planned to include a clause to enable the king to recall the courts whenever he pleased. There were objections that this would lead to corruption, with litigants bribing courtiers to hasten the settlement of their lawsuits.

More significantly, it represented yet further crown interference in the judiciary, continuing the unwelcome precedent set under Lauderdale, with fears that this was a design to subtly extend the royal prerogative. In the face of such simmering resentment, the disputed clause was quietly dropped from the final act.[90] Disquiet was also voiced over an act asserting the royal prerogative in points of jurisdictions, in which the king was granted the right to nominate a crown-appointed lieutenant to observe magistrates at work. It was looked upon by the advocates of the house, noted Fountainhall, as 'a mighty extension and streatch towards arbitrarie government'. The crown eventually gave up on attempts to make the court of justiciary alone competent to deal with the four pleas of the crown (murder, rape, robbery and arson) since it was regarded as an attack on hereditary jurisdictions.[91] Other more subtle innovations also attracted criticism. An act for encouraging trade and manufactories, which traditionally invited tradesmen from other countries to come and set up in business, pointedly omitted the word 'Protestant' strangers, an obvious sign, wrote Fountainhall, of the 'present government under a popish commissioner'.[92]

A number of government proposals were altogether rejected by parliament. An act altering the regulations for selling grain, a usury clause in the act concerning bills of exchange allowing merchants to borrow or lend money at 1 per cent per month and a change in the law relating to civil legal processes in cases of inhibition were all 'rejected by the plurality of voices'. A grant of half a month's cess in favour of the University of St Andrews was allegedly carried in the negative, but, through false marking of votes, was given royal assent.[93] However, a number of complaints directly instituted by members of parliament were also refused, such a motion by the duke of Hamilton against the town of Edinburgh's imposition of two pence on a pint of ale. An indictment handed in by twelve citizens of Edinburgh against the former provost, James Roughead, for 'lease-making of them to the king' was declined, as was a proposed act limiting the provost of Edinburgh to a term of two years maximum.[94] The case of Sir Andrew Ramsay of Abbotshall, provost of the town for twelve continuous years at the behest of Lauderdale, had shown how useful it was to have control of the leading vote in parliament; allowing more freedom in elections was therefore not in the interest of the crown.

An unprecedented amount of private warrants and ratifications were the last items to be considered before parliament was adjourned.

Numbering over 120 in total, this exceeded in quantity even the 1661 session, which had sought to rebalance over ten years of independent rule by rewarding loyal royalists with numerous grants of titles, land and privilege.[95] James was, in effect, seeking to buy support to shore up his new administration in the post-Lauderdale era. However, Rosehaugh, as king's advocate, threatened to formally protest against all of them, declaring he had no specific instructions from the king regarding what should pass. The design, argued Fountainhall, was that individuals would be forced to consult Rosehaugh for approval individually, a privilege for which they would have to pay handsomely.[96]

The 1681 session of parliament was adjourned on 17 September, with a new session appointed to convene on 1 March 1682.[97] James's first session of parliament had granted all that had been demanded: the lineal succession of the throne was assured, an extended grant of taxation had been approved, enabling more troops to be raised to deal with the ever-present problem of conventicles, and additional restrictions had been placed on all public officials by the new Test act. As an added bonus, all these measures had been passed with relatively little opposition from the gathered estates.

The royal burghs' compliance had been assured with a guarantee given before parliament that if they voted loyally with the crown, their trading privileges (removed in 1672) would be fully restored. On 4 August, the convention of royal burghs granted full power to those burgesses who sat in the articles to seek an act rectifying their present situation.[98] A series of draft acts rescinding the controversial statute of 1672 were prepared in response to a petition given in to the articles by the royal burghs on 15 August, but were never presented to the full parliament. The draft acts that the royal burghs hoped would restore their ancient privileges instead placed further limitations on their freedom of trade.[99] On 13 September, addressing the convention, the provost of Edinburgh reported the dire news that the articles had debated the issue of trading privileges for a considerable time. All the concessions offered, however, were 'bot ane further strenthning of the said act 1672 and further restricting of the burrows and putting them altogither out of hopes to recover their antient privileges which they had befoir the act 1672'. As Fountainhall noted, this was the 'reward the burrows got for ther cheap service to the court'.[100]

Those who were prepared to vote against the crown's proposals undoubtedly suffered from a lack of leadership, with the duke of Hamilton and the majority of his previous Party allies astutely deciding against another period of exile in the political wilderness. Prior to parliament, this coalition temporarily fell apart, split by bitter recriminations between those who had accepted the spoils of office under the duke of York and those who had continued to spurn attempts at reconciliation. Many of the nobility no doubt had ambitions of succeeding to the positions that had been held by Rothes, who fortuitously died the day prior to parliament. Indeed, as Burnet recounts, there were 'many pretenders' who competed for the vacancy 'by the most compliant submission and the most active zeal'.[101]

Throughout the session, James, in his role of king's commissioner, had a minimal input to proceedings, in total contrast to his predecessor. This, however, did not escape criticism. 'Some wise men observed', wrote Fountainhall, 'that the duke of York might have honestie, justice and courage eneugh and his father's peremptorinesse, but that he had naither great conduct nor a deep reach in affairs, but was a silly man.'[102] As he had done in the privy council in 1680–1, James was quite content to glorify in his titular role but less enthusiastic to take part in debates and provide actual leadership. His greatest asset was his position as heir to the throne. Although the duke of Lauderdale, the dominant master of parliament for over a decade, was absent, there were plenty of like-minded individuals who filled his place. The vocal minority who dared to voice opposition in the presence of the heir to the throne instead faced the wrath of Sir George Mackenzie of Rosehaugh, king's advocate, who assumed the role of guardian of the crown's interest. It was a considerable transformation from the 'factious young man' that had hectored Lauderdale at every turn in the 1669 session of parliament.[103]

Careful manipulation of parliamentary procedure and time also aided the success of the crown's legislative programme. Lauderdale's personal involvement in the packing of key committees had always been well known and conspicuous, but in 1681, more subtle measures were used to influence and restrict debate. Discussion within the full chamber was kept to a minimum and debate outwith the articles actively discouraged. Acts were often abruptly advertised before being voted on in full by a depleted chamber. Opponents were further discouraged by the imprisonment of those who had initially dared to question specifics of the legislation brought before the estates.

Within parliament itself, there was minimal resistance to the various acts sought by the crown. When these came to be implemented, however, there was little such concurrence. The controversial Test act had been drawn in such a manner as to exclude all crown opponents from sitting in future parliaments. Its effect, however, was only to create a broader dissident opposition, united in defence of Protestantism against a Catholic monarch. The extensive religious persecution of the early to mid–1680s, the infamous 'Killing Times', in which summary executions were inflicted on radical presbyterians who refused to recognise the royal supremacy, alienated even the most conforming of subjects.

On his accession as king in February 1685, James grew more confident, pursuing not only liberty of conscience and freedom of worship for Catholics but actively promoting them to public office and positions of power. By the time the Scottish parliament met once more in April 1685, there was a groundswell of opposition against the Catholic king and his unpopular policies of toleration. Although the first session of parliament was relatively obsequious, approving without controversy the majority of measures outlined in the king's instructions, the joint risings of the earl of Argyll and the duke of Monmouth in the summer of 1685 indicated the extent of hostility towards James in the nation at large. Both rebellions were successfully repressed but the hysteria against a general toleration of Catholics only grew, brought to new heights in October 1685 by Louis XIV's revocation of the Edict of Nantes, which guaranteed the rights of French Protestants. For contemporaries, it was confirmation, if any were needed, that Catholicism was inexorably linked to absolutism.

James increasingly concentrated power in the hands of a few trusted individuals. Both Hamilton and Queensberry were supplanted by a previous adherent of their opposition party, the earl of Perth, who was appointed chancellor in 1684. Joining Perth was his brother John Drummond, first earl of Melfort, as secretary of state and the earl of Moray, promoted to king's commissioner for the 1686 session of parliament. All three had recently converted to Catholicism. Even without the controversy surrounding James's religion, limiting his power-base in such a manner and excluding other influential nobles had echoes of the Lauderdale era, with all its unwelcome connotations.

When parliament met for its second session in April 1686, James instructed Perth and Moray to get an act passed relaxing the civil disabilities on Scottish Catholics. The estates, however, proved less than obliging, rejecting the royal proposal despite the tempting incentive of free trade with England. Parliament was thus adjourned on 15 June 1686 without the promised act, leaving James to institute toleration by edict rather than with consent of the estates. However, an unforeseen consequence of James's recourse to the royal prerogative was the forging of an unlikely alliance between episcopalians and radical presbyterians united in the common defence of Protestantism. It was an inauspicious beginning to the new king's reign, arousing tensions that ultimately resulted in the rejection of James as monarch in favour of the Protestant William of Orange. When James fled to the continent after William's landing at Torbay in December 1688, the Scottish parliament exerted its ancient and independent right to bestow the crown on whomsoever it pleased. The Revolution saw the abolition of the lords of the articles, the removal of the bishops, reducing the crown vote, and the royal prerogative superseded by the rule of law. The Scottish parliament witnessed a new constitutional settlement – one that was radically different from that enacted at Charles II's restoration in 1660.

Notes

1 *CSPD, 1678*, p. 291.

2 *CSPD, 1678*, pp. 292, 312.

3 *CSPD, 1678*, pp. 477, 559; *Extracts from the records of the burgh of Edinburgh, 1665–1680*, pp. 355–6.

4 BL, Additional Mss 23243, f. 5.

5 Mackenzie, *Life and Times of Lauderdale*, pp. 459–61.

6 Buckroyd, *Church and State*, pp. 129–30; Buckroyd, *Life of James Sharp*, pp. 106–16; Cowan, *Scottish Covenanters*, pp. 94–9; *Lauderdale Papers*, iii, pp. 162–4; *RPCS*, third series, vi, pp. 160–7, 174–8, 180, 207–8, 218–19. For Monmouth's instructions regarding his treatment of the rebels, see C. S. Terry, 'The duke of Monmouth's instructions in 1679', *The English Historical Review*, 20, 77 (1905), pp. 127–9.

7 See Public Record Office, Shaftesbury Papers, vi b, 428, printed by J. R. Jones as 'The Scottish Constitutional Opposition in 1679', *SHR*, 37 (1958), pp. 37–41. Hamilton, Tweeddale, Queensberry and other prominent nobles are included, but the anonymous writer of the list picks out for special mention those who have continually refused to subscribe the declaration of public trust, suggesting that there was a significant body of opposition that operated outside the public arenas.

8 Anon., *Some particular matter of fact relating to the administration of affairs in Scotland under the duke of Lauderdale* (London?, 1679); NAS, Hamilton Muniments, GD406/2/635/10; *CSPD, 1678*, p. 468; Lee, 'Government and politics in Scotland, 1661–1681', p. 276.

9 HMC, *Supplementary report of the manuscripts of the Duke of Hamilton*, pp. 99–100; BL, Additional Mss 23244, ff. 20–7; Wodrow, *Sufferings of the Church of Scotland*, iii, pp. 168–71; Lang, *Sir George*

Mackenzie, pp. 177–9; Mackenzie, *Life and Times of Lauderdale*, pp. 473–5. After the conference, the king wrote a letter to the council exonerating the judicatories and especially Lauderdale from the complaints raised against them by certain members of the nobility. That Lauderdale, who lived the majority of the time in London, should be blamed for all the actions of the council tended only 'to defame your persons and administrations'. *RPCS*, third series, vi, pp. 280–1.

10 *RPCS*, third series, vi, pp. 271–2.

11 Anon., *Some farther matter of fact relating to the administration of affairs in Scotland under the duke of Lauderdale, humbly offered to his majesties consideration* (London?, 1679).

12 Lang, *Sir George Mackenzie*, pp. 178–9; Hutton, *Charles II*, p. 376.

13 *RPCS*, third series, vi, pp. 264–5, 278. Burnet claimed that the indulgence and indemnity for the rebels involved at Bothwell Brig were Monmouth's own initiatives, although a second source states that Monmouth's instructions were in fact drafted by Lauderdale. See Burnet, *History*, ii, p. 239 and *CSPD, 1679*, p. 175.

14 Drumlanrig Castle, 'Transcripts of Queensberry letters', no.56; Buckroyd, *Church and State*, pp. 130–1; Mackenzie, *Life and Times of Lauderdale*, pp. 475–6.

15 *Lauderdale Papers*, iii, pp. 181–2; BL, Additional Mss 23245, ff. 3–5.

16 *Lauderdale Papers*, iii, pp. 183–5; Wodrow, *Sufferings of the Church of Scotland*, iii, p. 175; *RPCS*, third series, vi, p. 344.

17 *RPCS*, third series, vi, pp. 273, 393; Burnet, *History*, ii, p. 305; Buckroyd, *Church and State*, p. 132; Hutton, *Charles II*, p. 387.

18 Lauder of Fountainhall, *Historical Observes*, p. 75.

19 BL, Additional Mss 23245, f. 81.

20 Mackenzie, *Life and Times of Lauderdale*, p. 483; Lauder of Fountainhall, *Historical Observes*, p. 75.

21 HMC, *The manuscripts of the duke of Buccleuch and Queensberry*, ii, Introduction, p. 5.

22 Buckroyd, *Church and State*, p. 134; Cowan, *Scottish Covenanters*, pp. 104–8; Hutton, *Charles II*, p. 388.

23 *Lauderdale Papers*, iii, p. 223.

24 *Lauderdale Papers*, iii, pp. 223–5; BL, Additional Mss 23248, f. 14.

25 Lauder of Fountainhall, *Historical Observes*, p. 42.

26 *CSPD, 1680–81* (London, 1921), p. 343. See Jackson, *Restoration Scotland*, pp. 48–53, for an account of the importance of hereditary right of succession in Restoration intellectual culture.

27 *CSPD, 1678*, p. 291.

28 NAS, PA2/31, ff. 1r–2r; *RPS*, 1681/7/2; *CSPD, 1680–81*, p. 343. For twenty-eight of the forty-three burgh candidates, this was their one and only appearance at a parliament or convention. The comparable figure for the shires was fourteen of twenty-four.

29 Both Polwarth and Broomhall were to return to the political stage at the Revolution as prominent members of the Club. In 1688, Broomhall was described by Colin Lindsay, third earl of Balcarres, as leader of the presbyterian and discontented party. C. Lindsay, *Memoirs Touching the Revolution in Scotland by Colin, earl of Balcarres, presented to King James II at St Germains*, 1690, Lord Lindsay (ed.), (Edinburgh, 1841), p. 12.

30 Burnet, *History*, ii, p. 309.

31 NAS, PA2/31, f. 3r; *RPS*, 1681/7/4; Lauder of Fountainhall, *Historical Notices*, i, p. 302; *Miscellany of the Maitland Club, consisting of original papers and other documents illustrative of the history and literature of Scotland, vol. iii, part 1* (Edinburgh, 1843), 'An act by his royall highness, his majesties high commissioner, and lords of the privy council establishing the order of the ryding etc. at the opening of the ensuing parliament, 25 July 1681', pp. 119–27.

32 NAS, PA7/11/8/2, 'Minutes of parliament, 28 July 1681 to 13 September 1681', f. 22; *RPS*, A1681/7/2; Sir John Lauder of Fountainhall, *Chronological Notes of Scottish Affairs, from 1680 till 1701, being chiefly taken from the diary of Lord Fountainhall*, W. Scott (ed.), (Edinburgh, 1822), p. 19.

33 Fountainhall records that 'some expected a motion on the reading of the duke of York's commission in the house, that it should have been objected against the commissioner that he was not so capable of so hy a dignity, not being a Protestant . . . that he ought to swear the allegiance and supremacy which no papist without a dispensation could weel doe', Lauder of Fountainhall, *Historical Observes*, p. 46. Burnet maintains that above forty members of parliament had promised to side with Hamilton if he would insist on the commissioner taking the required oaths. When he refused, 'many who were offended at it complained of duke Hamilton's cowardice'. Burnet, *History*, ii, p. 308.

34 NAS, PA2/31, ff. 3r–v; *RPS*, 1681/7/5; Lauder of Fountainhall, *Historical Observes*, pp. 44–5.

35 NAS, PA2/31, ff. 3v–4r; *RPS*, 1681/7/6.

36 NAS, PA7/11/8/2, ff. 21–2; *RPS*, A1681/7/2. For the membership, see *NAS*, PA2/31, f. 4r; *RPS*, 1681/7/7.

37 NAS, PA2/31, f. 4v; *RPS*, 1681/7/10. For the account of the revival of the act in 1678, see Lauder of Fountainhall, *Historical Observes*, p. 277.

38 Ochiltree was the second son of the earl of Dundonald and his strong covenanting views were well known. His commission to the convention of estates in 1678 was disallowed but he accompanied Hamilton to London later that year. Present at the battle of Bothwell Brig, he was later implicated in the Rye House Plot, fleeing to Holland, only to return at the time of Argyll's rebellion. *Scots Peerage*, iii, p. 346; Young (ed.), *Parliaments of Scotland*, i, pp. 127–8.

39 NAS, PA7/11/8/3, f. 23; *RPS*, A1681/7/4.

40 NAS, PA7/11/96/1, 'Minutes of the lords of the articles, 28 July–16 September 1681', f. 303; *RPS*, C1681/7/1; Lauder of Fountainhall, *Historical Notices*, i, p. 306. For the membership of the committee of disputed elections, see NAS, PA2/31, ff. 4r–v; RPS, 1681/7/8.

41 NAS, PA7/11/8/3–4, ff. 23–6; *RPS*, A1681/7/6.

42 See NAS, PA7/25/85/6/1–8, 'Papers relating to disputed election in North Berwick', especially PA7/25/85/6/4, 'Protestation of council against Suittie'.

43 NAS, PA7/11/8/3–4, ff. 23–6; *RPS*, A1681/7/6. Bargany had been imprisoned on a charge of high treason in 1679 for plotting to assassinate the duke of Lauderdale. He successfully secured royal favour and was released in May 1680. The duke of York took steps to prevent his case being heard before parliament in 1681. *Scots Peerage*, ii, pp. 29–31.

44 NAS, PA7/11/8/4, ff. 24–5; *RPS*, A1681/7/6.

45 Lauder of Fountainhall, *Historical Notices*, i, p. 310.

46 NAS, PA7/11/8/4, f. 26; *RPS*, A1681/7/6.

47 NAS, PA7/11/8/4–5, ff. 26–7; *RPS*, A1681/7/8. It is not clear why the cases of Lochmaben and Annan were referred to the articles, as matters were still being remitted to the committee of debatable elections as late as 27 August. See NAS, PA7/11/8/7, f. 32; *RPS*, A1681/7/16.

48 Parliament's report on the matter can be found at NAS, PA7/11/25, 'Resolves of parliament anent the election of commissioners for the parliament, 1681'.

49 NAS, PA2/31, ff. 16r–17r; *RPS*, 1681/7/45. See Rait, *Parliaments of Scotland*, pp. 212–13 and William Ferguson, 'The electoral system in the Scottish counties before 1832', in *Miscellany II*, Stair Society Publications no. 35, D. Sellar (ed.), (Edinburgh, 1984), pp. 268–72 for further discussion of this act and its implications for future voting contests.

50 This is arguably the defect of the calculations made by Colquhoun (and subsequently repeated by Harris) in which extant commissions have been used to determine the average number of voters in shire elections in 1681, estimated at sixteen. This figure, however, takes no account of electors subscribing defeated commissions. Colquhoun, ' "Issue of the late civill wars": James, duke of York and the government of Scotland, 1679–1689', p. 117; Harris, *Restoration*, p. 23. Moreover, an average figure is largely meaningless, given the wide disparity in size of shires. Kinross-shire, one of the smallest shires, perhaps had an electorate of well within single figures, whilst Aberdeenshire or Ayrshire may have reached into the hundreds. See Terry, *Scottish Parliament*, pp. 39–41, for a discussion of voting figures in 1788, which highlights these wide variations between shire electorates.

51 For an extended account of burgh and shire electorates in the Revolutionary period, confirming a rise in participation, see D. J. Patrick,

'People and parliament in Scotland, 1689–1702' (University of St Andrews, Ph.D., 2002), chs. 3–4.

52 Aberdeenshire: 1681 commission, NAS, PA7/25/2/9; 1685 commission and Test act, NAS, PA7/25/2/10/1–2. Fifeshire: 1681 commission, NAS, PA7/25/14/10; 1685 commission and Test act, NAS, PA7/25/14/11/1–2. Dumfries-shire: 1681 commission, NAS, PA7/25/11/9; 1685 commission and Test act, NAS, PA7/25/11/10/1–2. Lanarkshire: 1681 commission, NAS, PA7/25/21/10; 1685 commission and Test act, NAS, PA7/25/21/11/1–2.

53 Lauder of Fountainhall, *Historical Notices*, i, pp. 306–7.

54 Lauder of Fountainhall, *Historical Notices*, i, pp. 301, 310–11. Cromlix seems to have escaped without punishment but the charges against him were almost certainly erroneous. He had been commissioner for Perthshire since 1669, his eligibility never previously being questioned. The cause of the dispute probably owed much to an earlier altercation with the duke of Lauderdale, for which Cromlix was imprisoned on Dumbarton Rock. Young (ed.), *Parliaments of Scotland*, i, p. 203.

55 *RPCS*, third series, vii, p. 256; Lauder of Fountainhall, *Historical Notices*, i, pp. 336–8.

56 NAS, PA7/11/9/5, f. 41; *RPS*, M1681/7/10; *CSPD, 1680–81*, pp. 410–11.

57 NAS, PA7/11/8/6, f. 29; *RPS*, A1681/7/11; NAS, PA2/31, f. 6r; *RPS*, 1681/7/17.

58 NAS, PA7/11/8/6, ff. 29–30; *RPS*, A1681/7/12; Lauder of Fountainhall, *Historical Notices*, i, pp. 322–3. For the report of the sub-committee of the articles anent the supply, see NAS, PA7/11/13, f. 66.

59 NAS, PA7/11/96/11, ff. 310–11; *RPS*, C1681/7/11–13; NAS, PA2/31, ff. 6v–8r; *RPS*, 1681/7/23.

60 NAS, PA7/11/8/7, f. 31; *RPS*, A1681/7/14.

61 NAS, PA7/11/96/12, f. 312; *RPS*, C1681/7/15. Both these overtures survive amongst the papers of the lords of the articles. See NAS, PA7/11/92–3.

62 NAS, PA7/11/8/7, f. 32; *RPS*, A1681/7/16; Burnet, *History*, ii, pp. 314–15. For the confession of faith as confirmed by parliament in 1567, see *RPS*, A1567/12/107.

63 NAS, PA7/11/8/8, f. 33; *RPS*, A1681/7/17; NAS, PA2/31, f. 8r; *RPS*, 1681/7/25; Lauder of Fountainhall, *Historical Notices*, i, pp. 307–8.

64 NAS, PA7/11/8/8, f. 33; *RPS*, A1681/7/17; W. Fraser (ed.), *The Chiefs of Grant*, 3 vols (Edinburgh, 1883), i, pp. 301–2.

65 Lauder of Fountainhall, *Historical Notices*, i, pp. 308, 316.

66 Cited from an unidentified source in Lang, *Sir George Mackenzie*, p. 220.

67 Lauder of Fountainhall, *Historical Notices*, i, pp. 309, 327.

68 *CSPD, 1680–81*, p. 517.

69 For more on the implications of the refusal of public officials to subscribe the Test, see *RPCS*, third series, vii, Introduction, pp. viii–xi.

70 J. D. Ford, 'James Dalrymple, first viscount Stair (1619–1695)', *Oxford Dictionary of National Biography*, vol. 14, pp. 988–94.

71 *RPCS*, third series, vii, pp. 233, 294–5.

72 *RPCS*, third series, vii, pp. 238, 242–3; Burnet, *History*, ii, pp. 319–23; Campbell, *The speech of the earl of Argyle at his trial on the 12th of December, 1681* (London, 1682), p. 2. For more on the use of oaths in the Restoration period and their implications for individual consciences, see Jackson, *Restoration Scotland*, pp. 147–55.

73 Hutton, *Charles II*, pp. 412–13.

74 Lauder of Fountainhall, *Historical Observes*, pp. 54–6.

75 Lang, *Sir George Mackenzie*, p. 219; *RPCS*, third series, vii, p. 239.

76 Burnet, *History*, ii, p. 318.

77 Acts discharging the summer session of the courts of justiciary, concerning the jurisdiction of the admiral court, the staple port and a petition of the royal burghs concerning their privileges were also laid open. NAS, PA7/11/9/18, f. 54; *RPS*, M1681/7/23; NAS, PA7/11/96/7–19, ff. 307–24; *RPS*, C1681/7/6–30.

78 NAS, PA7/11/96/7, f. 307; *RPS*, C1681/7/6; NAS, PA7/11/96/11, f. 310; *RPS*, C1681/7/11.

79 For more on the articles in 1685–6, see A. J. Mann, 'James VII, King of the Articles: political management and parliamentary failure', in Brown and Mann (eds), *The History of the Scottish Parliament, volume II: Parliament and Politics, 1567–1707*, pp. 188–207.

80 NAS, PA7/11/8/8, f. 33; *RPS*, A1681/7/17.

81 NAS, PA7/11/8/5, f. 28; *RPS*, A1681/7/9; Lauder of Fountainhall, *Historical Notices*, i, p. 314.

82 Lauder of Fountainhall, *Historical Notices*, i, pp. 313–14. For the 1661 and 1663 acts concerning the constitution of the articles, see NAS, PA2/26, ff. 8–10; *RPS*, 1661/1/13 and NAS, PA2/28, f. 79v; *RPS*, 1663/6/5. There were additional instances of parliamentary committees disregarding petitions given in by members. On 27 August, Sir Hugh Campbell of Cawdor complained that the committee for disputed elections had taken 'no notice' of a list of incapable commissioners he had submitted and unsuccessfully attempted to have these discussed in full parliament. On 29 August, Cawdor made the same request and was again rebutted, with the lord advocate alleging that it was intended only to delay the passage of the Test act. NAS, PA7/11/8/7–8, ff. 32–3; *RPS*, A1681/7/16–17.

83 NAS, PA7/11/96/13, f. 314; *RPS*, C1681/7/19. Lauder of Fountainhall states the earl of Haddington and Lord Blantyre were amongst those who made the request. *Historical Notices*, i, pp. 314–15.

84 NAS, PA2/28, f. 3v; *RPS*, 1662/5/6.

85 NAS, PA2/32, f. 150v; *RPS*, 1685/4/13.

86 Lauder of Fountainhall, *Historical Notices*, i, pp. 313–14.

87 Burnet, *History*, ii, p. 310.

88 NAS, PA2/31, f. 11r; *RPS*, 1681/7/31.

89 NAS, PA7/11/96/15, f. 317; *RPS*, C1681/7/22; Lauder of Fountainhall, *Historical Notices*, i, p. 314; *CSPD, 1680–81*, p. 440. For the 1593 'Act for puneisement of thame that trublis the parliament, sessioun and uther jugementis', see NAS, PA2/15, f. 13r; *RPS*, 1593/4/41.

90 Lauder of Fountainhall, *Historical Notices*, i, p. 316; NAS, PA7/11/8/8, f. 33; *RPS*, A1681/7/18. For the act as passed by parliament, see NAS, PA2/31, f. 11r; *RPS*, 1681/7/30. The town of Edinburgh protested against any such change to the sessions of the justice courts, but the petition of Sir James Dick of Priestfield, provost of Edinburgh, to the articles was rejected. The loss in revenue to the town from the reduction in trade over the summer months was estimated at £10,000 sterling annually. NAS, PA7/11/96/15, f. 316; *RPS*, C1681/7/21; *CSPD, 1680–81*, p. 447.

91 Lauder of Fountainhall, *Historical Notices*, i, pp. 320–1; NAS, PA2/31, f. 15v; *RPS*, 1681/7/42.

92 NAS, PA2/31, ff. 12r–13v; *RPS*, 1681/7/36; Lauder of Fountainhall, *Historical Notices*, i, pp. 318–19.

93 Lauder of Fountainhall, *Historical Notices*, i, pp. 321–2; NAS, PA2/31, f. 17v; *RPS*, 1681/7/47.

94 Lauder of Fountainhall, *Historical Notices*, i, pp. 311–12, 324; BL, Additional Mss 23248, f. 18.

95 NAS, PA2/31, ff. 31r–142v; *RPS*, 1681/7/88–216. See Mann, 'James VII, King of the Articles: political management and parliamentary failure', in Brown and Mann (eds), *History of the Scottish Parliament*, pp. 194–5 for a breakdown of public and private legislation passed from 1669–86.

96 Lauder of Fountainhall, *Historical Notices*, i, p. 323.

97 NAS, PA2/31, ff. 142v–143r; *RPS*, 1681/7/218. The planned 1682 session never met.

98 *Records of the Convention of the Royal Burghs of Scotland*, iv (1677–1711), p. 26.

99 NAS, PA7/11/96/7–8, ff. 308–9; *RPS*, C1681/7/10; NAS, PA7/11/87, 'Petition of the royal burghs'; NAS, PA7/11/88–91, 'Draft acts in favour of the royal burghs'.

100 *Records of the Convention of the Royal Burghs of Scotland*, iv (1677–1711), p. 27; Lauder of Fountainhall, *Historical Notices*, i, pp. 323–4. The privileges of the royal burghs were not restored until 1690. See NAS, PA2/34 ff. 49r–v; *RPS*, 1690/4/61.

101 Burnet, *History*, ii, p. 310.

102 Lauder of Fountainhall, *Historical Notices*, i, p. 327.

103 Mackenzie, *Memoirs*, p. 173.

Chapter 8

THE RESTORATION SCOTTISH PARLIAMENT IN A EUROPEAN CONTEXT

⟨∼⟩

Until relatively recently, histories of early modern representative assemblies, particularly comparative European studies, have often been too eager to pass judgment on the relative success or failure of individual institutions.[1] In doing so, there have been attempts to elucidate a number of general trends to account for the otherwise inexplicable demise or decline of various parliamentary institutions, such as the rise of royal absolutism in the late seventeenth century.[2] However, a Whiggish tendency to judge the importance and significance of early modern assemblies by the standards of a later age results in an often distorted view. Whilst many European assemblies shared common institutional characteristics, such as function, structure and membership, each developed differently to represent a diverse range of social and local interests and to meet the particular needs of specific political structures. Arguably, whilst a general comparative study of early modern European representative assemblies has its place, it seems more useful to assess the relative success or failure of institutions by examining how effectively each fulfilled its own peculiar function in the context of what contemporaries expected their assemblies to achieve.

There exists no standard or archetypal framework for the structure of early modern European parliaments. A widely diverse body of representative assemblies existed, from one- to four-chamber institutions, each attended by a variety of different interest groups. Parliaments were, however, royal institutions, summoned by monarchs (often with distinctly monetary motives) to assist in the business of government. No assembly could truly be called a democratic meeting of the realm, despite contemporaries often advancing a myth of an entirely representative assembly of the people. The majority instead reflected the basic organisation of European society into estates, with the politically significant orders (in most cases headed by the nobility) gaining admittance. In this respect, the Scottish parliament conforms to its European counterparts.[3]

In common with the parliament of Naples and the estates-general of France until 1560, the seventeenth-century Scottish parliament was a unicameral assembly, attended by three or four estates depending on political circumstance. Numbers in attendance in the early modern period could vary greatly, from a minimum of twenty-nine in April 1641 to a maximum of 232 in the parliament of June 1705.[4] Represented therein were the clergy and the nobility, who sat by right of summons, and the two elected estates, the commissioners of the shires and the burghs. To solve the procedural dilemma of an absentee monarch after the regal union in 1603, increasingly the crown was epitomised by the royal commissioner, an individual appointed for the duration of parliament to preside in the absence of the king. The monarch's interest was further augmented by the officers of state, numbering on average seven or eight, who sat by right of nomination from the crown.[5] Except for the revolutionary period of 1641–60, officers of state gained ex officio admittance to elected committees and thus served as reliable defenders of the royal supremacy. After the re-establishment of episcopacy in 1662, the bishops were entirely dependent on the crown; the nobility less so, although newly promoted peers could consistently be relied on to demonstrate loyalty for at least a short period of time. In the Restoration period in particular, there was widespread and unprecedented crown interference in shire elections and burgh councils, to varying degrees of success. Each combined to shape a chamber predisposed to the king's interests, with this augmented further by a genuine royalist reaction to the restoration of the monarchy in 1660.[6]

On Charles II's restoration, as described in the first chapter of this study, it was the committee of estates rather than parliament that was first convened to oversee the first steps in the revival of monarchical authority. This specialised interval committee, first instituted by the covenanters in 1640 as a temporary expedient to deal with the demands of military and diplomatic involvement in the civil wars in addition to the domestic administration of Scotland at times when parliament was not sitting, operated on a regular basis until 1651. At the Restoration, the committee from 1651 was recalled to act as a provisional government until English affairs were settled and preparations could be made for a meeting of the Scottish parliament.[7] A similar standing committee existed in the states-general of the United Provinces to carry out the ordinary executive and administrative work of provincial government. In Holland, the *gecommitteerde raden* or 'commissioned councillors' sat continuously, its main task

Figure 8.1 An illustration of the 'riding of parliament', the colourful ceremonial procession held at the opening and closing of each session, as depicted in Nicolas de Guedeville's Atlas Historique, ou Nouvelle Introduction à l'Histoire à la Chronologie & à la Géographie Ancienne & Moderne, 3 vols (Amsterdam, 1708). In the background is the only surviving image of the Scottish parliament in session. (© The Trustees of the National Museums of Scotland.)

being to administer the enforcement of edicts and decrees by the states-general at a provincial level, to control finances and oversee military preparations.[8] Standing committees were also prominent in the Iberian peninsula. The role of the *diputación del reino*, although being much smaller than its Scottish counterpart, consisting of only eight members, was broadly similar: to ensure that legislation passed by the *cortes* of Aragon was put into operation and to provide a means of administration between sessions of the full assembly. In the Catalan *cortes*, the *diputació* had a similar function, taking on the additional role of defending the principality's privileges in the Catalonian revolt of 1640.[9]

Unique to the Scottish parliament was the steering committee known as the lords of the articles. Instituted at the beginning of each session, the articles were the primary means by which legislation was vetted and drafted prior to being sent to the full chamber for approval. Effective royal control is supposed to have been achieved by the peculiar manner of election to the committee, in which the bishops, all royal appointees, elected the members of the nobility, who, along with the bishops, then chose the representatives of the other two estates.[10] Thus, the articles have long been viewed simply as a tool of the crown, echoing contemporary complaints of the committee's dominance and the limited involvement of the rest of the gathered estates in the making of acts. Although the committee (with its restrictive election procedure) was revived in 1661–3 precisely with this role in mind, it was seldom the case that the crown was able to push through unopposed or unaltered its entire legislative agenda.[11] In the Restoration period, the effectiveness of the articles in its original role of a preparatory committee undoubtedly suffered from the parliamentary management of the duke of Lauderdale, king's commissioner, who blatantly packed the committee with trusted allies and actively sought to keep their discussions secret. Under the brief commissionership of James, duke of York, in 1681 (as described in Chapter 7), the articles partly resumed its original function, operating relatively adeptly and with a membership containing a breadth of opinion not previously seen in the Restoration period.

The articles' closest approximation in European terms was the *sekreta utskott* or 'secret committee' of the Swedish *riksdag*, in which a select group of nobles, clerics and burghers (the peasants were excluded entirely) sat separately, with a similar preparatory and co-ordinating function to the Scottish lords of the articles. Committee members were appointed by the government, although nominations for representatives were often sought from the three upper estates. From its inception in 1627 to the late seventeenth century, the secret committee's remit was primarily restricted to foreign policy, but, in the crucial session of 1680 that laid the groundwork for the formal acceptance of Swedish royal absolutism, a carefully managed committee was consulted on the best means of raising money for an extensive programme of military reorganisation. In subsequent sessions, as absolutism became more established, the secret committee gained a much wider remit as the crown actively sought to bypass the plenary sessions of the *riksdag*. As with its Scottish counterpart in the Restoration period, decision making was effectively carried out in the committee, with the estates reduced to the subordinate role of ratifying their deliberations.[12]

At the beginning of each session of the *riksdag*, the secret committee received specific instructions from the king outlining the parliamentary agenda for the current session. The gathered estates also received a less detailed summary of the proposed issues requiring redress and were free to debate these separately, negotiating with the other estates and with the king until consensus was reached. Thus the course of business was largely determined by the crown, although a means of presenting grievances, either individually or on behalf of specific interest groups (usually one of the four estates), developed throughout the seventeenth century.[13] Such procedure mirrored that of the Scottish parliament, where, with the advent of absentee monarchy, legislative agendas frequently had to be fixed in advance to provide the king's commissioner with directions on how to proceed. Members of the articles were often used as a sounding board to gauge the possible reaction to controversial legislation, and, as was the case with the abortive proposal to issue the names of union commissioners in 1669 through the great seal and the rejected overture to abolish the summer session of the courts of judiciary in 1672, could reject proposals outright before they even reached the rest of the estates.

Until the reign of James VII, instructions to the lord commissioner from the king were relatively broad in scope or limited to a few defined issues. Considering the distance from Edinburgh to London, problems inevitably arose. As examined in the second chapter of this study, in 1663, after the embarrassment of the billeting affair, the earl of Middleton was dismissed as king's commissioner for passing acts without royal consent and operating too independently from the crown. Subsequent instructions issued to Middleton's successors were more detailed and, unlike his predecessor, Lauderdale made full use of his contacts at court to liaise with the king directly regarding draft acts prior to these being put before the gathered estates. Despite this, it is clear from Lauderdale's private instructions that Charles implicitly trusted his judgement and the commissioner was given considerable freedom to proceed as he thought best. James, duke of York's interest in the minutia of parliamentary procedure was evident when he assumed the role of commissioner to his brother in 1681, and on his accession he, as king, issued a profusion of detailed instructions, some of which were entirely superfluous.[14] Whilst there were obvious benefits in clearly setting out the reasons for which parliament had been summoned, therein lay the danger of this being interpreted as an unwelcome interference in the deliberative processes of the estates and further evidence of absolutist tendencies. Indeed, after the

Revolution, the crown promoted a more inclusive approach, actively consulting the major political figures prior to the drafting of royal instructions.[15]

In common with the majority of seventeenth-century European assemblies, the Scottish estates were frequently summoned for the purpose of granting taxation to subsidise the crown's often inadequate ordinary income. To do so, the monarch had the option of calling either a full meeting of parliament or, alternatively, a convention of estates. Another peculiarly Scottish institution, a convention could be called on only twenty days' notice rather than the forty required for parliaments, and was restricted in its deliberations to what was contained in the summons, primarily, in the later seventeenth century, requests for taxation.[16] By the Restoration period, there was no discernible difference in the membership between parliaments and conventions: both consisted of the same people (the four estates) and numbers in attendance often matched or exceed full sessions of parliament.[17] However, the restricted remit of conventions to only consider those issues explicitly mentioned in the royal letter of summons was a useful means by which the crown could secure taxation without having to first redress grievances. As such, conventions were often favoured in preference to parliaments at times when opposition to crown demands was to be feared, such as in 1665 and 1667 for grants of supply to fund the unpopular Anglo-Dutch war and in 1678, when discontent over the autocratic ministry of the duke of Lauderdale was approaching its peak.

The Restoration settlement of 1661 sought to provide the crown with a generous long-term provision of £40,000 sterling yearly for life, although, in common with many European monarchs, the pressures of expansionist colonial warfare and internal strife soon scuppered any plan for the king to live within his own means. The estates proved to be remarkably co-operative in providing future grants of taxation, even though the money raised was often disbursed on a number of unpopular ventures, such as to fund the expenses of commissioners for negotiating closer union with England in 1670 or to increase the size of a standing army to suppress religious dissent in 1678. Other European assemblies were less obliging, forcing their rulers to find alternative avenues for raising essential funds. Throughout the sixteenth century, the estates-general of France was often reluctant to produce the desired subsidies for the crown; thus it was summoned on only five occasions between 1560 and 1615 and thereafter not again until 1789. The estates-general's inability to establish relationships with the more regular meetings of the provincial estates ultimately contributed to its long absence from the political scene for much of the seventeenth century.[18] Local representation was well developed in France and fiscal power was invested in many provincial legislatures. Although a number of assemblies in areas such as Provence, Dauphiné and Normandy fell into abeyance in the seventeenth century, others flourished. The estates of Languedoc and Brittany met frequently and had a major role in regional administration, controlling the imposition and collection of subsidies. In these provincial assemblies, the crown was forced to negotiate the redress of grievances before grants of taxation could successfully be secured.[19]

A similar need for careful negotiation on behalf of the monarch in order to obtain an appropriate supply is evident in the *cortes* of Castile, which established a system in the late sixteenth century of explicitly conditional taxation.[20] By 1601, the *cortes* and the eighteen cities it represented could effectively block the raising of the *millones*, a tariff on foodstuffs and other essential commodities, thus depriving the crown of fiscal autonomy. During the reign of Philip III, as the price for approving new subsidies, the *cortes* successfully exercised administrative control over taxation, imposed budgets to ensure that money raised was spent in the public good and demanded legislative restrictions on the royal prerogative. Such pretences to independence from monarchical authority were brought to an end by the late 1630s when Philip IV wrestled back control of the administration of the *millones*, breaking the dependence of the *cortes* on the cities. From 1643, the crown began to bypass the *cortes* altogether, going directly to each city for consent for taxation. Deprived of its fiscal role, the Castilian assembly no longer served any useful function and it ceased to be summoned after 1665.[21] The initial success of the Castilian *cortes* and similarly the French provincial assemblies in achieving considerable jurisdiction in the collection and administration of taxation was largely due to the flimsy framework of royal authority in the localities. Yet, when monarchs made determined steps to establish or improve direct links with provincial government, previously significant central institutions were left superfluous.[22]

The principle of redress before supply was not unique to Castile, although therein it was more explicitly enshrined in actual legislation than in any other European country.[23] In 1650, the Swedish *riksdag* insisted that its grievances should be addressed prior to the granting of taxation.[24] In both England and Scotland (despite the king being provided a supply for life from customs receipts), direct taxation was granted only for a limited time, thus necessitating the recall of the estates once the supply had expired. In Restoration England, there was strong resistance to a proposed general excise on inland commodities, mainly due to fears that the crown might become over-funded, thereby negating the need for regular meetings of the estates.[25] Although the restrictions inherent in conventions of estates should have meant that raising subsidies in Scotland was relatively painless, the crown often faced strong resistance to demands for further taxation. In the late sixteenth century, conventions of estates in 1578, 1583 and 1586 all proved unco-operative. Plans to augment the crown's impoverished finances were thrown into turmoil by the refusal of four successive conventions in 1599–1600 to concur with James VI's requests for money.[26] In the Restoration period, the king's demands were largely met, although in 1667 and in 1672 the crown was forced into amending the intended means of collection after complaints about the unfairness of the distribution of the taxation burden.

The ability of the crown to raise money by other means, without recourse to national representative assemblies, has been inexorably linked to the rise of royal absolutism. Impatient with the obstructionism and parochialism of estates and taxpayers, monarchs either refused to summon assemblies or coerced others into voting automatically whatever was demanded of them. The financial pressures of war and military expansionism, common to nearly all of Europe at some point in the seventeenth century, stimulated the establishment of absolutism as a means of government, but it was the acceptance of such rule by influential groups within society, such as nobles eager for advancement at any price, that dictated whether absolute monarchy gained a foothold.[27] As with all attempts to establish one overriding theory to explain what appears to be a general historical trend, there are exceptions that stubbornly refuse to conform to any pattern. The diversity of European representative institutions already remarked upon decreases the likelihood of ordering it all into any neat and manageable arrangement.

An increase in royal authority and the resultant demise of many European assemblies came in many guises. Scandinavian absolutism was largely consensual and initially aimed at reducing aristocratic power. In Denmark, frustrated with the staunch intractability of the nobility and their refusal to share the burden of taxation, the *rigsdag* of 1660–1, dominated by representatives of the clergy and the towns, voted for the abolition of an elective monarchy in favour of a hereditary one. Frederick III was then granted a wide range of powers

appropriate to his new status.[28] Social tension in Sweden was prominent in the 1650s, again directed towards the privileges of the nobility, and this came to the fore after the Scanian war of 1675–9, which
reduced already scant crown resources to its bare minimum. The continued refusal of the nobility to negotiate on the resumption of crown
lands, previously conveyed to them in lieu of payment for services
rendered, eventually soured relations with the other estates who bore
the brunt of taxation. When the *riksdag* in 1680 constitutionally
downgraded the aristocratic council, which had grown considerably
in power during Karl XI's minority, they effectively handed over the
reigns of government to the monarch. This was confirmed in the
session of 1682–3 when the estates were successfully persuaded to
issue a declaration acknowledging the divine right of the king to legislate at will. In doing so, the *riksdag* renounced the very reason for
its existence.[29]

Absolute monarchy became established in other European countries for entirely different motives and with contrasting fortunes. In
Habsburg Austria, Leopold I's attempt to impose Catholicism on his
subjects was as much for reasons of political expediency as for spiritual concerns. A uniform religion would act as a cohesive force,
uniting the many variant states, nations and cultures that existed
under the umbrella of the Austrian monarchy. Despite resistance,
Bohemia and Lower Austria had been largely converted by Leopold's
predecessors, Ferdinand II and III. Hungary, however, consistently
resisted attempts at enforced conversion, eventually leading to the
outbreak of open revolt in 1670. The ensuing military occupation,
with its renewed attempts at stamping out Protestantism, met with
strong opposition from an increasingly rebellious population. As a
result, Leopold was forced into accepting the compromise of a multi-
denominational state in return for Hungarian acknowledgment of the
Habsburg right of succession. The recalled Hungarian *diet*, now a
potent symbol of national identity, only grew in power and status in
the later years of the seventeenth century, operating autonomously
and with considerable fiscal independence.[30] The establishment of
absolutism in Germany was also a picture of contrasts. The estates of
Brandenburg-Prussia were effectively emasculated by the Elector
Frederick William in the 1650s and 1670s when he sought taxation
without their consent. The estates of Württemberg, however, proved
much more resilient, refusing to countenance the establishment of a
standing army out of fear that its adoption would alter the duchy's
political structure.[31]

Both Scottish and English representative assemblies experienced many of the same problems as their European counterparts in the seventeenth century, such as expensive involvement in unpopular foreign wars, but largely escaped what is termed absolute monarchy. Relations between the crown and estates certainly deteriorated at key points, leading to constitutional revolution first in the 1640s and again in 1688–9, but throughout the estates played a central role and revolution only strengthened their power. Indeed, it was in parliament that opponents to royal absolutism found a platform to express their views.[32] Charles II's return as king in 1660, however, was enthusiastically welcomed since it brought to an end an imperial experiment that, in Scottish terms, had meant little more than military occupation. In 1661–3, at its first meeting for ten years, the Scottish parliament willingly surrendered most of the constitutional gains achieved by the estates in the 1640s in favour of stability and order under a strong monarchy. Nevertheless, despite a comprehensive reassertion of royal power, some of the ideology behind the covenanting rebellion survived. In both England and Scotland there remained a widely held belief that the estates should be regularly consulted by the monarch. Thus, resistance inevitably arose when attempts were made to circumvent parliament or when their ancient liberties were perceived to have been infringed.

The emergence of an organised opposition in Scotland in 1669 was directed largely towards the authoritarian management of the estates by the duke of Lauderdale and his packing of lucrative offices with relatives or close allies, as outlined in Chapters 4 and 5. Disappointed noble rivals provided the initial impetus for the beginnings of an organised movement, later termed by contemporaries an actual party, and although there were the nascent beginnings of an alternative political agenda that sought limitations on royal power, ideas which were to mature in the country party agenda of the 1688–9 revolutionary period, it was against the ministry of Lauderdale in particular that opposition was directed. Indeed, aside from the activities of presbyterian religious dissenters, Scotland remained overwhelmingly loyal to the crown, even initially to the administration of the Catholic James, duke of York as parliamentary commissioner in 1681 and as king in 1685. However, after 1686, when James sought to impose unpopular Catholicising polices by proclamation rather than through parliament, limiting his powerbase to such an extent that he alienated significant figures in his own privy council, opposition inevitably arose. In 1689, parliament declared James VII to have explicitly 'forefaulted' the throne, demonstrating that Scottish political obedience to monarchy was not unconditional.[33]

Measured against the yardstick of its European counterparts rather than the traditional comparison with its English neighbour, the Scottish parliament in the late seventeenth century stands out as a relatively powerful institution. Indeed, whilst contemporaneous representative assemblies in Denmark, Norway, France, Castile, Germany and Sweden were being sidelined or dissolved by their respective rulers, in Scotland there remained an enduring parliamentary dimension to political culture. The estates were politically significant and active throughout the later seventeenth century, sitting in session on average for forty days per year in the period 1660–1707.[34] For the crown, parliament remained a necessary evil, for it was the source not only of legislation but of essential taxation necessary for the running of government.

Yet the Restoration settlement of 1661–3 has traditionally been viewed as the complete surrendering of the hard-won constitutional gains of the 1640s by an entirely submissive chamber, powerless at resisting a complete reassertion of monarchical authority. In contrast, however, with a number of European assemblies, the augmentation of the royal prerogative was at least consensual and largely in reaction to the disastrous republican experiment of the 1650s. In Scotland, the estates, led by nobles eager to resume their traditional role at the head of society, willingly consented to a reduction in their power since it was believed that a compliant parliament and a strong monarchy would be the best means to guard against a repeat of revolution from below.

Thus the totality of crown control in parliament has generally been overstated. If it was truly the case that the Scottish estates were left powerless by the constitutional settlement enacted at the Restoration (as has been the dominant argument of much of the output on later seventeenth-century Scotland), one wonders not only why countless nobles, bishops and shire and burgh commissioners actually bothered to turn up for the meetings of a body in which they had little or no influence, but did so in increasing numbers throughout the reign of Charles II. At every meeting of the estates in the Restoration era, dissent and opposition was voiced either against crown policy or towards the means by which parliament was managed, this despite the limitations on free speech inherent in the structure of parliament, such as the controlling aspect of the lords of the articles and the restrictions placed on conventions of the estates. The duke of

Lauderdale's infamous remark to Charles that 'never was a king soe absolute as you are in poor old Scotland'[35] was largely hyperbole and shown to be such by the continued activities of presbyterian dissenters in the localities and by the emergence of an organised opposition within parliament. Throughout the Restoration period, meetings of the estates had to be carefully managed to ensure a compliant membership: in a weak institution, this would not have been necessary. Even so, after 1674, the duke of Lauderdale could risk no more meetings of parliament under his leadership for fear of dissent. The recourse to more manageable conventions of estates for essential grants of taxation was precisely because parliament had become too difficult to control.

The traditional unfavourable assessment of the historical significance of the early modern Scottish parliament, such as that promoted by Rait's extensive thematic study of the institution, assumes that the sole function of parliament was to resist the demands of an absolutist monarch. Yet, as a recent study into the Portuguese *cortes* has convincingly demonstrated, this 'crown versus parliament' interpretation often fails to take account of what contemporaries expected from parliamentary sessions. In early modern Portugal, the actual act of the political community coming together was in itself of great symbolic value.[36] Thus, in concentrating on supposed constitutional defects, it is easy to overlook the fact that in many European countries parliament was the main arena in which the most influential men of the realm came together to debate issues of common interest. Parliament had a vital role of legitimising the monarch's authority by approving his demands, but it was also a place where much other business, both private and public, was done.

It has been the incorporating union of 1707 that has defined the historical reputation of the early modern Scottish parliament. Similar to other European institutions that were either done away with or constitutionally downgraded by their rulers, the fact that these assemblies ceased to exist in an independent form has been taken as ample evidence of their weakness or unimportance. However, throughout the seventeenth century, unlike many of its continental counterparts, the Scottish parliament successfully resisted the implementation of royal absolutism and continued to possess the vital consent required for monetary supplies. The vociferous opposition towards the heavy-handed management of the estates and crown interference in their deliberations, a prominent feature of parliament in the Restoration era, was precisely because this was not normal procedure. Throughout its history, from medieval times until its final meeting in 1707, the Scottish parliament played an integral role in government, being consulted on a broad range of subjects and often exercising its right to resist and defeat proposition by the crown with which it disagreed. It says much about the power of the Scottish estates in a European context that when parliament was absorbed into a British institution in 1707, it was by their choice and with their consent, not by royal diktat.

Notes

1. See, for example, H. G. Koenigsberger, *Estates and Revolutions: Essays in Early Modern European History* (Ithaca, 1971), pp. 6–8 and A. R. Myers, *Parliaments and Estates in Europe to 1789* (London, 1975), pp. 91–2, for a damning assessment of the significance of the Scottish parliament.

2. J. Miller (ed.), *Absolutism in seventeenth-century Europe* (Basingstoke, 1990); G. Parker and L. M. Smith (eds), *The General Crisis of the seventeenth century* (London, 1978).

3. M. Graves, *The Parliaments of early modern Europe* (Harlow, 2001), pp. 159–65. For a comprehensive survey of the basic structure of the seventeenth-century Scottish parliament in a European context, see Young, 'The Scottish parliament in the seventeenth century: European perspectives', pp. 139–49.

4. NAS, PA2/22, f. 61r; *RPS*, 1641/4/2; NAS, PA2/39, ff. 1r–2v; *RPS*, 1705/6/2.

5. Occasionally the officers of state present at parliamentary sessions could exceed eight, although, in obedience to an act of 1617, eight was the maximum who could vote in proceedings. See NAS, PA2/19, f. 3r; *RPS*, 1617/5/11.

6. Rait, *Parliaments of Scotland*, pp. 278–83, 326–7; Terry, *Scottish Parliament*, pp. 1–9; K. M. Brown and A. J. Mann, 'Parliament and politics in Scotland, 1567–1707', in Brown and Mann (eds), *The History of the Scottish Parliament, volume II: Parliament and Politics, 1567–1707*, pp. 11–12, 28–9.

7. Young, *Scottish Parliament*, pp. 23, 26–9, 305–9; NAS, PA2/22, ff. 37r–39r; *RPS*, 1640/6/43.

8. J. L. Price, *Holland and the Dutch Republic in the Seventeenth Century: the Politics of Particularism* (Oxford, 1994), pp. 131–3; J. I. Israel, *The Dutch Republic: its Rise, Greatness and Fall, 1477–1806* (Oxford, 1995), pp. 279–81; Young, 'The Scottish parliament in the seventeenth century: European perspectives', p. 149.

9. Myers, *Parliaments and Estates in Europe*, pp. 30–1; R. Bonney, *The European Dynastic States, 1494–1660* (Oxford, 1991), pp. 219–21; Young, 'The Scottish parliament in the seventeenth century: European

perspectives', p. 150; X. Gil, 'Crown and *cortes* in early modern Aragon: reassessing revisionisms', *PER*, 13 (1993), pp. 120–1.

10 The method of election to the articles prior to 1603 is largely unknown, but the later reputation of the seventeenth-century committee has tended to attach itself to the entire history of the articles. It has been suggested that prior to the Restoration, the election procedure outlined above operated only in 1621 and 1633. Stevenson, *The Scottish Revolution*, pp. 167–8.

11 In a number of recent studies it has convincingly been argued that before the early seventeenth century, the monarch rarely, if ever, achieved total domination of the articles. When James VI eventually forced his own nominees on an intractable parliament in 1621, the outrage this caused indicated this was not normal procedure. See MacDonald, 'Deliberative processes in parliament', pp. 40–50 and Tanner, 'The lords of the articles before 1540', pp. 189–212.

12 G. Rystad, 'The estates of the realm, the monarchy and empire, 1611–1718', in M. F. Metcalf (ed.), *The Riksdag: A History of the Swedish Parliament* (New York, 1987), pp. 101–2; A. F. Upton, 'The *riksdag* of 1680 and the establishment of royal absolutism in Sweden', *The English Historical Review*, 102, 403 (1987), pp. 283, 293; A. F. Upton, 'Sweden', in Miller (ed.), *Absolutism in seventeenth-century Europe*, pp. 114–15; A. F. Upton, *Charles XI and Swedish Absolutism, 1660–1697* (Cambridge, 2001), pp. 32, 34–7.

13 Rystad, 'The estates of the realm, the monarchy and empire', pp. 98–101; Young, 'The Scottish parliament in the seventeenth century: European perspectives', pp. 154–5.

14 For examples of royal instructions to commissioners, see *Lauderdale Papers*, i, pp. 39–40 (1660), 103–5 (1662), 296–8 (1662), ii, pp. 184–7 (1670), 223–4 (1672), 234–6 (1673) and iii, p. 1 (1673). James's instructions as king in 1685 can be found in HMC, *The Manuscripts of the Duke of Buccleuch and Queensberry*, i, pp. 90–8.

15 See Mann, 'Inglorious revolution', pp. 134–40, for a detailed discussion of royal instructions to commissioners from the Restoration until the union.

16 A convention of estates in 1575 uniquely passed a diverse range of acts, albeit these were regarded as explicitly temporary legislation, to be confirmed in a future parliament. See NAS, PC1/7, pp. 295–313; *RPS*, A1575/3/1–15 and J. Goodare, 'The Scottish Parliament and its early modern "rivals"', *PER*, 24 (2004), pp. 149–50. Conventions, however, came to be regarded as meetings summoned for the sole purpose of granting taxation due to the dangerous precedent set by the 1643 meeting, which formally entered into a revolutionary alliance with the English parliament against Charles I. Young, *Scottish Parliament*, pp. 63–70 and Young, 'The Scottish parliament in the seventeenth century: European perspectives', pp. 142–3.

17 Rait, *Parliaments of Scotland*, pp. 154–8.

18 Bonney, *European Dynastic States*, pp. 322–3; Myers, *Parliaments and Estates in Europe*, pp. 102–4.

19 W. Beik, *Absolutism and Society in Seventeenth-century France: State Power and Provincial Aristocracy in Languedoc* (Cambridge, 1985), pp. 128–30, 140–6; Myers, *Parliaments and Estates in Europe*, p. 104; Bonney, *European Dynastic States*, pp. 327–8.

20 J. I. Fortea Pérez, 'The *cortes* of Castile and Philip II's fiscal policy', *PER*, 11 (1991), pp. 128–38; C. Jago, 'Crown and *cortes* in early modern Spain', *PER*, 12 (1992), pp. 181–5.

21 C. Jago, 'Habsburg absolutism and the *cortes* of Castile', *The American Historical Review*, 86 (1981), pp. 310–11, 314–22; I. A. A. Thompson, 'The end of the *cortes* of Castile', *PER*, 4 (1984), pp. 127–33; I. A. A. Thompson, *Crown and Cortes: Government, Institutions and Representation in early modern Castile* (Aldershot, 1993), pp. 42–5. See, however, C. Jago, 'Parliament, subsidies and constitutional change in Castile, 1601–1621', *PER*, 13 (1993), pp. 123–37, which puts forward the argument that the autonomous nature of consensual taxation was imperfectly realised and that many of the conditions imposed on the crown by the *cortes* were seldom met. A similar state of affairs existed in the *cortes* of Aragon, where the estates were free to present grievances for redress prior to the granting of subsidies. However, the crown frequently pressured or bribed individuals to withdraw their petitions. Gil, 'Crown and *cortes* in early modern Aragon', p. 115.

22 Graves, *Parliaments of early modern Europe*, p. 193.

23 The king formally accepted the taxation with the proviso, contained within the actual act, it was granted 'for as long as the conditions of this contract are observed and if any of them are broken it shall *ipso facto* cease'. I. A. A. Thompson, 'Castile', in Miller (ed.), *Absolutism in seventeenth-century Europe*, pp. 80–1.

24 Rystad, 'The estates of the realm, the monarchy and empire', pp. 102–4.

25 M. J. Braddick, *The Nerves of State: Taxation and the Financing of the English State, 1558–1714* (Manchester, 1996), pp. 148–51.

26 Goodare, 'Parliamentary taxation in Scotland', pp. 42–5, 49–52.

27 J. Miller, 'Introduction', in Miller (ed.), *Absolutism in Seventeenth-century Europe*, pp. 1–20.

28 K. J. V. Jespersen and E. L. Petersen, 'Two revolutions in early modern Denmark', in E. I. Kouri and T. Scott (eds), *Politics and Society in Reformation Europe: Essays for Sir Geoffrey Elton on his sixty-fifth Birthday* (London, 1986), pp. 488–98; Bonney, *European Dynastic States*, pp. 255–6, 358–9; Graves, *Parliaments of early modern Europe*, pp. 131–2.

29 Rystad, 'The estates of the realm, the monarchy and empire', pp. 73–9; Upton, 'Sweden', pp. 108–9, 114–15; Upton, 'The *riksdag* of 1680', pp. 285, 288–9, 293, 297–301.

30 J. Bérenger, 'The Austrian lands: Habsburg absolutism under Leopold I', in Miller (ed.), *Absolutism in seventeenth-century Europe*, pp. 158–9, 166–73; Graves, *Parliaments of early modern Europe*, pp. 137–9.

31 Myers, *Parliaments and Estates in Europe to 1789*, pp. 107–10; H. W. Koch, 'Brandenburg-Prussia', in Miller (ed.), *Absolutism in seventeenth-century Europe*, pp. 144–6; P. H. Wilson, 'The power to defend, or the defence of power: the conflict between duke and estates over defence provision, Württemberg, 1677–1793', *PER*, 12 (1992), pp. 25–45.

32 Goodare, 'The Scottish parliament in its British context, 1603–1707', p. 23.

33 NAS, PA2/33, f. 33r; *RPS*, 1689/3/94.

34 The estates met on average every two years between 1661 and 1688. Brown and Mann, 'Parliament and politics in Scotland, 1567–1707', pp. 11, 41.

35 *Lauderdale Papers*, ii, p. 164.

36 P. Cardim, 'Ceremonial and ritual in the *cortes* of Portugal (1581–1698)', *PER*, 12 (1992), pp. 1–15.

CONCLUSION

When the first session of the newly restored Scottish parliament came to a close in July 1661, Charles II could look back on recent events in his northern kingdom with considerable satisfaction. The right of the monarch to choose his own ministers, officers of state and privy councillors, to make war and peace, to summon and prorogue sessions of parliament and the revival of the key preparatory committee, the lords of the articles, had been granted with little more than a murmur of complaint from the gathered estates. Yet this state of affairs was by no means a foregone conclusion when Charles was restored to the throne in 1660 after twenty years of constitutional upheaval. Even the most optimistic royalist could never have predicted that in little over a year the crown would have achieved such a complete recovery of its powers. Nor could it have been anticipated that a chamber staffed by significant numbers of individuals who had previously sided with the covenanters would so readily agree to the revival of the prerogative powers necessary to keep parliament in check. The most contentious measure of the session was the rescissory act, which attempted to imagine away the years of revolution by abolishing all covenanting innovations and the more controversial reforms of Charles I. Yet even the group who voted against its passage (about forty in number) caused little meaningful disturbance. Those few who left the chamber rather than subscribe an oath of loyalty to the crown did not attempt to disrupt the rest of the proceedings or raise disorders in the localities. Instead, the majority slipped into political obscurity for the rest of the reign.

Only a small group of radical ministers made much fuss about the subsequent restoration of episcopal church government in the following session of parliament. Blamed for the mistakes of 1649–51 that had led to subjugation at the hands of Cromwell, they had been increasingly sidelined since the recalled committee of estates in 1660 took action against their rival meetings. Presbyterianism had become associated with rebellion and later disorders did little to dispel such suspicions. Episcopacy was thus revived not for theological reasons but because it was intrinsically more compatible with monarchical authority and the preservation of civil order than presbyterianism. Accepting an episcopalian established church did not mean acknowledging *jure divino* claims about divine authority, consenting to episcopal jurisdiction as per the English model or approval of enforced modes of liturgical discipline. Fearful of a repeat of the theocracy of the late 1640s, the political establishment promoted a more erastian religious settlement, confirmed by the 1669 act of supremacy that explicitly ratified the king's prerogative right to order the external government and policy of the church as he saw fit. The political impotence of the newly restored bishops was made clear by the policies of accommodation and indulgence offered to religious dissenters throughout the late 1660s and into the 1670s, which were pursued against the will of many of the episcopal clergy. Amid escalating unrest by religious non-conformists, it was in practical rather than doctrinal terms that episcopacy was defended. As a result, the failure of the established church to develop a convincing theological case for its existence, combined with a rise in secular anti-clericalism amongst the ranks of the nobility in particular, meant that by the revolutionary period of 1688–9 episcopal church government was all too easily dispensed with in favour of a return to presbyterianism.

For the Scottish nobility, an alliance with the crown was the best way of recovering their power, wealth and privileges lost to the covenanters and latterly to Cromwell. The nobles dominated negotiations with General Monck in 1659–60 and successfully ensured that their chosen method of interim government, the committee of estates from 1651, was reinstated. The key posts in the new administration went to individuals who had remained loyal to the crown throughout the last decade, even though almost all had been active in the covenanting regime at some point in their political career. In the localities, many of those who had been ousted from their positions after the failure of the Engagement were reinstated. There is evidence of managed elections for the first parliamentary session, but it is also true that there was a genuine royalist reaction within Scotland. Accepting Charles as monarch meant, in the short-term at least, an end to the quartering of English soldiers, to the levy of cess and to the general disorder of the last decade in particular. Scotland had played a subordinate role in the republican regime and the prospect of advancement in a new administration was not just tempting for ambitious members of the nobility. Positions in councils across the land were up for grabs and the best way of securing such offices was to demonstrate loyalty to the crown. In parliament, the delayed implementation of an indemnity act helped to obtain the support of those who feared retribution for past behaviour. One covenanting innovation survived: the system of oaths to demonstrate loyalty. Those who refused to subscribe both an oath of fealty and declaration of public trust were not just removed from parliament but from all positions of authority.

The scramble for public office blighted the first few years of the newly restored parliament's existence. Factional divisions and corruption proliferated under the earl of Middleton, who soon became increasingly obsessed with ensuring that it was he alone who dominated Scottish affairs. The ease by which Middleton persuaded the gathered estates to enact the audacious billeting plot to oust his main rivals was ample evidence of the initial submissiveness of parliament. However, Middleton made a disastrous miscalculation, operating too independently from the absentee monarch, and he paid with his job. Parliament was quick to change its allegiances, however. At the command of Lauderdale, they renounced their former actions in order to preserve royal favour. It seemed that whatever the king's commissioner asked, the estates were quick to grant.

Two conventions of estates were summoned in the mid-1660s solely for monetary reasons, despite crown claims that the more than generous yearly annuity of £40,000 sterling granted to the king in 1661 would mean an end to such future grants of taxation. As in England, the crown over-estimated its finances and the resulting shortage was compounded by a serious downturn in trade. Although the conventions were assembled to provide a supply for English military action against the Dutch, it was the perpetual problem of religious dissent that necessitated first a standing army, then a large militia, to ensure order in the localities. The government had few problems securing generous fiscal grants from the two conventions, which were once more eager to express their loyalty to the crown, but the imposition of successive taxes to pay for the expansion in manpower (and the use of troops to collect these funds) made the royalist administration more unpopular in certain localities than ever. Armed rebellion broke out in 1666 because the government had underestimated the strength of feeling against such quartering of troops and especially the submissiveness of those ministers who had been forcibly removed from their parishes by the ecclesiastical legislation of 1663. As the royalist administration was to learn from bitter experience, repressive religious policies only bred discontent.

Despite contemporary claims to the contrary, the Pentland rising was never a serious threat to the stability of the Scottish government. Its main consequence was that it exposed the limits of the regime's authority in the localities. Lauderdale's commanding position at court depended on the illusion that all was well north of the border and such a high profile demonstration of the ineptitude of some of his deputies in Scotland provided the excuse for their removal. The bishops, headed by Archbishop Sharp, were forced into accepting the royal supremacy in church matters and new policies of toleration. The earl of Rothes was demoted to the post of chancellor and the large numbers of troops, the power-base of his support, were disbanded. A standing army, something no other monarch had possessed, had been appointed as a means of crushing any opposition to the restitution of royal power, to prevent any popular uprising such as that of the covenanters. Yet providing for permanent troops was something for which the Scottish economy was never designed. The army proved to be a massive drain on resources and, with a significant depression in trade caused by war and continuing disagreements with England over commercial tariffs, the Scottish economy languished in the doldrums throughout the reign of Charles II.

Finally unencumbered by any political rivals, Lauderdale was appointed royal commissioner to parliament in 1669. The deputies he appointed to oversee business in Scotland after Rothes's fall, the earl of Tweeddale and Sir Robert Moray, had few ambitions to succeed to Lauderdale's position. Indeed, Moray could only be persuaded to stay a year before he returned to his scientific studies in London. Tweeddale had initial success, especially in curbing some of the corruption that had flourished under Middleton and Rothes, and he spearheaded a number of new initiatives, the most significant being the idea of closer political ties with England. Some form of union had initially been suggested as a means of bringing both countries to a trade agreement and negotiations for political union began largely as a result of the failure of these talks. There were benefits for everyone except crucially the English. The king believed union would wean his northern kingdom away from their traditional commercial and political associations with the Dutch, with whom the English were currently at war, and that he could make use of Scottish votes in a British parliament; the leading Scottish politicians were assured of promotion and an end to the trading restrictions enshrined in the navigation acts. Yet, when parliament met to approve the proposals, it became clear that there was no broad support for such an initiative: Lauderdale recognised as much when he refused to allow the chamber to vote on the membership of a commission to treat with English representatives. A number of vocal opponents constantly challenged the government's plans, and, after consultation with key members of the articles, even Lauderdale was forced to admit to the king that such a measure could not be pushed though an unwilling chamber.

Despite the recent erosion of parliamentary powers and the submissiveness of previous sessions to crown demands, there still existed a widespread belief that parliament had a right to be consulted on a frequent basis by the king, especially on a proposal that would have resulted in a reduction in its powers or, ultimately, its demise. Within the next few years, after the failure of the abortive union scheme, the summoning of regular parliamentary sessions was a familiar demand of the fledgling parliamentary opposition that emerged in response to the authoritarian ministry of the duke of Lauderdale. Parliament had an essential role in legitimising monarchical government and attempts to rule through the privy council or by proclamation alone were strenuously opposed. However, the Restoration settlement had granted the king the sole right to summon and prorogue parliament. Thus, in practice, beyond numerous appeals to the monarch to convene a new session, the estates were effectively powerless to see their demands met.

Although the subsequent failure of the union proposal initially quietened opposition, when parliament reconvened in 1672 a number of other perceived constitutional abuses ignited further protests. A measure removing the monopoly of trading rights from the royal burghs was interpreted as an attack on their ancient privileges, and the advocates, many of whom represented burgh seats in parliament, were enraged by the unprecedented advancement of a number of uneducated men to their ranks. Regardless of the government's true intentions, both these initiatives were regarded as ill-disguised attempt at subjugation. Lauderdale's personal behaviour as royal commissioner in parliament was also significant. His paranoia that any opposing view was a threat to his own standing and that of the crown roused further discontent amongst the estates.

Despite the emergence of some disquieting voices of dissent within the previously submissive parliament, the crown faced problems only when opposition became widespread over the estates. The growing discontent of the burghs, and to a lesser extent the shires, found leadership in the guise of the duke of Hamilton. Consistently overlooked for government position, Hamilton seems to have been motivated mainly by his exclusion from political favour. He found sympathy with the earls of Tweeddale and Kincardine, who had both been cast aside by Lauderdale on little more than a whim. In 1673, genuine discontent over monopolies provided the excuse for making a broader attack on Lauderdale's ministry. This was unexpected since Lauderdale believed that the restrictions of the Restoration settlement prevented such opposition from being elected. Crucially, there was no such restriction on members of the nobility, who exploited existing disgruntlement amongst the other estates against the monopolies in particular. The lesser estates paid severely for their involvement. To purge those implicated in the attack on Lauderdale, restrictions on burgh elections were rigorously enforced and attempts to regulate advocates led to a long and bitter dispute. Cases of controverted elections, a rare occurrence at the beginning of the reign, multiplied, necessitating the regular establishment of a special parliamentary committee to settle the disputes. It was ample evidence of increasing discontent in the localities; a worrying development since, aside from the activities of presbyterian religious dissenters in mainly Lowland regions, most areas had remained remarkably co-operative with crown demands.

Hamilton and his supporters made their protests known in parliament because it was believed that this was the arena in which grievances could be redressed. It is clear that the royalist administration did not share this view. When the opposition's attempts failed, they were forced to journey to court to represent their complaints directly to the monarch. This too had little success. Lauderdale, from the beginning of the Restoration, had realised that real influence depended on having the king's ear. Even when he was absent from London, he had a channel of communication open that the opposition could not hope to rival. It was he and often he alone who kept Charles informed of events in his northern kingdom, giving some idea of the importance the king placed on Scottish events. As long as there was no danger of insurgency in Scotland, the king was content to delegate responsibility for its government to his chief minister.

After the events of 1673, there was a marked reduction in the role of the estates. Lauderdale became increasingly tired with parliament because it was too difficult to control and too dangerous, especially when he was facing similar hostility from south of the border. Requests for a new meeting were consistently ignored until the financial situation necessitated a further grant of taxation. A convention of estates was again called in 1678 because it was limited only to discussions on tax. Yet Hamilton and his 'party' of followers, benefiting from increased organisation, managed to turn the issue of controverted elections into another attack on the commissioner. Although the opposition did not disrupt the passage of the supply, their repeated attacks on Lauderdale's personal conduct within parliament were highly damaging. This, coupled with the military debacle of the Highland Host, combined to make Lauderdale's position as chief Scottish minister increasingly untenable.

Since the Restoration, partly as a result of the practical difficulties caused by an absentee monarch, it had been the royal commissioner to the Scottish parliament that wielded effective political power rather than the king. As a result, opposition was no longer restricted to criticism of the monarch himself but increasingly came to be directed against individual officers of state or the executive. Lauderdale's refusal to demit the office of king's commissioner in the intervening period between parliamentary sessions attracted censure, but it was the perceived deficiencies in his personal character and his authoritarian conduct in parliament that were most controversial. Linked to this was concerns about general constitutional abuses within parliament and a tendency for the king to vest power in the hands of what some contemporaries regarded as a potential dictatorship, bypassing established institutions such as parliament and privy council and answerable only to the crown. Ironically, in his later dealings with parliament, James was frequently criticised for arbitrariness when Lauderdale had often been guiltier. The significant difference, however, was that whereas a crown-appointed minister could be removed, the heir to the throne could not.

The meeting of the convention of estates in 1678 was Lauderdale's last as royal commissioner. Although his influence had been reduced somewhat due to ill health, in 1680 the English parliament achieved what their Scottish counterparts could not: securing Lauderdale's retirement from politics. English opposition to the continuance of Lauderdale's rule was crucial. It is unlikely that Charles would have removed his foremost Scottish minister on the demands of parliament alone. Indeed, Hamilton had been seeking as much for a decade without result. It was only when opposition both north and south of the border was in likelihood of uniting did the king act. It was Charles's fear of English, not Scottish, disaffection that led him to seek conciliatory policies. When this occurred, Lauderdale was at once as disposable as both Middleton and Rothes had been.

With Lauderdale's retirement ended a form of government that had dominated Scotland since the Restoration. No individual was ever to match his twenty-year supremacy over the Scottish administration, nor was any other Scot able to succeed to his enviable position as the king's closest advisor. Moderates and radicals alike on both sides of the border may have hated Lauderdale precisely for these reasons, but his legacy for succeeding commissioners of parliament was to reveal the true potential of the office. The duke of York, for one, understood that Lauderdale's longevity as secretary and commissioner lay in his control of the flow of information to the monarch. Thus, when James succeeded to the post of commissioner left vacant by Lauderdale's departure in 1681, he followed his predecessor's example and set up a secret council staffed by seven leading councillors. This process continued when he was created king: vital decision-making was carried out at court and power was concentrated in the hands of a few key individuals.

James's short period of exile in Edinburgh after Lauderdale's retirement was at first successful, partly because few dared to voice discontent about the heir to the throne in his presence, especially criticism regarding his Catholic faith, and because many of the noble leaders of the parliamentary opposition were initially satisfied with court patronage. Yet many of the old tensions remained. In complete contrast to Lauderdale, James played a minimal role in parliament. Nevertheless, this did not mean that there was no need to control the chamber and there were familiar attempts to stifle debate. Although the membership of the articles was opened up to reflect a breadth of opinion not previously seen in the Restoration period, blatant attempts were made to push through their decisions with the minimum of discussion or amendment from the rest of the chamber. Yet, despite further determined efforts to restrict the estates' input into legislation, it was in parliament that James's intended toleration for Scottish Catholics in 1686 was comprehensively defeated. In spite of the numerous restrictions on who could elect and be elected and the attempted suppression of free debate that had been prominent features of parliament throughout the Restoration era, the estates were not entirely impotent, as James found to his cost.

What did the fledgling parliamentary opposition that emerged during the Restoration era represent? For one, it felt no affinity with the presbyterian dissenters that were involved in armed rebellion against the crown. Indeed, the duke of Hamilton, the noble leader of the nascent political party that emerged in the 1670s, had often advocated more repressive measures against religious non-conformists, hoping to benefit financially from the involvement of his troops. The parliamentary opposition also remained consistently loyal to the crown, even initially to James VII as a Catholic monarch, and it was inconceivable that those who sided with Hamilton would go to the lengths of an armed struggle. It was hostility to the long tenure of the duke of Lauderdale and exclusion from political office that first galvanised noble involvement, but it is clear that not all of those involved by 1678 could have hoped to personally benefit from the removal of one deeply unpopular minister. Nevertheless, by restricting their complaints to mainly constitutional issues, Hamilton's party manifestly lacked a popular dimension that could attract widespread public support. Unlike the earl of Shaftesbury and the developing Whig party south of the border who exploited the emotive issue of anti-Catholicism in the exclusion crisis that gripped England from the late 1670s, the reluctance of Hamilton and his allies to forge closer links with the established radical presbyterian opposition ultimately restricted what they could hope to achieve.

Despite such limitations, as was evident in the union debates of 1669 and in later disputes when requests for the recall of the estates were refused, there existed a fairly universal belief that parliament had a significant role to play in the ruling of the country, even if the crown was often reluctant to acknowledge it. Yet this was in conflict with the system of government revived by the Restoration settlement. With the comprehensive reassertion of the royal prerogative and the restitution of the lords of the articles, the estates were purposefully left with little input into the drafting of legislation, and, under Lauderdale in particular, any suggested alterations to the pre-planned legislative programme were positively discouraged. Nevertheless, at almost every meeting of the estates there was resistance to this means of government. Few remnants of the covenanting era survived the Restoration but it is clear that some of the ideology behind the constitutional revolution of the 1640s endured. The escalating problem of religious non-conformity, leading eventually to armed rebellion, was ample demonstration of the continuation of covenanting beliefs. Amongst sections of the political elites some aspects of covenanting political thought survived, albeit in a watered down form. For, even after the unprecedented reassertion of monarchical power in 1661, it was still believed that parliament had a role in limiting unrestrained royal authority.

This was especially true towards the end of the reign of Charles II, when discontent towards the increasingly arbitrary rule of Lauderdale reached its peak and concerns over the succession of the throne to a Catholic heir grew. The publication of Sir James Dalrymple of Stair's *Institutions of the Law of Scotland* in 1681, with its emphasis on the

divine and natural basis of law and its superiority over the royal prerogative, articulated theories which had a long historical pedigree.[1]
Harking back to the political philosophy of the sixteenth-century the-
orist and historian George Buchanan and the ideology expounded by
committed covenanters such as Samuel Rutherford, radical presbyterians in the Restoration era justified their armed struggle against the
king on the grounds that subjects had a right to resist a tyrannical
monarch. Even amongst moderates within the political community, a
contractual monarchy, with a significant role for national institutions
such as parliament, privy council and the court of session, was celebrated as the best means of royal government.[2]

Such theories of the limited nature of kingship and the constitutional importance of institutions such as parliament became the basis
for a new political agenda that can be followed through to the 1688–9
Williamite revolution and beyond. The growth in discontent after the
parliament of 1685–6 was dissolved demonstrated that the opposition that had first appeared in the reign of Charles II was not centred
against one particularly dominant individual, such as Lauderdale, but
rather against a belief that parliament was a subservient body, with a
minimal role to play in policy. When James VII was deposed, the
Scottish crown was offered conditionally to William and Mary.
Subsequently, throughout the 1690s, the country party, led by
Andrew Fletcher of Saltoun, sought to reduce crown powers. As
detailed in his famous policy of limitations, Fletcher's concept of a
constitutional monarchy subject to an annual parliament that had
powers to appoint committees and officers of state was the complete
antithesis of parliament's role as defined in the constitutional settlement enacted at the Restoration.

Notes

1. Sir James Dalrymple of Stair, *The Institutions of the Law of Scotland,
   deduced from the originals and collected with the civil, canon and feudal
   laws, and with the customs of neighbouring nations* (Edinburgh, 1681).
2. To counter such theories and coinciding with James, duke of York's presence in Scotland from 1679–82, there was a new flourishing of royalism,
   best seen in Sir George Mackenzie of Rosehaugh's treatise on absolute
   monarchy, *Jus Regium: or the just and solid foundations of monarchy in
   general, and more especially of the monarchy of Scotland, maintain'd
   against Buchannan, Naphtali, Dolman, Milton, &c.* (Edinburgh, 1684).
   For further discussion on this tract, see Jackson, *Restoration Scotland*,
   pp. 54–9.

BIBLIOGRAPHY

Manuscript Sources

British Library, London

Additional Mss

Lauderdale Papers, c.1647–82
Add Mss 23113–23138
Add Mss 23242–23245
Add Mss 23247–23248
Add Mss 35125

Drumlanrig Castle, Thornhill, Dumfries

Buccleuch Muniments

Transcripts of letters addressed to William Douglas, earl of Queensberry.

National Register of Archives for Scotland

Drumlanrig Castle, Survey 1275, Bundle 1176, 'Coppie minuts of parliament holden at Edinburgh, 23 Aprile 1685'.

Glasgow Archives and Special Collections, Mitchell Library, Glasgow

Stirling family of Keir Muniments

T-SK 11/1, various correspondence, 1613–1791.

Stirling-Maxwell family of Pollok Muniments

T-PM 108, 109, 113, 114, various correspondence, 1659–78.

Glasgow University Library, Glasgow

Special Collections
Mss Gen 210, letter book of Archbishop James Sharp.

National Archives of Scotland, Edinburgh

Acts of the Parliaments of Scotland

PA2/26–32, parliamentary register, 1 January 1661–15 June 1686.
PA7/8–12, supplementary warrants and parliamentary papers, 1650–89.
PA8/1, acts etc. of the conventions of estates, 1665–78.
PA11/12, registers and minute books of the committee of estates, 23 August–13 October 1660.
PA11/13, minute book of the committee of estates, 9 October–8 December 1660.
PA7/25, parliamentary commissions.

Exchequer Papers

E6/1, Sederunt books, 8 July 1667–8 March 1672.
E6/2, Sederunt books, 11 June 1672–26 February 1676.
E6/3, Sederunt books, 21 November 1676–13 April 1682.
E9/3, Warrants of the Treasury register, January–December 1669.

Gifts and Deposits

GD6/1108, Biel Muniments, 'The calling and proceedings of the convention of estates holden at Edinburgh, the 26 Junii 1678, by the duke of Lauderdale, his majesties commissioner'.
GD31/121, Papers of the family of Fea of Clestrain, Orkney, correspondence of A. Gibson to Henry Graham of Breckness.
GD45/14/110, Papers of the Maule Family, earls of Dalhousie, letters from Lord Brechin at London to his father.
GD90/2/260, Yule Collection, Scroll warrant book of the secretary for Scotland, 20 August 1660–4 July 1670.
GD97/3/150 (RH4/124/1), Papers of the Edmonstone Family of Duntreath.
GD406/1, Papers of the Douglas Hamilton family, dukes of Hamilton and Brandon, correspondence of the dukes of Hamilton, 1563–1712.
GD406/2 and GD406/M1 and M9, Uncatalogued Hamilton Papers.

National Library of Scotland, Edinburgh

Advocates' Manuscripts

Adv Mss 25/6/9, 'Note on decisions in parliament regarding controverted elections'.

Almack Collection

Mss 3922, Correspondence of the Maitland family, 1598–1679.

Customs Accounts

Mss 2263, 'A History of Events, 1635–62'.

Dalrymple Collection

Mss 3423, Lauderdale correspondence, 1656–62.
Mss 3424, Lauderdale correspondence, 1663–65.

Miscellaneous Collections

Mss 9375, Complaints against the duke of Lauderdale, December 1674.
Mss 5049–50, Correspondence of Sir Robert Moray to Alexander Bruce, second earl of Kincardine, 1658–65.

Papers of Charles Kirkpatrick Sharpe

Mss 2512, Letters to John Maitland, duke of Lauderdale from Archbishops Sharp and Burnet.

Watson Collection

Mss 595, Miscellaneous papers.
Mss 597, Papers of the earls of Lauderdale, 1641–97.

Wodrow Manuscripts

Quarto XXXV, Miscellaneous papers, 1660–78.
Quarto LXIII, 'A brief narration of the coming in of prelacie againe in this kirk' by Robert Douglas.
Octavo XI, Miscellaneous, including letters of the duke of Lauderdale to Archibald Primrose, clerk register, 1651–74.

Yester Papers

Mss 7001, Catalogue of the Yester Papers.
Mss 7003–9, Correspondence, 1661–84.
Mss 7023, Lauderdale letters, 1664–72.
Mss 7024–5, Letters of John Hay, earl of Tweeddale, 1660–96.
Mss 7033–4, Miscellaneous papers, 1660–79.
Mss 7121, Letters of Gilbert Burnet to the earl of Tweeddale, 1669–76.
Mss 14403, Correspondence, 1666–88.
Mss 14406, Correspondence, 1645–74.

Mss 14414, Political papers, 1666–1703.
Mss 14417, Letters of Andrew Hay, son of John Hay, clerk register, 1672–99.
Mss 14488, Political papers, 1660–97.
Mss 14489–90, Papers relating to public affairs, 1660–78.
Mss 14492, 'The proceedings of the commissioners of both kingdoms, 1667–68'.

Yule Collection

Mss 3134, 'Memorial on the differences between the earl of Tweeddale and the duke of Lauderdale from 1666 to 1682'.
Mss 3136, Lauderdale letters, principally to John Hay, earl of Tweeddale, 1659–72.
Mss 3177, Transcripts of letters from Sir George Mackenzie, 1670–89.

PRINTED PRIMARY SOURCES

Airy, Osmund (ed.), 'Letters addressed to the earl of Lauderdale', in *The Camden Miscellany*, vol. 8 (London, 1883), pp. 1–43.
Airy, Osmund (ed.), *The Lauderdale Papers*, 3 vols (London, 1884–5).
Anon., *To His Grace His Majesties High Commissioner and the High Court of Parliament, the humble address of the synod of Aberdeen* (Aberdeen?, 1661).
Anon., *Some farther matter of fact relating to the administration of affairs in Scotland under the duke of Lauderdale, humbly offered to his majesties consideration* (London?, 1679).
Anon., *Some particular matters of fact relating to the administration of affairs in Scotland under the duke of Lauderdale, humbly offered to your majesties consideration, in obedience to your royal command* (London?, 1679).
Anon., *The Declaration of the Rebels in Scotland* (Edinburgh, 1679).
Baillie, Robert, *The letters and journals of Robert Baillie, principal of the University of Glasgow, 1637–1662, edited from the author's manuscripts*, D. Laing (ed.), 3 vols (Edinburgh, 1841–2).
Burnet, Gilbert, *A History of His Own Time*, O. Airy (ed.), 2 vols (Oxford, 1897–1900).
Burnet, Gilbert, *A Supplement to Burnet's History of My Own Time*, H. C. Foxcroft (ed.) (Oxford, 1902).
Calendar of State Papers, Domestic Series, March 1st to October 31st, 1673, F. H. Blackburne Daniell (ed.) (London, 1902).
Calendar of State Papers, Domestic Series, November 1st, 1673 to February 28th, 1675, F. H. Blackburne Daniell (ed.) (London, 1904).
Calendar of State Papers, Domestic Series, March 1st, 1677 to February 28th, 1678, F. H. Blackburne Daniell (ed.) (London, 1911).

Calendar of State Papers, Domestic Series, March 1st, 1678 to December 31st, 1678, with addenda 1674 to 1679, F. H. Blackburne Daniell (ed.) (London, 1913).

Calendar of State Papers, Domestic Series, January 1st, 1679 to August 31st, 1680, F. H. Blackburne Daniell (ed.) (London, 1915).

Campbell, Archibald, *My Lord Marquis of Argyle, his speech upon the Scaffold, the 27 of May 1661* (Edinburgh, 1661).

Campbell, Archibald, *The speech of the earl of Argyle at his trial on the 12th of December, 1681* (London, 1682).

Clerk of Penicuik, Sir John, *History of the Union of Scotland and England by Sir John Clerk of Penicuik*, D. Douglas (ed.) (Edinburgh, 1993).

Dalrymple, Sir David, *A Catalogue of the Lords of Session, from the Institution of the College of Justice in the year 1532, with Historical Notes* (Edinburgh, 1794).

Douglas, Robert, *A sermon preached at the down-sitting of the Parliament of Scotland, January 1 1660/1* (Edinburgh?, 1661).

Extracts from the records of the burgh of Edinburgh, 1655–1665, M. Wood (ed.) (Edinburgh, 1940).

Extracts from the records of the burgh of Edinburgh, 1665–1680, M. Wood (ed.) (Edinburgh, 1950).

Extracts from the records of the burgh of Glasgow, vols ii–iv, J. D. Marwick and R. Renwick (eds) (Edinburgh, 1876–1911).

Firth, C. H. (ed.), *The Clarke Papers*, 4 vols (London, 1901).

Fraser, William (ed.), *The Stirlings of Keir and their Family Papers* (Edinburgh, 1858).

Fraser, William (ed.), *Memoirs of the Maxwells of Pollok*, 2 vols (Edinburgh, 1863).

Fraser, William (ed.), *The Chiefs of Grant*, 3 vols (Edinburgh, 1883).

[Hickes, George], *Ravillac Redivivus, being a Narrative of the late Tryal of Mr James Mitchell, a Conventicle preacher, who was executed the 18 of January, 1677 for an attempt which he made on the sacred person of the Archbishop of St Andrews* (London, 1678).

Historical Manuscripts Commission, *The manuscripts of the duke of Hamilton (Eleventh Report, appendix, part vi)* (London, 1887).

Historical Manuscripts Commission, *The manuscripts of his grace the duke of Buccleuch and Queensberry, preserved at Drumlanrig Castle (Fifteenth Report, appendix, part viii)*, 2 vols (London, 1897–1903).

Historical Manuscripts Commission, *Report on the Laing manuscripts preserved in the University of Edinburgh (Seventh Report)*, 2 vols (London, 1914).

Historical Manuscripts Commission, *Supplementary report of the manuscripts of the duke of Hamilton (Twenty-First Report)* (London, 1932).

Hyde, Edward, *The life of Edward, earl of Clarendon . . . written by himself*, 3 vols (1759).

Innes, Cosmo and Thomas Thomson (eds), *The Acts of the Parliament of Scotland*, vols v–viii (Edinburgh, 1820, 1870).

Lauder of Fountainhall, Sir John, *Chronological Notes of Scottish Affairs, from 1680 till 1701, being chiefly taken from the diary of Lord Fountainhall*, W. Scott (ed.) (Edinburgh, 1822).

Lauder of Fountainhall, Sir John, *Historical Observes of Memorable Occurrents in Church and State, from October 1680 to April 1686, by Sir John Lauder of Fountainhall*, D. Laing and A. Urquhart (eds) (Edinburgh, 1840).

Lauder of Fountainhall, Sir John, *Historical Notices of Scotish Affairs, selected from the manuscripts of Sir John Lauder of Fountainhall, Bart., one of the Senators of the College of Justice*, D. Laing (ed.), 2 vols (Edinburgh, 1848).

Lauder of Fountainhall, Sir John, *Journals of Sir John Lauder of Fountainhall, with his Observations on Public Affairs and other Memoranda, 1665–1676*, D. Crawford (ed.) (Edinburgh, 1900).

'Letters from John, earl of Lauderdale, and others, to Sir John Gilmour, president of session', in Scottish History Society, Henry M. Paton (ed.), *Miscellany of the Scottish History Society*, v (Edinburgh, 1933), pp. 109–94.

'Letters from John, earl of Lauderdale to John, second earl of Tweeddale and others', in Scottish History Society, Henry M. Paton (ed.), *Miscellany of the Scottish History Society*, vi (Edinburgh, 1939), pp. 113–240.

Lindsay, Colin, third earl of Balcarres, *Memoirs Touching the Revolution in Scotland by Colin, earl of Balcarres, presented to King James II at St Germains, 1690*, Lord Lindsay (ed.) (Edinburgh, 1841).

Mackenzie of Rosehaugh, Sir George, *Memoirs of the Affairs of Scotland from the Restoration of Charles II*, T. Thomson (ed.) (Edinburgh, 1821).

Maidment, James (ed.), *A Book of Scottish Pasquils, 1658–1715* (Edinburgh, 1868).

Miscellany of the Maitland Club, consisting of original papers and other documents illustrative of the history and literature of Scotland, vol. iii, part 1 (Edinburgh, 1843).

Nicoll, John, *A diary of public transactions and other occurrences, chiefly in Scotland, from January 1650 to June 1667*, D. Laing (ed.) (Edinburgh, 1836).

Paterson, John, *Tandem Bona Causa Triumphat, or Scotland's Late Misery bewailed, and the Honour and Loyalty of this Ancient Kingdom asserted in a Sermon preached before His Majesties High Commissioner, and the Honourable Parliament of the Kingdom of Scotland. At Edinburgh the 17 day of February 1661* (Edinburgh, 1661).

Records of the Convention of the Royal Burghs of Scotland, with extracts from other records relating to the affairs of the burghs of Scotland, 1295–1711, vols iii–iv, J. D. Marwick (ed) (Edinburgh, 1878–80).

The Records of the Parliaments of Scotland to 1707, K. M. Brown et al. (eds) (St Andrews, forthcoming).

The Register of the Privy Council of Scotland, third series, i (1661–64), P. Hume-Brown (ed.) (Edinburgh, 1908).

The Register of the Privy Council of Scotland, third series, ii (1665–69), P. Hume-Brown (ed.) (Edinburgh, 1909).

The Register of the Privy Council of Scotland, third series, iii (1669–72), P. Hume-Brown (ed.) (Edinburgh, 1910).

The Register of the Privy Council of Scotland, third series, iv (1673–76), P. Hume-Brown (ed.) (Edinburgh, 1911).

The Register of the Privy Council of Scotland, third series, v (1676–78), P. Hume-Brown (ed.) (Edinburgh, 1912).

The Register of the Privy Council of Scotland, third series, vi (1678–80), P. Hume-Brown (ed.) (Edinburgh, 1914).

The Register of the Privy Council of Scotland, third series, vii (1681–84), P. Hume-Brown (ed.) (Edinburgh, 1915).

The Register of the Privy Council of Scotland, third series, viii (1683–84), P. Hume-Brown (ed.) (Glasgow, 1915).

The Register of the Privy Council of Scotland, third series, ix (1684), H. Paton (ed.) (Edinburgh, 1924).

The Register of the Privy Council of Scotland, third series, x (1684–85), H. Paton (ed.) (Edinburgh, 1927).

Sharpe, C. K. (ed.), *Letters from the Lady Margaret Kennedy to John, duke of Lauderdale* (Edinburgh, 1828).

Sharpe, C. K. and Sir G. Sinclair (eds), *Letters from Archibald, earl of Argyll to John, duke of Lauderdale* (Edinburgh, 1829).

[Stewart of Goodtrees, Sir James], *An Accompt of Scotland's grievances by reason of the duke of Lauderdale's ministrie, humbly tendered to his majestie* (Edinburgh, c.1674).

[Stewart of Goodtrees, Sir James and John Stirling], *Naphtali, or, The wrestlings of the church of Scotland for the kingdom of Christ, contained in a true and short deduction thereof, from the beginning of the reformation of religion, until the year 1667* (Edinburgh, 1667).

Terry, Charles S. (ed.), *The Cromwellian Union: Papers relating to the Negotiations for an Incorporating Union between England and Scotland, 1651–1652, with an appendix of papers relating to the negotiations in 1670* (Edinburgh, 1902).

'Thirty-four letters written to James Sharp by the duke and duchess of Lauderdale', in Scottish History Society, *Miscellany of the Scottish History Society*, i (Edinburgh, 1893), pp. 229–92.

Turner, Sir James, *Memoirs of His Own Life and Times*, T. Thomson (ed.) (Edinburgh, 1829).

Wodrow, Robert, *The History of the Sufferings of the Church of Scotland from the Restoration to the Revolution*, R. Burns (ed.), 4 vols (Glasgow, 1828–30).

PRINTED SECONDARY SOURCES

Airy, Osmund, 'The Lauderdale Mss in the British Museum, 26 vols', *The Quarterly Review*, 57 (1884), pp. 407–39.

Airy, Osmund, 'Lauderdale, 1670–82', *The English Historical Review*, 1, 3 (1886), pp. 445–69.

Allan, David, *Philosophy and Politics in later Stuart Scotland: Neo-Stoicism, Culture and Ideology in an age of crisis, 1540–1690* (East Linton, 2000).

Beik, William, *Absolutism and society in seventeenth-century France: state power and provincial aristocracy in Languedoc* (Cambridge, 1985).

Bonney, Richard, *The European Dynastic States, 1494–1660* (Oxford, 1991).

Braddick, Michael J., *The Nerves of State: Taxation and the Financing of the English State, 1558–1714* (Manchester, 1996).

Brown, Keith M., 'The vanishing emperor: British kingship and its decline, 1603–1707', in Roger A. Mason (ed.), *Scots and Britons: Political Thought and the Union of 1603* (Cambridge, 1994), pp. 58–87.

Brown, Keith M. and Alastair J. Mann (eds), *The History of the Scottish Parliament, volume II: Parliament and Politics, 1567–1707* (Edinburgh, 2005).

Brown, Keith M. and Roland J. Tanner (eds), *The History of the Scottish Parliament, volume I: Parliament and Politics, 1235–1560* (Edinburgh, 2004).

Brunton, George and David Haig, *An Historical Account of the Senators of the College of Justice from its Institution in 1532* (Edinburgh, 1832).

Buckroyd, Julia, 'The dismissal of Archbishop Alexander Burnet, 1669', *Records of the Scottish Church History Society*, 18 (1973), pp. 149–55.

Buckroyd, Julia, '*Mercurius Caledonius* and its immediate successors, 1661', *The Scottish Historical Review*, 54 (1975), pp. 11–21.

Buckroyd, Julia, 'The Resolutioners and the Scottish nobility in the early months of 1660', *Studies in Church History*, 12 (1975), pp. 245–52.

Buckroyd, Julia, *Church and State in Scotland, 1661–1681* (Edinburgh, 1980).

Buckroyd, Julia, 'Anti-clericalism in Scotland during the Restoration' in Norman Macdougall (ed.), *Church, Politics and Society: Scotland 1408–1929* (Edinburgh, 1983), pp. 167–85.

Buckroyd, Julia, 'Bridging the gap: Scotland, 1659–1660', *The Scottish Historical Review*, 66 (1987), pp. 1–25.

Buckroyd, Julia, *The Life of James Sharp, Archbishop of St Andrews, 1618–1689: A Political Biography* (Edinburgh, 1987).

Cardim, Pedro, 'Ceremonial and ritual in the *cortes* of Portugal (1581–1698)', *Parliaments, Estates and Representation*, 12 (1992), pp. 1–15.

Clarke, Aidan, *Prelude to Restoration in Ireland: The End of the Commonwealth, 1659–1660* (Cambridge, 1999).

Cowan, Ian B., 'The Covenanters: a revision article', *The Scottish Historical Review*, 47 (1968), pp. 35–52.

Cowan, Ian B., *The Scottish Covenanters, 1660–1688* (London, 1976).

Davies, Godfrey and Paul Hardacre, 'The restoration of the Scottish episcopacy, 1660–1661', *The Journal of British Studies*, 1 (1961), pp. 32–51.

Davies, J. D., 'International relations, war and the armed forces', in L. K. J. Glassey (ed.), *The Reigns of Charles II and James VII & II* (Basingstoke, 1997), pp. 211–33.

Dow, F. D., *Cromwellian Scotland* (Edinburgh, 1979).

Elder, John R., *The Highland Host of 1678* (Glasgow, 1914).

Ferguson, William, *Scotland's Relations with England: a survey to 1707* (Edinburgh, 1977).

Ferguson, William, 'The electoral system in the Scottish counties before 1832', in *Miscellany II*, Stair Society Publications no. 35, D. Sellar (ed.) (Edinburgh, 1984), pp. 261–94.

Ford, J. D., 'James Dalrymple, first viscount Stair (1619–1695)', in *Oxford Dictionary of National Biography* (Oxford, 2004), vol.14, pp. 988–94.

Gardner, William B., 'The later years of John Maitland, second earl and first duke of Lauderdale', *The Journal of Modern History*, 20 (1948), pp. 113–22.

Gil, Xavier, 'Crown and *cortes* in early modern Aragon: reassessing revisionisms', *Parliaments, Estates and Representation*, 13 (1993), pp. 109–22.

Glendinning, Miles (ed.), *The Architecture of Scottish Government: from Kingship to Parliamentary Democracy* (Dundee, 2004).

Goldie, Mark, 'Divergence and union: Scotland and England, 1660–1707', in Brendan Bradshaw and John Morrill (eds), *The British Problem, c.1534–1707* (Basingstoke, 1996), pp. 220–45.

Goodare, Julian, 'Parliamentary taxation in Scotland, 1560–1603', *The Scottish Historical Review*, 68 (1989), pp. 23–52.

Goodare, Julian, 'The estates in the Scottish parliament, 1286–1707', *Parliamentary History*, 15 (1996), pp. 11–32.

Goodare, Julian, 'Scotland's Parliament in its British context, 1603–1707', in Harry T. Dickinson and Michael Lynch (eds), *The Challenge to Westminster: Sovereignty, Devolution and Independence* (East Linton, 2000), pp. 22–32.

Goodare, Julian, *The Government of Scotland, 1560–1625* (Oxford, 2004).

Goodare, Julian, 'The Scottish Parliament and its early modern "rivals"', *Parliaments, Estates and Representation*, 24 (2004), pp. 147–72.

Graves, Michael, *The Parliaments of early modern Europe* (Harlow, 2001).

Harris, Tim, *Restoration: Charles II and his Kingdoms, 1660–1685* (London, 2005).

Hewison, James K., *The Covenanters: a History of the Church of Scotland from the Reformation to the Revolution* (Glasgow, 1908).

Hughes, E., 'The negotiations for a commercial union between England and Scotland in 1668', *The Scottish Historical Review*, 24 (1926), pp. 30–47.

Hutton, Ronald, 'The making of the secret treaty of Dover', *The Historical Journal*, 29 (1986), pp. 297–318.

Hutton, Ronald, *Charles II: King of England, Scotland and Ireland* (Oxford, 1991).

Hutton, Ronald, 'John Maitland, duke of Lauderdale (1616–1682)', in *Oxford Dictionary of National Biography* (Oxford, 2004), vol. 36, pp. 218–25.

Hyman, Elizabeth H., 'A church militant: Scotland, 1661–1690', *Sixteenth Century Journal*, 26 (1995), pp. 49–74.

Israel, J. I., *The Dutch Republic: its Rise, Greatness and Fall, 1477–1806* (Oxford, 1995).

Jackson, Clare, 'The paradoxical virtue of the historical romance: Sir George Mackenzie's *Aretina* and the civil wars', in John R. Young (ed.), *Celtic Dimensions of the British Civil Wars* (Edinburgh, 1997), pp. 205–25.

Jackson, Clare, 'Restoration to Revolution: 1660–1690', in Glenn Burgess (ed.), *The New British History: founding a modern state, 1603–1715* (London, 1999), pp. 92–114.

Jackson, Clare, *Restoration Scotland, 1660–1690: Royalist Politics, Religion and Ideas* (Woodbridge, 2003).

Jago, Charles, 'Habsburg absolutism and the *cortes* of Castile', *The American Historical Review*, 86 (1981), pp. 307–26.

Jago, Charles, 'Crown and *cortes* in early modern Spain', *Parliaments, Estates and Representation*, 12 (1992), pp. 177–92.

Jago, Charles, 'Parliament, subsidies and constitutional change in Castile, 1601–1621', *Parliaments, Estates and Representation*, 13 (1993), pp. 123–37.

Jespersen, Knud J. V. and E. Ladewig Petersen, 'Two revolutions in early modern Denmark', in E. I. Kouri and Tom Scott (eds), *Politics and Society in Reformation Europe: Essays for Sir Geoffrey Elton on his sixty-fifth Birthday* (London, 1987), pp. 473–501.

Jones, James R., 'The Scottish constitutional opposition in 1679', *The Scottish Historical Review*, 37 (1958), pp. 37–41.

Jones, James R., *Charles II: Royal Politician* (London, 1987).

Keith, Theodora, 'The economic causes for the Scottish Union', *The English Historical Review*, 24, 93 (1909), pp. 44–60.

Keith, Theodora, *Commercial Relations of England and Scotland, 1603–1707* (Cambridge, 1910).

Keith, Theodora, 'The trading privileges of the Royal Burghs of Scotland, part I', *The English Historical Review*, 28, 111 (1913), pp. 454–71.

Keith, Theodora, 'The trading privileges of the Royal Burghs of Scotland, part II', *The English Historical Review*, 28, 112 (1913), pp. 678–90.

Kidd, Colin, *Subverting Scotland's Past: Scottish Whig Historians and the Creation of an Anglo-British Identity, 1689–c.1830* (Cambridge, 1993).

Koenigsberger, Helmut G., *Estates and Revolutions: Essays in early modern European History* (Ithaca, 1971).

Lamb, J. A., 'Archbishop Alexander Burnet, 1614–84', *Records of the Scottish Church History Society*, 11 (1955), pp. 133–48.

Lang, Andrew, *Sir George Mackenzie, His Life and Times, 1636–1691* (London, 1909).

Lawson, Roderick, *The Covenanters of Ayrshire: Historical and Biographical* (Paisley, 1887).

Lee Jr, Maurice, *The Cabal* (Urbana, 1965).

Lynch, Michael, 'Response: old games and new', *The Scottish Historical Review*, 73 (1994), pp. 47–63.

Macaulay, Thomas B., *The History of England from the Accession of James II*, 6 vols (London, 1913–5).

MacDonald, Alan R., ' "Tedious to rehers?" Parliament and locality in Scotland c.1500–1651: the burghs of North East Fife', *Parliaments, Estates and Representation*, 20 (2000), pp. 31–58.

MacDonald, Alan R., 'Deliberative processes in parliament, c.1567–1639: Multicameralism and the lords of the articles', *The Scottish Historical Review*, 81 (2002), pp. 23–51.

Macinnes, Allan I., 'Repression and conciliation: the Highland dimension, 1660–1688', *The Scottish Historical Review*, 65 (1986), pp. 167–95.

Macinnes, Allan I., 'Early modern Scotland: the current state of play', *The Scottish Historical Review*, 73 (1994), pp. 30–46.

Macinnes, Allan I., 'Politically reactionary Brits? The promotion of Anglo-Scottish union, 1603–1707', in Sean J. Connolly (ed.), *Kingdoms United? Great Britain and Ireland since 1500* (Dublin, 1999), pp. 43–55.

MacIvor, Ian and Bent Petersen, 'Lauderdale at Holyroodhouse, 1669–70', in David J. Breeze (ed.), *Studies in Scottish Antiquity, Presented to Stewart Cruden* (Edinburgh, 1984), pp. 249–68.

MacKechnie, Aonghus, 'Housing Scotland's Parliament, 1603–1707', *Parliamentary History*, 21 (2002), pp. 99–130.

Mackenzie, W., *The Life and Times of John Maitland, Duke of Lauderdale* (London, 1923).

Mann, Alastair J., 'Inglorious revolution: administrative muddle and constitutional change in the Scottish Parliament of William and Mary', *Parliamentary History*, 22 (2003), pp. 121–44.

Mann, Alastair J., 'The Scottish Parliaments: the role of ritual and procession in the pre-1707 parliament and echoes in the new parliament of 1999', in Emma Crewe and Marion G. Müller (eds) *Rituals in Parliaments: Political, Anthropological and Historical Perspectives on Europe and the United States* (Frankfurt, 2006), pp. 135–58.

Mathieson, W. L., 'The Scottish parliament, 1560–1707', *The Scottish Historical Review*, 4 (1907), pp. 49–62.

McCoy, F., *Robert Baillie and the Second Scots Reformation* (California, 1974).

McCrie, Thomas (ed.), *The life of Mr Robert Blair, minister of St Andrews, containing his autobiography, from 1593 to 1636; with supplement to his life, and continuation of the history of the times to 1680, by his son in law, Mr William Row* (Edinburgh, 1848).

Miller, John (ed.), *Absolutism in seventeenth-century Europe* (Basingstoke, 1990).

Myers, A. R., *Parliaments and Estates in Europe to 1789* (London, 1975).

Parker, Geoffrey and Lesley M. Smith (eds), *The General Crisis of the seventeenth century* (London, 1978).

Paterson, Raymond Campbell, *King Lauderdale: the Corruption of Power* (Edinburgh, 2003).

Paterson, Raymond Campbell, 'King of Scotland: Lauderdale and the Restoration north of the border', *History Today*, 53, 1 (London, 2003), pp. 21–7.

Patrick, John, 'The origins of the opposition to Lauderdale in the Scottish parliament of 1673', *The Scottish Historical Review*, 53 (1974), pp. 1–21.

Patrick, John, 'A union broken? Restoration politics in Scotland', in Jenny Wormald (ed.), *Scotland Revisited* (London, 1991), pp. 119–28.

Pérez, José I. Fortea, 'The *cortes* of Castile and Philip II's fiscal policy', *Parliaments, Estates and Representation*, 11 (1991), pp. 117–38.

Price, J. L., *Holland and the Dutch Republic in the Seventeenth Century: the Politics of Particularism* (Oxford, 1994).

Rait, Robert S., *The Parliaments of Scotland* (Glasgow, 1924).

Robertson, Alexander, *The Life of Sir Robert Moray* (London, 1922).

Rystad, Göran, 'The estates of the realm, the monarchy and empire, 1611–1718', in Michael F. Metcalf (ed.), *The Riksdag: a History of the Swedish Parliament* (New York, 1987), pp. 61–108.

Seaward, Paul, *The Cavalier Parliament and the Reconstruction of the Old Regime, 1661–1667* (Cambridge, 1989).

Seaward, Paul, *The Restoration* (Basingstoke, 1991).

Smellie, Alexander, *Men of the Covenant: the Story of the Scottish Church in the Years of the Persecution* (London, 1909).

Smout, T. C., 'The Anglo-Scottish Union of 1707: the economic background', *The Economic History Review*, new series, 16 (1964), pp. 455–67.

Stevenson, David, 'The financing of the cause of the Covenants, 1938–51', *The Scottish Historical Review*, 51 (1972), pp. 89–123.

Stevenson, David, *The Scottish Revolution, 1637–44: the Triumph of the Covenanters* (London, 1973).

Stevenson, David, *The Revolution and Counter-Revolution in Scotland, 1644–1651* (London, 1977).

Szechni, Daniel, 'Constructing a Jacobite: the social and intellectual origins of George Lockhart of Carnwath', *The Historical Journal*, 40 (1997), pp. 977–96.

Tanner, Roland J., 'The lords of the articles before 1540: a reassessment', *The Scottish Historical Review*, 79 (2000), pp. 189–212.

Tanner, Roland J., *The Late Medieval Scottish Parliament: Politics and the Three Estates, 1424–1488* (East Linton, 2001).

Terry, Charles S., 'The duke of Monmouth's instructions in 1679', *The English Historical Review*, 20, 77 (1905), pp. 127–9.

Terry, Charles S., *The Pentland Rising and Rullion Green* (Glasgow, 1905).

Terry, Charles S., *The Scottish Parliament: its constitution and procedure, 1603–1707* (Glasgow, 1905).

Thompson, I. A. A., 'The end of the *cortes* of Castile', *Parliaments, Estates and Representation*, 4 (1984), pp. 125–33.

Thompson, I. A. A., *Crown and Cortes: Government, Institutions and Representation in early modern Castile* (Aldershot, 1993).

Thomson, Edith E. B., *The Parliament of Scotland, 1690–1702* (Oxford, 1929).

Upton, A. F., 'The *riksdag* of 1680 and the establishment of royal absolutism in Sweden', *The English Historical Review*, 102, 403 (1987), pp. 281–308.

Upton, A. F., *Charles XI and Swedish Absolutism, 1660–1697* (Cambridge, 2001).

Walker, Patrick, *Biographia Presbyteriana*, 2 vols (Edinburgh, 1827).

Willcock, John, *A Scots Earl in Covenanting Times: being Life and Times of Archibald, 9th Earl of Argyll (1629–1685)* (Edinburgh, 1907).

Wilson, Peter H., 'The power to defend, or the defence of power: the conflict between duke and estates over defence provision, Württemberg, 1677–1793', *Parliaments, Estates and Representation*, 12 (1992), pp. 25–45.

Woodward, D., 'Anglo-Scottish trade and English commercial policy during the 1660s', *The Scottish Historical Review*, 56 (1977), pp. 154–74.

Yould, G. M., 'The duke of Lauderdale's religious policy in Scotland, 1668–79: the failure of conciliation and the return to coercion', *Journal of Religious History*, 11 (1980), pp. 248–68.

Young, John R., *The Scottish Parliament, 1639–1661: a Political and Constitutional Analysis* (Edinburgh, 1996).

Young, John R., 'Seventeenth-century Scottish parliamentary rolls and political factionalism: the experience of the Covenanting movement', *Parliamentary History*, 16, 2 (1997), pp. 148–70.

Young, John R., 'The Scottish parliament in the seventeenth century: European perspectives', in A. I. Macinnes, T. Riis and F. G. Pederson (eds), *Ships, Guns and Bibles in the North Sea and the Baltic States, c.1350–c.1700* (East Linton, 2000), pp. 139–72.

Young, Margaret D., (ed.), *The Parliaments of Scotland: Burgh and Shire Commissioners*, 2 vols (Edinburgh, 1992).

UNPUBLISHED THESES

Colquhoun, Kathleen M., ' "Issue of the late civill wars": James, duke of York and the government of Scotland, 1679–1689' (University of Illinois at Urbana-Champaign, Ph.D., 1993).
Lee, Ronald A., 'Government and politics in Scotland, 1661–1681' (University of Glasgow, Ph.D., 1995).
Lennox, Roy W., 'Lauderdale and Scotland: a study in Restoration politics and administration, 1660–1682' (University of Columbia, Ph.D., 1977).
Patrick, Derek J., 'People and parliament in Scotland, 1689–1702' (University of St Andrews, Ph.D., 2002).

WORKS OF REFERENCE

Balfour-Paul, Sir James (ed.), *The Scots Peerage*, 9 vols (Edinburgh, 1904–14).
Black, George F., *The Surnames of Scotland* (New York, 1946).
Cheney, C. R. and M. Jones (eds), *A Handbook of Dates*, revised edition (London, 2000).
Fryde, E. B., D. E. Greenway, S. Porter and I. Roy (eds), *Handbook of British Chronology*, third edn (Cambridge, 2003).
Groome, Francis H., *Ordnance Gazetteer of Scotland: a Survey of Scottish Topography, Statistical, Biographical and Historical*, 6 vols (Edinburgh, 1882–5).
The Ordnance Gazetteer of Great Britain, third edn (London, 1987).

INDEX